A
Community of
Writers

A Community of Writers

TEACHING WRITING
IN THE JUNIOR AND SENIOR
HIGH SCHOOL

Steven Zemelman
ROOSEVELT UNIVERSITY

Harvey Daniels
NATIONAL COLLEGE OF EDUCATION

Heinemann
Portsmouth, NH

Heinemann
A Division of Reed Publishing (USA) Inc.
361 Hanover Street, Portsmouth, NH 03801-3912
Offices and agents throughout the world

The following have generously given permission to use quotations from copyrighted works:

Chapter 2, pages 18–19: Table by Janet Emig reprinted with permission of Macmillan Publishing Company from *Encyclopedia of Educational Research*, 5th edition, Volume 4, Harold E. Mitzel, Editor in Chief. Copyright © 1982 by American Educational Research Association.

Chapter 3, pages 34–38: Ernest Hemingway, "Hills Like White Elephants," from *Men Without Women.* Copyright 1927 Charles Scribner's Sons; copyright renewed 1955 Ernest Hemingway. Reprinted with the permission of Charles Scribner's Sons, an imprint of Macmillan Publishing Company.

Figure 4–1: Reprinted from Philip G. Hanson, *Learning Through Groups.* San Diego, CA: University Associates, Inc., 1981. Used with permission.

Chapter 7, Figure 7–2 and pages 97–98: From Nancie Atwell, *In the Middle: Writing, Reading and Learning with Adolescents.* Copyright © 1987 by Boynton/Cook Publishers, Inc. Used with permission.

Chapter 9, page 119: Essay question from *English Composition Test in Achievement Test from Admission Testing Program* 1971, December administration. Reprinted with permission of Educational Testing Service.

Chapter 9, pages 128–30: Mike Royko column, *Chicago Tribune*, Monday, February 2, 1987, reprinted by permission: Tribune Media Services.

Figure 17–2: From Paul Diederich, *Measuring Growth in English.* Copyright © 1974 by the National Council of Teachers of English. Reprinted by permission of the publisher.

Chapter 18, pages 242–47: From *The Discoverers* by Daniel J. Boorstin. Copyright © 1983 by Daniel J. Boorstin. Reprinted by permission of Random House, Inc.

Figure 18–1: From the *Chicago Reader*, October 8, 1987. Reprinted by permission of Chicago Reader, Inc.

Figure 18–2: From *India Abroad*, December 11, 1987. Reprinted by permission of the publisher.

Figure 19–1: From Frances Zaniello, based on a talk by Gordon Pradl. Reprinted with permission.

Library of Congress Cataloging-in-Publication Data
Zemelman, Steven.
    A community of writers : teaching writing in the junior and senior high school / Steven Zemelman, Harvey Daniels.
      p.   cm.
    Bibliography: p.
    Includes index.
    ISBN 0-435-08463-1
    1. English language—Composition and exercises—Study and teaching (Secondary) I. Daniels, Harvey, 1947–   II. Title.
PE1404.Z4 1988   88-790
808'.042'0712—dc19   CIP

Front-cover photo by Wladislaw Finne; back-cover photo by Bob Tanner.
Designed by Wladislaw Finne.
Printed in the United States of America.
10 9 8 7 6

Contents

Acknowledgments

The first book we wrote together, *A Writing Project*, grew out of our effort to create and nurture a program of teacher development in writing and peer leadership among teachers. That book describes what we do in intensive in-service workshops for teachers. Our Illinois Writing Project has been running for ten years now, and *this* book reflects what we've learned from all the teachers who have joined in our programs—from all the writing and talking and hashing over, the planning and trying out and recounting and refining. Teachers in hundreds of workshops have unceasingly challenged us to listen and understand their schools, their kids, and their work as clearly and as empathically as we could. They've demanded better and more useful explanations of the activities we've recommended. But they've also accepted our invitation to take initiative, and every suggestion we've made they've returned tenfold. At conferences and in-service days again and again we've heard ideas we once may have mentioned, now metamorphosed into elaborate, artful approaches far beyond anything we had imagined. This has reminded us how much joy a true professional community can generate.

In this book, we've tried to gather ideas on all aspects of teaching writing, and so we owe much to our colleagues throughout the country, even when we sometimes disagree with parts of what they've said. We're especially indebted to a number of our field's intellectual mentors. James Britton built the conceptual framework that underlies much of what we believe. Janet Emig first called people's attention to the complex processes students follow as they write. Peter Elbow gave us deep psychological insights into writers' minds. Donald Graves has been thanked by many authors, but rarely for what we consider his greatest qualities—his gentleness, his encouraging manner, and his ability to build community among teachers wherever he goes.

Other sites of the National Writing Project—particularly the New York City and the Milwaukee Projects—have provided invaluable thoughts and encouragement. Recent writings about whole language by Ken Goodman and Judith Newman have helped us connect our efforts to a broader perspective. Work in the neighbor discipline of group dynamics, especially by David and Roger Johnson, Richard and Patricia Schmuck, and Philip Hanson, has provided essential insights.

We're especially thankful to our children, Mark and Dan, Nick and Marny, whose lives and love overflow with pleasurable language, and whose ups and downs with growth and school have made all our thinking much more real for us. Our wives, Susan and Elaine, in their own work, their involvement with education, and their delight with words, have been cherished fellow travellers.

At the heart of this book are specific teaching ideas we've taken from eighteen of our colleagues in the Illinois Writing Project. Each of these gifted teachers appears later in the text, and their school addresses are listed in the appendix for anyone who wishes to correspond with one of them directly. But many other teachers have influenced this book just as powerfully, in deep and diffuse ways. Dagny Bloland probably knows the literature of literacy better than the rest of us put together. Tom and Kathy Daniels have nourished us in every way and sustained our hope for Chicago. Jura Harris, Roxanne Henkin, and Cara Keller are elementary school colleagues who have taught us much about working with writers of any age. Keith Fuerst and Maria Palumbo have developed the Project's gradual reach across the curriculum. This past year, Joanne Trahanas demonstrated how a brave teacher can change. Terry Shepherd represents the Writing Project in "the rest" of Illinois, while Doug Temkin handles our West Coast affairs with aplomb. To the hundreds of other teachers who've contributed their energy to the work of the Project and to the flavor of this book, we are deeply grateful.

Some of the people already mentioned have read and commented on this book at different stages of its growth. Because so many of these friends are also expert writing teachers, the quality of the feedback and guidance has been superb. Roxanne Henkin in particular helped us to see some grave weaknesses, lovingly buffering her corrections with generous, unearned praise. Jackie Kaster, Harvey's graduate assistant at National College, cheerfully and effectively searched through the manuscript to organize the bibliography, index, and permissions.

Again, we're fortunate to have Philippa Stratton as our editor. Our field is blessed by her deep commitment to the centrality of language and community in education. We believe that the list of books she has edited for Heinemann in the past several years is the single most important printed resource for reading and writing teachers in this country. Further, Philippa's humor, encouragement, and calm can carry authors through even the most frantic stages of creating a book.

We're grateful for our own partnership, which has grown through our work on this book while at the same time we've managed to remain separate individuals. Our families have patiently endured the interminable nightly 10:00 P.M. phone calls that have kept us going.

Special thanks, finally, to our institutions—Roosevelt University, which gave Steve a semester's leave when much work was done; and National College of Education, where Harvey's colleagues enact an abiding concern for the lives of teachers. Those who wish to correspond with us can write to either school: Roosevelt University, 430 S. Michigan Avenue, Chicago, IL 60605; or National College of Education, 2840 Sheridan Road, Evanston, IL 60201.

Part I

Process and Paradigm

Chapter 1

The Challenge

Junior and senior high school students want to write, can write, and do write. They write school assignments: book reports, essays, term papers, literary criticism, laboratory notes, character sketches, five-paragraph themes, answers on ditto sheets, and articles for the school newspaper, the yearbook, and the literary magazine. They also write thank-you notes to their grandmothers, messages for the family refrigerator, meticulously folded notes full of hilarious or cruel gossip, college and job application essays, love letters, dreamy poems, secret diaries, pretend newspapers, satires of TV shows, personal wish lists, and—just for fun—stories of romance, science fiction, and adventure.

As Eric Erickson and others have shown, identity formation is the consuming developmental task for adolescents; and writing comes closer to these kids' urgent personal concerns than any other school subject. After all, in learning to write, students are invited—compelled, really—to make sense of the world, to weigh ideas, to explore values, to find their own connections, to invent voices, styles, personae on a page—and then to test everything out by communicating with others, sharing writing and exchanging responses.

For teachers, writing is the most wonderful and meaningful subject to teach because it invites us to know each of our students in a deeply personal way. After all, our job is to stimulate and then respond to students' written expression. And as kids offer us this work, they are sharing pieces of the self they are creating. Often these writings reflect volatile, tentative, fragile, transient, and embryonic selves—but what a privilege for the teacher, what a remarkable relationship of intimacy and trust. And what an unmatched opportunity to be a person of consequence in students' academic and personal growth.

But for many of us who have worked with kids in grades six through twelve, these are strange statements. We are much more familiar with students' resistance to writing, their groans when we make assignments, their prideless craftsmanship, the failure of their writing to reveal any genuine purpose or any real voice, their stubborn refusal to look back and revise what they have written. Indeed, as teachers of junior and senior high school, we have inherited many students whose work has been completely severed from personal significance, the meaning-making and self-creation that writing makes possible. These students do not want to write, and sometimes they either cannot or will not try.

This is hard for us teachers, and we get discouraged too. We begin to think that all these elevated uses for writing are just idealistic daydreaming, that it can't happen in our classrooms, not with *these* kids. But this is wrong, and we didn't become English or language arts teachers because we are defeatists. The fact is that writing has been taught so badly in our schools and kids have been compelled to waste their writing on so many trivial and demoralizing purposes that their urge to write has often been stunted. Now we face an uphill struggle in reconnecting our students and ourselves with all the possibilities for learning and exploration that writing offers.

This book is about some tools that can help meet this challenge. It gathers from many classroom teachers, from theoretical and practical publications, and from our own experience, fresh ways of teaching that can bring alive the magic of writing as a tool of thinking and personal growth. The task for us as teachers is a large one, and it cannot be accomplished with just a few neat tricks or clever assignments. It means reconsidering our understanding of students themselves, re-seeing the possibilities in the classroom, reordering some traditional elements of the curriculum, changing some familiar, perhaps cherished patterns of instruction. Admittedly, the goal is lofty: to show our students their power to think and tell and create with words and, in so doing, to recapture the spirit of our own calling to be teachers. But the spread of writing projects and other new composition programs around the country shows that the goal is reachable. Dedicated, innovative teachers are making it happen every day.

THE PROCESS PARADIGM

By now, almost everyone working in schools—not just English and language arts teachers—has heard that we have a new way to teach writing. Over the past fifteen years, an alternative model of writing instruction has emerged, one that is far more effective than the traditional approach most of us were led through as students and have practiced as teachers. Some enthusiasts say this new way of teaching writing is so radically different from the old product-centered view that it reflects a genuine paradigm shift, a change of intellectual models parallel to the historic shift from the Ptolemaic picture of the earth as a flat body at the center of the universe to the Copernican model we now accept. If such analogies apply, we are indeed talking about some pretty big changes here.

The term "writing process" has slid with ease, if not necessarily understanding, into the working vocabulary of countless students, teachers, administrators, board members, textbook publishers, book salespeople, and even—where enthusiasm runs especially high—parents. In other guises, this new approach is sometimes called the "workshop" or "studio" method. Sometimes it's called (with less than complimentary intentions) the "natural process" approach; at the other extreme, some guru-hungry teachers call it the "Donald Graves program" and talk with each other about the extent to which they "teach Graves." It is perhaps testimony above all to the impact of the National Writing Project and its nearly 150 sites that a general awareness of the process model of writing instruction has spread so widely over the past fifteen years.

In the next chapter, we will give a detailed explanation of just what this new paradigm entails and how it differs from the old one. However, as a place to start, we want to outline here a list of fifteen key methods or conditions associated with the process paradigm.

In process-oriented classrooms, students enjoy:

1. Teachers who understand and appreciate the basic linguistic competence that students bring with them to school, and who therefore have positive expectations for students' achievements in writing.

2. Regular and substantial practice at writing.

3. Instruction in the process of writing—learning how to work at a given writing task in appropriate phases, including prewriting, drafting, and revising.

4. The opportunity to write for real, personally significant purposes.

5. Experience in writing for a wide range of audiences, both inside and outside of school.

6. Rich and continuous reading experience, including both published writing and the work of peers and teachers.

7. Exposure to models of writing in process and writers at work, including both classmates and skilled adult writers.

8. Collaborative activities that provide ideas for writing and guidance in revising drafts in progress.

9. One-to-one writing conferences with the teacher.

10. Inquiry-oriented classroom activities that involve students with rich sets of data and social interaction, and that focus on specific modes or elements of writing.

11. Increased use of sentence-combining exercises which replaces instruction in grammatical terminology.

12. Mechanics of writing taught in the context of students' own compositions, rather than in separate exercises and drills.

13. Moderate marking of the surface structure errors in student papers, focusing on sets or patterns of related errors.

14. Flexible and cumulative evaluation of writing that stresses revision. The teacher's written comments include a mixture of praise and criticism, with praise predominating.

15. Writing as a tool of learning in all subjects across the curriculum.

These are some of the key teaching methods and principles associated with the process model, ideas that have emerged during the last two decades of intense experimentation, research, and theory building in composition. Obviously, there is still some explaining left to do. And frankly, we think there are some problems with the idea of a paradigm shift and some questions about what different people mean when they describe the "new" and the "old" approaches. The amount of change that's actually occurred in school writing programs to date may not be quite Copernican in its impact. But for now we'll simply assert that we think the shift is at least potentially an important one and that this book is about making it come true.

ELEMENTARY-SCHOOL APPLICATIONS

The process approach to writing instruction has been adopted widely and has had great impact at the elementary level. In the Chicago area, where we work, we've seen scores of elementary classrooms where writing instruction has been transformed by teachers following this new approach. Across the country, the story is the same: by taking Writing Project workshops, by reading the books of Donald Graves or Lucy Calkins, by experimenting on their own, many teachers have taken a whole new direction with beginning writers. Instead of being drilled in the presumed "subskills" of writing—spelling, punctuation, grammar—their students write whole texts every day, keep folders of their work, revise their pieces regularly, read aloud to each other, collaborate in groups, publish their best work for outside readers, and most delightfully of all, love to write. Indeed, these process-oriented teachers are always swapping stories about kids' indignant protests whenever daily writing time has to be shortened or omitted. Writing, in almost all of these classrooms, has become the children's favorite subject.

The products of these elementary-school writing workshops are beautiful and inspiring expressions of individual children and their encounter with the power of language: stories, poems, reports, narratives, personal autobiography, illustrated cartoon tales, and dictionary entries. Indeed, to visit one of these classrooms and listen to children reading their work aloud or to explore hallways papered with lavishly illustrated reports is to be awed by the power of even the youngest schoolchildren to make meaning with language. It's always exciting to be reminded of how much kids can accomplish when they are set free and guided.

In districts where outcomes are measured closely, the official results of the process writing approach parallel those of Graves in his pioneering 1982 study: when young children are taught writing with this approach, they achieve just as well as other students in all the "subskills" of composition as well as in reading achievement—while their actual writing performance, not surprisingly, is clearly superior.

YES, BUT . . .

Unfortunately, the process approach has not been translated so widely or successfully to the higher grades. We know of fewer junior-high or high-school classrooms where the process approach has been fully and successfully implemented. There are a number of good reasons for this. We need to understand those reasons, those problems, and find ways of overcoming them.

So what hurdles do we face? To begin with, junior-high and high-school subjects are usually departmentalized, which among other things means that teachers see each of their students for forty to sixty minutes per day instead of the five hours that elementary teachers usually enjoy. This makes it much harder for the teacher to know each student well, and since daily contact is so short, it takes the teacher more days, more weeks into the year to come to know each kid. Also, when subjects are departmentalized, each teacher's total student load rises to 125 or 150, instead of the 25 or 30 pupils usually found in a self-contained elementary classroom. Obviously, it's much harder for a teacher to establish personal connection and a sense of audience with such a large and shifting cast of characters. At best, the teacher has to create not one but five or six communities of writers, each of which will need to have some of its own special ways of operating. But even then, the teacher may not be able to keep these communities together for the whole year, as elementary teachers customarily do; semester-long courses are normal in many high schools, and classes may change as often as every six or eight weeks.

The difference in volume of work cannot be overlooked, either. It's tough to read and respond to the papers of 150 writers who, unlike a class of 30 primary-grade kids, produce huge stacks of complex, or at least lengthy, text. This means, for example, that it is not easy for a secondary teacher who circulates through a roomful of student writers to effectively monitor developing pieces simply by glancing over shoulders or having two-minute "process conferences." The greater volume and complexity of the writing presents all kinds of challenges, not the least of which is budgeting time. One sobering calculation: a secondary teacher with a typical class load who takes just ten minutes to work with a paper from each of her students will invest something like *twenty hours* of her own out-of-class time.

Though plenty of elementary teachers would disagree, it does seem that they have more discretion and flexibility in how they use their daily instructional time than secondary teachers have, or feel that they have. In junior high or high schools, those forty-five-minute periods seem to carry the implication that every moment should directly advance some curriculum goal. The process approach to writing is an inherently holistic, inductive, nonmechanistic approach that requires large chunks of class time for writing and responding to writing. Secondary teachers for whom such activity isn't formally installed in the curriculum don't have a full day from which to steal the minutes needed for such workshop time. Elementary teachers can also embed writing activities in their own non–language-arts lessons—all they have to do is infuse writing activities into science, social studies, art, or math units. High-school language-arts teachers, on the other hand, can only depend on the goodwill of other teachers, who almost invariably feel that teaching kids to write (or even using writing as a tool of learning) is solely the English Department's job.

All this talk about trying to sneak writing practice into the classroom implies that the status of writing in high-school curriculum guides is not congenial to the process approach, and indeed it often isn't. To begin with, the kinds of writing specifically prescribed in the district curriculum may differ significantly by grade levels. In the elementary grades the curriculum often calls for expressive and narrative activities that entice students with their personal-ness, but in secondary school the guidelines generally call for concentration on the more formal and expository forms of writing—reports, explanations, arguments, essays, research writing, term papers—genres that may be less immediately attractive and motivating to students. In many high schools, the curriculum guide may be pretty specific about *not* taking a holistic, workshop approach to writing.

Secondary curricula (and teachers) typically show little confidence that students can learn the mechanics of writing from practicing writing; instead, much time and many costly textbooks are allocated to the purpose of "directly teaching" the presumed subskills of composing in drills or exercises. As a result, most secondary teachers feel they have to spend class time "using the books," separately teaching spelling, grammar, usage, mechanics, vocabulary, manuscript formats, and the like.

Then there are the differences in the kids themselves. Most elementary students—especially primary kids—approach school with enthusiasm and a deep, intrinsic desire to unlock the puzzle of literacy. It is no coincidence that the work of Donald Graves has been most popular and successful with first- and second-grade teachers and children; indeed, a good deal of this success comes simply from taking advantage of (rather than stifling) some of the natural developmental fireworks of six- and seven-year-olds. The pace of growth in the early grades can be dazzling. Think, for example, of the tremendous growth between the average kindergarten writing sample and the typical piece of third-grade writing. Elementary teachers often see prompt and tangible results in their students' work—in fluency, length of writing, attempts at revision, and so forth—and this kind of change gives teachers tremendous encouragement to continue with their efforts. This is just another reminder of something educators often forget: that kids in elementary school simply develop at a faster rate, cognitively and linguistically, than do high-school students.

At the other end of the school spectrum, things happen much more slowly. Most secondary-school students do not attack schoolwork with the powerful, innocent gusto of first graders. After all, they are veterans, the youngest of whom have been at it for at least seven years, and their fundamental, if imperfect, literacy has long since been achieved. School has lost its newness, or has proven itself to be uninspiring; in any case, adolescents certainly do not act as though they expect any fresh excitement from another day on the work farm. Many have become jaded and bored: good students will work only if paid in the coin of grades, while poorer students often won't work whatever the pay.

The implications of all this for upper-grade writing instruction include both slow growth and attitude problems. It is often impossible to tell freshman and senior papers apart at all; in fact, in a research study we conducted about five years ago, we found that the average high-school writer in the Chicago metropolitan area grew *not at all* as a writer throughout the four years of high school. And when students, for whatever reasons, have learned to hate writing, the teacher faces a situation that's far different from the elementary teacher whose kids erupt in protest if writing is *not* allowed.

In summary: two of the things that encourage teachers to try new methods are seeing students make swift progress and seeing them enjoy the work—results that are harder to achieve among adolescents than they are among primary schoolers. Secondary teachers must learn how to create the right conditions and must also learn to take their satisfaction from subtler, less spectacular gains.

The psychosocial issues facing junior-high and high-school students sometimes seem to make writing instruction harder at this age level. Adolescents are often fearful of exposing themselves, sharing their thoughts and their feelings, or making themselves vulnerable to the prying eyes of peers or adults. Thus, many of the best ways we know to make writing real, largely by creating a close-knit community of writers, seem prohibited. In a sense, the kids are right to be skittish; nothing makes us feel quite so vulnerable as when we release a piece of our writing, a frozen chunk of our self, to the world. Ironically, it is much easier for a bunch of six- or seven-year-olds, who have little experience in handling the uncertainties of a broader public audience, to risk this than kids five or ten years older. The adolescents may feel much more threatened by writing, even though they are actually much shrewder about discourse, more experienced with a wide variety of audiences, and much better equipped to protect themselves than the younger kids.

Teachers at the different levels of school have their own issues, too, because the training and orientation of elementary- and secondary-school teachers are different. Elementary teachers tend to embrace the idea of teaching the "whole child" (whatever they may mean by this) and are comfortable with a developmental and holistic approach to developing literacy. Secondary English teachers tend to be more subject-matter loyalists, feeling that they are experts on literature and language and that their job is to convey this content to the students. High-school teachers often feel more immediately accountable to the public and the "real world" than teachers at the lower grade levels. They can no longer tell parents or administrators, "Don't worry, Johnny will get it next year," because finally there will be no next year. As kids approach graduation and college or work beyond, there's a feeling of ultimate responsibility on the part of their teachers: that we have to buckle down and teach all those basics that haven't already been perfectly mastered—things like grammatical terminology, term-paper formats, and the like.

YES

The good news is, despite all these challenges and difficulties, the process paradigm can work and does work for junior-high and high-school teachers and students. Across the country, many teachers have found not just a more effective way of teaching the skill of writing, but also a way to use writing as a powerful tool for learning the subject matter of school. And they have discovered that using writing in this way creates a deeply needed and supremely valuable island of community, sharing, and collaboration for adolescents.

In the most effective of these classrooms, writing is pervasive. Students write every day, share their words with others, and listen. They write for their own intellectual and affective purposes—to learn, to think, to organize, to plan, to explore. Because they have taken control of writing as a tool for thinking, their learning of the subject matter of school is more efficient and more self-aware and critical. They write for out-of-school purposes and audiences, to get things done in the real world. They exercise a great degree of choice and discretion over what they write, even for course assignments. They take pride in their work, exhibiting careful craftsmanship. They feel ownership and authorship of their own words, and they are sensitive and insightful critics of their classmates' work. In short, they behave as writers and as communities of writers.

So the new model, the fad, does work. The challenge is to significantly adjust, revise, and translate the new paradigm to make it effective with secondary-school kids. We cannot just steal Graves' or Calkins' approach and use it on teenagers. Too many things are different. And that's what this book is about—translating the new paradigm, the process model of writing instruction, to the junior and senior high school setting, where the kids, the logistics, the curriculum, the teachers, the social dynamics, and the expectations of parents and public are different in a number of critical ways from the lower levels of schooling.

And just to be absolutely clear, we'll go one step further: we believe it is *harder* to implement the process approach to writing at the junior-high and high-school level. It calls for more struggle, more work, more upstream swimming by the teacher. But it is also potentially even more valuable at this level, because this is the part of school we most desperately need to reform.

We are writing this book directly on the heels of a spate of national commission reports about the sorry state of American education, an outpouring of angst that has unanimously tabbed the junior and senior high schools as the weakest link in a fragile chain of educational institutions. Completely aside from debating the merits of this dire picture, we have been struck by the fact that all the reams of recommendations from the various panels of experts—businesspeople, scientists, politicians, financiers, school administrators (but very few classroom teachers, of course) —really boil down to one simple thing: do the same things harder, longer, faster. Schools are exhorted to teach more courses, add more requirements, give more tests, have a longer school day and year, train teachers more and longer, pay teachers more, and so on. In other words, all this "criticism" can actually be seen as a kind of bizarre, backhanded *endorsement* of the status quo. It all says that if we just do the same things better, kids will learn. In this alleged wave of school reform, the fundamental assumptions and processes of American education have not been called into question.

We see things differently. We agree that schooling in the United States is in many ways a disappointment, but we don't think this is because kids and teachers don't try hard enough. We think it is because *we are doing some wrong things and we should do something else.* Unlike all of these national commissions, we want to challenge some fundamental ideas and practices. Here's just one small example. A unanimous article of faith of all these reports is that in teachers' training, pedagogical studies are worthless and should be replaced by more content instead—more courses in the subjects teachers might eventually be called upon to teach. We think this is totally wrong; we think pedagogy is one of the critical weaknesses of the educational system and needs to be radically improved. We feel that the process by which learning is organized and presented is of transcendent importance to the outcomes of schooling. If I, as a teacher, spend the class period telling you rules for good writing, I am doing something profoundly different from what I do if I engage you as an active participant in a writing workshop, a growing community of writers. These are not minor differences of pedagogical styles; they are the essence of the matter.

So this book is concerned with the processes, the structures, the relationships in teaching writing as much as with any particular content, rules, or principles. This book is not about doing the same things harder, longer, stronger. It's about trying different things until we find methods that work, and then developing these. It's about doing something different. And in the processes and structures of this new approach to teaching writing there is a pattern, a pattern for teachers who want to use it, for transforming relationships in the classroom in a way that points toward a profoundly revitalized kind of learning in school.

But we're getting ahead of ourselves. The first thing we need to do is to explain the process paradigm itself. That's the work of the next chapter.

Chapter 2

Defining
the Process
Paradigm

This new paradigm, which we conveniently call "process writing," isn't actually new, of course. One can look back into history and find teachers from almost any age employing methods that sound much like our modern process approach. The Roman rhetorician Marcus Fabius Quintillian advised that students should "practice composition and be constantly employed in that enterprise" and stated that their teachers shouldn't stress correctness so much as "boldness" and "exuberance." Go easy on the evaluation, Quintillian warned writing instructors in 91 A.D.: "Youthful minds sometimes give way beneath the weight of correction excessively severe, become despondent and grieve and in the end . . . in their fear of blundering everywhere, attempt nothing."

Closer to home, a number of nineteenth-century American educators struggled to teach language arts in ways that seem fully contemporary; in their time, of course, they were called romantics. Barrett Wendell, a professor of rhetoric at Harvard in the 1890s, wrote of his frustrations and his deepening appreciation of what it means to teach writing:

Bewildering, depressing, maddening, debasing, I should have found this work years ago, but for the growing conviction, which strengthens as the years go by, that the meanest of these works [student papers] if we will only let ourselves see it truly, is a very marvelous thing. Careless, thoughtless, reckless as these [students] so often are, the most careless, the most thoughtless, the most reckless of all, has put before me an act of the creative imagination for which . . . one can find no lesser word than divine. All unknowing, and with the endless limitations of weakness and perversity, he has looked for himself into the great world of immaterial reality, which, just as he knows it, no other human being can ever know; and with these strange, lifeless conven-

tions we call words he has made some image of what he has known in that world which is all his own; and that image begins by and by to arouse within me some conception of what life has meant to him.

—English Composition (*New York: Charles Scribner's Sons, 1903*), p. 304

Reading this heartfelt testimony a century later, we can almost hear Wendell's harder-boiled Harvard colleagues chuckling in the background at his naive idealism. But we know that Wendell was right about writing and about students. We recognize that Wendell's eagerness to care for his students, to see the world through their eyes, to appreciate their strengths, to exult in their tiniest steps of exploration, in a very real sense to love them, reflects one of the oldest, and certainly the best, elements of our profession's true ideals and traditions.

THE WHOLE LANGUAGE MOVEMENT

So even if today's enthusiasm for process writing superficially resembles a fad, it is vital to recognize its deep roots. This view of language learning is part of an old and evolving set of ideas that may eventually prevail over other models and more permanently guide our teaching of literacy. In recent years, the term *whole language* has come to designate this broader, historically evolving philosophy of language-arts instruction, of which the process approach to writing is only a part.

As Mark Clarke of the University of Denver explains, whole-language teaching means, first of all, that reading and writing teachers use "complete texts in communicative situations, as contrasted with focused skills practice or the use of 'phonics' or isolated language drill."

Teachers in such classrooms emphasize the use of "real" texts (i.e., newspapers, children's books, school memos, notes to and from home, etc.) for the teaching of reading rather than basal readers or publisher packets or textbook series. They reason that children do better when they are attempting to understand something they have chosen to read, rather than when they are trying to make sense of a book which the teacher has chosen for them. Similarly, writing instruction is based on the children's attempts at communicating with someone else. The kids are encouraged to experiment with the language in order to get it to express what they want it to express. Relatively little isolated practice takes place in such traditional activities as spelling, word lists, grammar and punctuation exercises, etc. The rationale is that the acquisi-

tion of conventions of print and grammar (i.e., spelling, punctuation, handwriting, etc.) will be taught when the child is ready to attend to accuracy in the course of producing a meaningful text. Whole language teachers have a strong philosophical commitment to the idea that errors are a natural part of learning. It is through a focus on meaning and revision that conventions of print and grammar are learned. In whole language classrooms children are encouraged to experiment with reading and writing strategies in order to communicate with others through print.

Figure 2–1 shows some of the roots of the whole-language approach, the intellectual heritage, if you will, of this movement. As you can see, this is not the diagram of some transitory fad, but rather of a group of closely related yet evolving ideas across a broad historical span.

The roots of the whole-language movement emerge from four different fields: the language-arts curriculum, linguistics, educational philosophy, and social psychology. The *language-arts curriculum* has always had both programs and theories that stress having students use real language for real purposes as a means of acquiring and stretching linguistic abilities. Over the past fifty years, *linguistics* has described children's language acquisition, providing us with an increasingly clear and generative model of how human beings undertake the incredibly complex task of learning, mostly unconsciously and untaught, the thousands of abstract rules that make up the grammar of their native language. In *educational philosophy*, there has long been a school of thought that stresses education as an active, inductive, social, and democratic experience. And in *social psychology*, our growing knowledge of group processes, and the centrality of communication in those processes, has long invited us to recognize and use the classroom group itself as the most powerful tool for teaching and learning.

In reviewing the diagram in Figure 2–1, note that the process approach to writing—the kind of writing this book is about—is just one corner of the whole language or integrated language-arts movement. It connects with everything teachers and kids can do with reading, speaking, listening, and other elements of the curriculum, but it is still only a part of the picture. We believe that this is how most teachers explore and take ownership of the larger model—by trying something from one corner and then growing out toward the others. Anyway, that's how it worked for us.

This set of ideas cycles in and out of education, repeatedly being pushed back by the traditional (Janet Emig calls them the "magical") approaches and then re-emerging. This may remind you of the often-used image in

---

Figure 2–1 *Origins of the Whole Language Movement*

LANGUAGE ARTS CURRICULUM

—Language experience
  reading
—"Process" writing
—Writing to learn across the
  curriculum
—Integrated language arts
—Reader response to literature

Using language and literacy
for real, personally meaningful
purposes as the key to growth.

INSTRUCTIONAL PHILOSOPHY
AND DESIGN

—Progressive-humanistic
  education
—Dewey: education as
  democracy
—Student-centered learning
—Inquiry learning
—Open classroom/integrated
  day

Learning through active,
experiential, inductive, social,
democratic processes.

**WHOLE
LANGUAGE**

LINGUISTICS AND
DEVELOPMENTAL PSYCHOLOGY

—Psycholinguistics: native
  oral language acquisition
—Emergent literacy studies
—Sociolinguistics: social base
  of language
—Developmental psychology:
  constructivist learning
  theory

Children's language
acquisition is our most
powerful model and metaphor
of complex learning.

GROUP DYNAMICS AND SOCIAL
PSYCHOLOGY

—Applications of group
  dynamics to classroom
  groups
—Stages in development of
  groups
—Collaborative learning,
  circles of learning
—Facilitation vs. teaching

The classroom as a complex
social community and
resource for learning.

education of a pendulum swinging back and forth; indeed, this seems to be the standard metaphor for changes in our field. How impartial and content-free this pendulum image is, tempting us to believe that the fluctuations in educational practice are merely the results of some pointless, random, eternal variation. In fact, this is no impartial pendulum swinging; it is more like the battlefront in a war that moves back and forth with assaults and retreats. This is a historical struggle of one set of ideas against another, continually being fought out in close relation to the social-political-economic issues outside of schools.

Process writing and whole language, when taught in their true, pure forms, are related to a specific set of educational ideas, ideas that are partisan, that are opposed to other ideas, and that contend with opposing models and paradigms. To refer to this continuing struggle as the vacillation of vacuous fads or the swinging of a pendulum cheapens the efforts of people who are working, often against much resistance, to put these ideas into practice and to show how they work. We believe that this struggle is crucially important. As we wrote on the final page of our last book:

Teaching writing is connected with democracy, with teaching and enacting respect for human beings, helping them to respect themselves—as opposed to worshipping the American Star and Hero System. . . . Teaching writing—if it's done in a good way and not just to put kids through their paces—is about helping kids see that all of them are the heroes in this country. They grow up to be the people who make it run, keep it afloat, sustain its values, suffer its deprivations and self-destructiveness, pick up its always reviving struggle for connection, for community, for joy and creation.

We think the cycle is really more like a spiral. Each time this set of ideas comes back it gains strength and coherence from the new research and practice that connects with it, and each time it appears it exerts more influence on the schools before it is once again suppressed. Today, we don't parse or diagram sentences as much as we once did, even though grammar still holds a central place in most curricula; we don't stress having students recite memorized poems or chunks of literature; we don't spend so much time having them copy over passages from books in order to practice penmanship; we don't spend energy on elocution exercises. As each of these unproductive practices is dropped, and as more effective, growth-producing methods prove themselves, we see gradual progress toward a better understanding of how human beings actually learn and acquire new uses of language.

DEFINING PROCESS WRITING

Now, having provided some of the context into which the process approach to writing fits, we need to return to writing itself—to the upper left-hand corner of the diagram in Figure 2–1—and to the problem of more clearly defining what process writing is. As John Dewey pointed out fifty years ago, innovators always bear a greater burden of explanation than traditionalists: "It is easier to walk in the paths that have been beaten than it is, after taking a new point of view, to work out what is practically involved in the new point of view." We first need to identify the key points of contrast between the old and new paradigms. As a place to start, here is an abridged version of Janet Emig's helpful graphic comparison of the polarities, which appears in the *Encyclopedia of Educational Research*:

OLD/TRADITIONAL VIEW	NEW/PROCESS VIEW
Writing is a product to be evaluated.	Writing is a process to be experienced.
There is one correct procedure for writing.	There are many processes for different situations, subjects, audiences, authors.
Writing is taught rather than learned.	Writing is predominantly learned rather than taught.
The process of writing is largely conscious.	Writing often engages unconscious processes.
The process of writing is essentially linear: planning precedes writing and revision follows drafting, etc.	Writing processes are varied and recursive.
Writers must be taught atomistically, mastering small parts and subskills before attempting whole pieces of writing.	Writers learn best from attempting whole texts.
Writing can be done swiftly and on order.	The rhythms and pace of writing can be quite slow, since the writer's actual task is to create meaning.

OLD/TRADITIONAL VIEW	NEW/PROCESS VIEW
Writing is a silent and solitary activity.	Writing is essentially social and collaborative.

Emig's chart provides a quick, schematic comparison of the new model and the older one. It also raises a number of tricky and important implications: for example, if writing is mostly learned rather than taught, what are teachers supposed to do? Emig's "Process View" column carries a few hints about teaching, and fortunately, over the past two decades, a great deal of thinking, testing, and research have fleshed out these ideas into a full, working definition of the process model. The fifteen principles for teaching writing that we outlined in Chapter 1 embody the major implications of this research, and we can begin to fill in Emig's sketch by discussing these principles in more detail.

But first, a brief word about the body of research supporting these principles. After being the stepchild of the three R's throughout the educational history of this country, writing has in recent years finally attracted the attention of many skillful, well-funded researchers. The results of this burst of empirical investigation have strongly endorsed the new process paradigm, and generally lent very little credence to the traditional pedagogical approaches. These research findings have been so consistent and powerful that they have helped to legitimize the new model in official public discourse about education.

While our list of principles draws upon many valuable sources, we want especially to credit a recent book by George Hillocks, *Research on Written Composition*. Hillocks has compiled the results of all the research studies in composition done over the period 1963–83 into one invaluable resource for both teachers and policymakers. Further, Hillocks employed a statistical technique called *meta-analysis*, which allows the results of many differently designed research studies to be combined and compared, so that the effectiveness of different types of treatments can be looked at overall. The result is that Hillocks' book provides the best available summary of what works in teaching writing. The only drawback of this important resource for both teachers and policymakers is Hillocks' personal prejudice against the National Writing Project, which he wrongly categorizes as promoting low-level and ineffective teaching strategies. Readers who recognize that most NWP sites *do* practice "environmental" methods of writing instruction (the most effective approach, according to

Hillocks) will be able to screen the text accordingly and enjoy its full benefit.

We return, then, to the fifteen teaching concepts that we introduced in Chapter 1, to offer some comments about and elaborations of each entry. This should provide a sufficient definition of the process model of writing instruction, so that we can go on to specific classroom strategies in confidence that we're all talking about the same paradigm. We want to caution as we offer this list that we are not implying "good" writing teachers must enact *all* of these ideas in their classrooms, or that this book will be telling you, the teacher-reader, that you should implement and master all of them. On the contrary, we've noticed that the very finest writing teachers we know have intuitively picked two or three or four methods on this list, ideas that somehow fit their own style of teaching, and then translated them in a highly personalized way for working with their own students. Even more on the contrary, we think a list like this can be dangerous if teachers or their supervisors view it as embodying all the necessary parts ("subskills") of ideal practice. To make this menu of possibilities into a checklist of requirements is to engage in an insidious kind of perfectionism.

The common thread in the list below is that in the supporting research summarized by Hillocks and others, *each of these fifteen practices is associated with growth in students' writing performance according to measures of overall quality or effectiveness.* Research shows that improvement in student writing performance is related to the following elements.

1. Teachers who understand and appreciate the basic linguistic competence that students bring with them to school, and who therefore have positive expectations for students' achievements in writing.

Educators have long been familiar with the "Pygmalion in the Classroom" research by Rosenthal and Jacobsen and others, which shows the tremendous power of teachers' expectations to condition the outcomes of student learning. We are now discovering the altogether unsurprising fact that teachers' expectations are also very powerful in writing instruction. As Perl and others have documented, kids seem to grow more rapidly as writers when their teachers take delight in what they can do with language, accept and appreciate the language kids bring to school, and think of their job as building upon a solid base. On the other hand, teachers who see students' language as crude, handicapping, underdeveloped, immature, incomplete, or stunted have far less success in nurturing successful writers. Obviously there is nothing startling about this finding—in a way, it simply recapitulates the old Peace Corps ad about the glass that's described as being either half full or half empty. Teachers who see student writers as half full stimulate more growth than those who see them as half empty.

2. Regular and substantial practice at writing.

Kids who write a lot get better at it. Not much news about that—but lack of practice is probably the single greatest reason for American students' dismal performance in writing. Kids in our schools simply don't write enough to grow as writers. Statistics from the National Assessment of Educational Progress, from reports like Arthur Applebee's, and from various individual states dramatically demonstrate that students write surprisingly little. According to NAEP, the average high school student in the United States completes a substantial piece of writing (which NAEP defines as one paragraph or more) about once a month. Now, how could anyone build competence at an activity so complex and demanding as writing by practicing only nine or ten times a year? Clearly, one of the main challenges to all teachers is to devote more student time, more learning time, to actually doing writing. There are really only two main ways of doing this: by reallocating instructional time presently used for other activities (many of which, like spelling, usage, or punctuation, can more effectively be taught through increased time-on-writing); or by using writing as a tool or method of teaching other subject matter content in the curriculum. We believe that both approaches can and should be used by teachers, and much of this book is about how.

3. Instruction in the process of writing—learning how to work at a given writing task in appropriate phases, including prewriting, drafting, and revising.

Perhaps the second most important finding of all this research—after the need for much more writing practice—is that students' writing improves when their teachers break the work into stages, instead of simply assigning topics and then grading the eventual products. In other words, teachers need to help students approach writing as a process, a series of steps or stages an author goes through to develop a piece of writing. Many students are unaware of this craftsmanlike view of writing; they believe that good writers magically spin a perfect product out of their heads in one try. Instead, teachers need to create the staged process in the classroom: first, to structure time and activities for prewriting to help students gather and organize material and prepare for writing; next, to structure time and space for drafting, providing good conditions and support for students as they generate first versions of a piece; then, to provide activities for revision, helping students to resee and rework their writing toward clearer and better-edited products; finally, to arrange for students' writing to reach a variety of audiences, outlets for the work that provide direction during the writing and feedback on the product. There is a great deal of research showing that when students internalize this process approach, learning to take time and effort with prewriting and revision, their writing grows much more than students who don't have such an awareness. But students will not begin using this staged approach simply because they are exhorted to, or because someone tells them about it. The teacher needs to institute the process in the classroom, structuring and sequencing activities so that students experience it firsthand and internalize the stages of the process.

4. The opportunity to write for real, personally significant purposes.

Where students often select their own subjects for writing, their writing grows more than in programs where the teacher always sets the topic. This finding is supported by the classroom studies of Donald Graves and others who observe that, at least some of the time, students need to exercise complete responsibility for the writing process from beginning to end. In order to appreciate the depth of this idea, we need to acknowledge the high degree of dependence upon the teacher that is created by the usual approach to teaching writing. Traditionally, the teacher decides on the topic; says what form or mode the writing is supposed to take; announces a length for the piece (or minimum number of words or pages, at least); offers some guidance about the tone, style, vocabulary, and other matters; and then, after the student has cranked out a piece according to these specifications, the teacher reviews the result against preset criteria and even locates each mechanical error for the student. In other words, the teacher has made all the important choices and decisions in the "writing," and has even done the clerical work of proofreading the final copy. If this is supposed to be rigorous, traditional instruction, how come it doesn't demand very much work from the students in terms of thinking, judgment, or responsibility? The research shows, on the contrary, that when students take more responsibility—we might even say authorship—from the very start, defining their own subjects and developing them through their own choices and decisions, their investment in writing increases.

5. Experience in writing for a wide range of audiences, both inside and outside of school.

One of the most important things skilled writers do is to anticipate and meet the needs of an unseen, and perhaps only partly known, audience. This complex and deeply embedded skill seems to develop not through listening to precepts offered by teachers, but by actually trying to communicate with a wide range of audiences and learning from the results. When students have opportunities to write for a variety of audiences other than the teacher, their writing seems to grow more than when their only outlet for the work is a teacher's in-box. We speculate that there are four reasons why using different audiences with kids is so powerful. For one thing, a real audience provides that little jolt of energy that comes with knowing that the work is real, and not just another school hurdle to jump through. Second, writing for real audiences gives authors some vital practice in thinking about their readers, trying to guess what they know, believe, understand, respond to, what language they recognize, what tone may be most effective with them, and so on. Third, audiences provide real feedback, priceless information about how effective a piece of writing really was, how it struck someone. Finally, writing for a real audience exerts upon the writer natural pressure to edit. If kids in school are writing to a clearly defined audience, perhaps one outside of the classroom in the "real" world, they easily recognize the importance of polishing the product, of taking pride in the form of their work—not because they'll get in trouble with the teacher or get their mechanics grade lowered, but because they don't want anything to compromise the effectiveness of their writing as communication. And this, of course, is the same reason real writers have for careful editing.

6. Rich and continous reading experience, including both published writing and the work of peers and teachers.

One of the least surprising findings from recent research on writing is the correlation between reading widely and well, and writing well. We adults probably recognize intuitively that a lot of what we know about writing we've learned from our reading; we have internalized vocabulary, sentence patterns, discourse types, even the underlying structures of whole genres of writing simply through the osmotic process of reading. Kids who have many opportunities to absorb these patterns learn in a very important way about how to write. One direct and more narrow implication of this idea is that kids must have a chance to read examples or models of the kinds of writing they are expected to produce in school. Too often, we ask students to produce highly conventionalized genres or forms of writing—research papers being the leading example—without their ever having had the chance to read and internalize the implicit patterns that characterize the genre.

7. Exposure to models of writing in process and writers at work, including both classmates and skilled adult writers.

Students need to see skilled writers at work, so that they can gain insight into the processes by which writing gets done. Unfortunately, many students have crippling misconceptions about writing. Many believe, for example, that "good" writers write it right the first time. They define good writers as those who work neatly and effortlessly, and make no mistakes. But students need to see the way it really is: that experienced writers develop a piece through stages and steps, that it usually isn't perfect at first, that writing doesn't get easier or neater as you get better at it. One key practice that helps students better understand mature writing is for the teacher to write with the students, and to talk about his mental processes with them. For many kids, their teacher may be the only adult they ever really see at work writing, using writing to get something important done for himself—so this modeling may be vitally important. Students can also learn much from studying early drafts from their classmates, teachers, or even famous writers so they can discover the various processes by which rough ideas are gradually revised and shaped into final works.

8. Collaborative activities that provide ideas for writing and guidance in revising drafts in progress.

The research strongly shows that social activities integrated into the writing process—such as prewriting discussions, collaborative drafting, peer editing groups, reading work aloud to the whole class or subgroups—can lead to better writing. These findings reflect an idea we discussed earlier: that writing is in fact a highly social act, and that past instructional practices mistakenly conceiving it as a solitary activity have been counterproductive. Even if drafting is done in solitary fashion, most real writing is part of a dialogue, one voice in an ongoing conversation in some larger community. When that conversation is aborted by having students simply write, turn in the paper, and get it back with a grade, we cut them off from a major portion of the available learning experience.

9. One-to-one writing conferences with the teacher.

Λ number of studies have shown that when the teacher takes time to conduct regular, individual conferences with students about their writing, this kind of feedback helps students grow. Conferences may be very short (two or three minutes, in some studies) and may be fairly widely spaced (once every two or three weeks, for example) and still have considerable impact. It seems clear that the direct, personal focusing that happens in a conference is what makes it one of the most powerful things a teacher can do to promote growth in writing. Most teachers have long acknowledged the value of this practice but found it difficult to manage—figuring out what to do with the other twenty-nine students while these one-to-one conferences are going on. Later, we explain how some teachers we know have solved the management problems and what they do in conferences.

10. Inquiry-oriented classroom activities that involve students with rich sets of data and social interaction, and that focus on specific modes or elements of writing.

Hillocks' research has contributed a couple of new terms to the literature of writing and writing research; one of them is *environmental* instruction. Hillocks identified four main approaches to teaching writing: presentational, individualized, natural process, and environmental. In his meta-analysis of research studies, he found the following differences in performance between treatment and control groups measured in terms of fractions of a standard deviation.

MODE OF INSTRUCTION	
EXPERIMENTAL/CONTROL EFFECTS	
Presentational	.02
Individualized	.16
Natural process	.18
Environmental	.44

In the *presentational* approach, the teacher lectures and conducts whole-class discussions about characteristics of good writing, sets students to work implementing these precepts, and gives written feedback on the results. On average, this approach results in essentially no measurable growth in students' writing performance. In fact, it was found that if the focus of the teacher's presentations is grammatical terminology, students' writing actually tends to deteriorate.

The next method, which Hillocks labels the *individualized* mode, uses the one-to-one teacher-student conference as its main instructional strategy. This model delivers about eight times the growth in student writing as the presentational approach. However, in Hillocks' meta-analysis, this change represents less than a fifth of a standard deviation, so this improvement is actually quite modest.

The next model, the *natural process* approach, is just about as effective as the individualized. It is characterized by free writing on topics of student interest followed by peer-group sharing and teacher comment, but little direct instruction. Although the essence of this model seems to be having the teacher stand aside and let the kids write, it is associated with a considerably higher level of growth in the overall quality of student writing than the traditional, presentational approach.

The final category of instruction is what Hillocks calls the *environmental*. This approach is more than twice as effective as either the individualized or the natural process models. In environmental instruction, the teacher re-enters the process not as a grammarian or rule giver, but as a structurer of time, materials, and activities. The environmental teacher organizes many of the factors in the classroom environment to provide rich and structured writing practice for students, focusing sequentially on specific aspects of the writing work at hand, and involving a wide range of social-collaborative processes to help move the work along. As we'll explain later, we call this sort of artful teaching "facilitation." And even though Hilloocks incorrectly tries to assign this latter term and this special teacher role to the natural process mode, this book aims to show why facilitation is the key to doing environmental-mode writing instruction in the classroom.

11. Increased use of sentence-combining exercises, which replaces instruction in grammatical terminology.

Probably the best-researched question in the history of composition instruction concerns the connection between the teaching of formal grammar—diagramming sentences, learning the names of the parts of speech, and the like—and skill at writing. The outcome of nearly a hundred years of study is essentially unanimous: there is no positive relationship between knowing formal grammar and writing well. As one article in a 1920 issue of *Elementary School Journal* matter-of-factly began, "We were shown a number of years ago that children who have studied formal grammar do not write any better or interpret literature any better than children who have not studied formal technical grammar." In fact, as Hillocks' more recent and more sophisticated study shows, focusing on grammar and mechanics in a writing class is the only approach that causes an average *worsening* in students' writing performance (about a third of a standard deviation in his meta-analysis). This doesn't mean that grammar is actually harmful, but simply that it is irrelevant to composition and steals instructional time from classroom activities more directly related to writing.

On the other hand, sentence combining, a type of exercise in which students combine several short "kernel" sentences into longer, more complex ones, is strongly associated with improved writing performance. Sentence combining works because it is a productive, not an analytic, activity; it works by helping students to tap into their oral language base, their latent knowledge of many complex sentence types, and then to practice transferring this oral knowledge to writing.

It is important that you, the reader, not confuse the messenger with the message here—especially since debates over the value of grammar are finally religious in nature. Both of us are quite fond of grammar and have a good deal of training in linguistics. We believe that the study of language is a vital element of a humanistic education. Indeed, if we were kings of the world, students would probably be studying a lot more grammar and descriptive linguistics than is currently the case: we'd have them learning about semantics and phonology and syntax, the origins and history of language, language change, social dialects and occupational jargons, attitudes toward language, and dozens of other fascinating subjects. But what we wouldn't do—based on what we've learned from the research and from our own work with real, live writers— is to expect grammatical terminology to help anyone learn how to write. So we wouldn't use writing time to teach grammatical terms or linguistic information.

12. Mechanics of writing taught in the context of students' own compositions, rather than in separate exercises and drills.

The research confirms what most teachers have already learned through long and painful experience: there's often little transfer between what kids can do in a controlled drill situation and on actual pieces of writing. Spelling is perhaps the most familiar example. Students who have scored 100 percent on the weekly spelling test will promptly misspell half the words from the very same list on a book report or in-class essay. This reminds us that teaching kids how to manifest subskills on a ditto is no guarantee of any transfer to consistent, productive use in actual writing.

The problem is that the cognitive task of getting correct answers on a one-skill test is totally different from the demands of a real writing situation, where an author must balance and attend to dozens of factors—content, audience, purpose, rhetoric, vocabulary, tone, mechanics of all kinds. Indeed, research offers little support for atomized drills in mechanics and instead points teachers toward addressing mechanics where they make the most sense: amid the texts kids create themselves.

13. Moderate marking of the surface structure errors in student papers, focusing on sets or patterns of related errors.

Much research has been devoted to teacher marking of student papers in order to find the "right" way for teachers to handle the problem of errors. The standard, traditional approach is for the teacher to mark every error in every paper every student ever writes with a red pen. While this is viewed by the public, most principals, and many teachers as the only responsible and appropriate kind of teacher feedback, the research does not validate its effectiveness. In fact, students do not seem to be able to learn very well from such a flood of red ink. They often cannot see through the welter of undifferentiated marks to notice what the related sets or patterns of errors are; in other words, the feedback is not clear and focused. Many students also experience such wholesale marking of their papers as a personal rejection and become discouraged from paying any further attention to the paper at all. Instead, the research recommends that teachers focus students' attention on one or two related patterns of error at a time, making sure the problem is mastered before directing their attention to another category of errors.

14. Flexible and cumulative evaluation of writing that stresses revision. The teacher's written comments include a mixture of praise and criticism, with praise predominating.

In some of the most effective writing programs recently studied, teachers separate evaluation from grading and hold off grading until late in the development of each assignment—or even until late in the term. This approach emerges from the insight that grades tend to kill off pieces of writing. Since students know that grades customarily mark the end of a piece of work in school, teachers who put grades on early drafts of writing often inadvertently terminate students' engagement with the work and cut off the possibility of revision. More effective teachers focus on giving students formative responses to early drafts, using this feedback to move students along into a process of revising.

One element of such responding is written comments on papers. The comparative value of different forms of these comments has been investigated. The conclusion: the most growth-inducing sort of comment is not all praise or all criticism, but a mixture of praise and criticism, with praise predominating. Of course this is a mixture that many skillful teachers have long since discovered for themselves: "I liked your story a lot because it was funny and full of details. I got a little bit confused in the middle where Abraham Lincoln and Janet Jackson were dancing on the roof, but then it all came together at the end, and the Easter Bunny's speech really summed things up nicely."

15. Writing as a tool of learning in all subjects across the curriculum.

Students grow not so much by practicing writing as by using it, applying writing as a tool for learning both in and out of school. One of the dangers, ironically, of the process-writing movement is that we want to make more time in the instructional day for writing—which, at one level, of course, is welcome. But we mustn't focus on writing just because we want to do a better job with a neglected element of the official school curriculum. The larger reason for learning to write—the reason that ought to be reflected in the time we spend on writing with kids—is that writing helps people get important things done: thinking, exploring, relating, and making connections. In school, we have unlimited opportunities to embed writing activities into the work of other content areas—literature, science, history, music, art, everything. In schools where writing is used across the curriculum, students' writing performance grows strongly. That's because kids are being shown, in countless ways every day, how they can take power over writing and, through writing, think for themselves and express themselves.

This, then, is the list of observations and recommendations researchers are continuing to refine. However, as we know, educational research too often fails to influence classroom practice very much, or for very long. While this may seem to be another manifestation of the fad/pendulum phenomenon, we believe that the history of obstacles and frustrations described in Chapter 1 offers a much better explanation of why this happens. In addition, researchers themselves are frequently quite unhelpful about translating their findings into usable classroom practices, and their lack of awareness of teachers' everyday working conditions hampers communication between the two groups. This book aims to improve the connection at the secondary level, using the tremendous resourcefulness of good teachers who have shared their ideas and strategies with us over the past ten years. In so doing, we hope to strengthen the cycle of progressive whole-language teaching, which forms the larger context for our effort, as it comes round once again in the ongoing battle for the soul of American schooling.

A NOTE ON PROPHETS, PARADIGMS, AND HOW TO READ THIS BOOK

The daughter of a friend of ours attends seventh grade at a fine local junior high school. Julianna's teacher has been through a couple of district-sponsored in-service programs on writing and has become a disciple of the writing-process approach. Among other things, this teacher enthusiastically pressures students to revise their writing, asking them to leave the trail of their revisions right in the work. "Don't worry about making it pretty," he says. "Let me see the scratch-outs, arrows, insertions, and other changes right on your paper." Julianna's personal composing process has comfortably accommodated the teacher's preferences. When she writes, Julianna still works, as she always has, in one essentially continuous and skillful draft. Then, when she's done, she looks back through the text for a few especially fine or sophisticated word choices. If she has written "gigantic," for example, she'll now erase it and write in "big." Then she crosses out "big" and writes "gigantic" above it. Once she's made a few more such "revisions," Julianna smudges up the corners of the paper and turns it in to her delighted teacher.

Sarah Freedman's research has uncovered similar instances. In a long-term ethnographic study of two California classrooms where peer response groups were being used, Freedman collected delightful transcripts of students in editing groups collaboratively subverting the teacher's instructions. The kids would negotiate ways of pretending to get the work done and to fake some peer feedback that the teacher would believe was genuine. The two teachers Freedman selected for the study were, like Julianna's teacher, highly respected veteran teachers reportedly dedicated to the new process paradigm. But both teachers admitted to Freedman their personal lack of belief in the strategy. Indeed, these teachers' management of the response groups—including inconsistent directions and the failure to provide systematic, staged training—dramatized how a teacher's halfhearted embrace of a half-understood idea can completely undermine a promising activity.

What Julianna and the students in California have done is to turn the new paradigm back into the old one: once again, students are grinding out disconnected writing to a teacher's specifications, rather than truly owning their words and work. This regression happens over and over when teachers don't implement and monitor their innovations deeply, congruently, thoughtfully, and self-critically. As we'll explain more in Chapter 4, there's no power like the power of violated expectations among students: when teachers try something unexpected in the classroom, even when it may be pleasant and valuable, kids have limitless ways of channeling things right back into the old, familiar ways. If a teacher is just mimicking the surface features of an ill-understood strategy, subversion and regression are inevitable.

We've seen many other disturbing cases where blind or shallow allegiance to the process paradigm has created classrooms just as rigid and uncreative as any that adhere to the traditional approach. We've seen teachers exhausted and demoralized from trying to publish handmade books or class magazines on the frantic timetable dictated by Graves. We hear from teachers who blame themselves for not being able to meet the conferencing schedule set forth by Calkins. We meet teachers who have been made to feel guilty, apologetic, and untrendy because they still give their students occasional writing assignments or, Graves forbid, have a whole class write on the same topic at the same time.

As Nancie Atwell says in a reflective moment in her book *In the Middle*, "I realize that I am running just as tight a ship as I ever did, it's just a different kind of ship." When we teachers fall in love with our own innovations, it's important to ask ourselves: How different is this ship? How tight? And how tight can it be and really be different from the traditional one?

We think that the process model, which we've just generally endorsed, is an important step ahead for our field. However, like any paradigm, it opens the door to blind allegiance, to rigidity, to loyalty tests, even to oppression. Some of these problems have already begun to afflict the process approach to writing. The ideas of a few key theorists—Graves, Calkins, Murray—have ossified into doctrine for too many teachers. But in writing, as in everything else, the map is not the territory, and the prophets are not the paradigm.

If a new paradigm starts to restrict teachers' choices, to narrow the range of things you're allowed to try in the classroom, something has gone astray. If the paradigm asks you to blindly follow the dictates of some guru, then it's no better than blindly following the dictates of dumb tradition. Indeed, how can we ask students to be responsible for their own work if we won't take responsibility for our own teaching?

The same principle applies in full to this book. In the coming chapters, we offer many concrete, explicit suggestions and activities for teaching writing. It's a complex and sensitive art, and only through specifics can we exemplify and elucidate what we're trying to say. However, readers should not mistake these suggestions for The Method of teaching writing, nor will wise teachers try to do all the things we mention. We hope that, instead, teachers will be inspired by one or more of these ideas to go ahead and create their own new activities for teaching writing, that they'll choose one or two aspects of the craft at a time to explore in more depth, and that they'll fill in the many gaps and blind spots we've neglected.

This book is not about becoming anyone's disciple or being converted to a pedagogical religion. It's about expanding your choices, your repertoire, your flexibility. We believe that teachers should have the widest possible range of strategies from which to draw in working with the students they have. While we do believe that some ideas and techniques are better than others—and we will continue to make our preferences clear—we recognize that for almost any imaginable situation with real kids in real schools, there will usually be several good ways for a teacher to behave. You don't have to possess the "right" technique; you just need one that works.

The danger we face in our field today, and it's now a serious threat, is the idea that there is only one right way to handle a given kid, a given grade level, a given chunk of curriculum, a given element of writing. This is not just wrong; it is profoundly, dangerously, insidiously wrong. It makes a joke of any connection we assert between kids' authorship of writing and our hopes that schools can build freedom, democracy, or liberation. If there's only one right way to teach writing, then all that's left for teachers to do is decide which church to join and then follow the doctrine.

Orthodoxy is the enemy. Donald Graves said this loud and clear a few years back, and what happened? Most people just ignored his warning and elevated *him* to the pantheon. So we'll say it again. Orthodoxy is the enemy. This is *our* one orthodoxy, but we sincerely hope it's the only one.

Chapter 3

A
Sample Integrated
Activity

We have said that if you practice the process model of writing in its pure form, you will inevitably be drawn into a more integrated, whole-language approach to teaching. You'll be designing and conducting classroom activities that aren't just writing, but that weave writing together with reading, speaking, listening, literature, and language study. You'll be creating integrated, holistic language activities that naturally implement many of the principles on the list of fifteen key ideas just outlined in Chapter 2.

We want to offer an example of one of these integrated activities right away, to show how some of these ideas can be brought together in the classroom. What follows is just an example (not an orthodoxy!), one of countless ways of manifesting the values and strategies of the process paradigm in teaching some real curriculum content to kids. The remainder of the book then breaks things down in more detail, showing how particular methods and conditions can be used to create rich and profitable writing experiences.

It's going to take a few pages to describe this activity. The fact is that the better activities, we've found, tend to be complex, involving a variety of materials and steps. In contrast, the school world is full of textbook writing assignments, story-starters and activity cards that are nothing if not brief: "You are a blob of whipped cream! Write about how you feel!" On a good day, a few kids may do brilliantly with such assignments, just by luck. But for most it's an unengaged exercise, filling up a page to someone else's specifications.

Integrated activities, on the other hand, are usually much more complicated, but they have the potential to engage students deeply in a topic and in a real exchange with other people about something that matters. Further, they truly demonstrate and enact the concept of writing as a tool of learning by creating a classroom environment of active, collaborative exploration.

If you are frustrated by short class periods and an overstuffed, sternly mandated curriculum, don't conclude that you can't possibly use such complex methods. Teachers are often very creative about coping with arbitrary and educationally unsound restrictions. Many parts of a larger activity are elastic and can be expanded or condensed to fit various time periods.

Actually, a number of these activities, on subjects across the curriculum, are described in the book. Chapter 6 includes one about writing and reading profiles of classmates; in Chapter 9, there's one on the AIDS epidemic; in Chapter 11, one explores the psychological issue of loss as a requirement of growth; Chapter 18 presents an integrated activity about some astronomical concepts and a social-science activity on the problem of loneliness in urban society. All of these activities follow underlying patterns and rhythms that will be readily apparent and adaptable to a wide variety of other content.

This initial example is simply a sequence of language activities for progressively deepening students' interest in and understanding of a piece of literature. We first learned this structure from Carla Asher and Marcie Wolfe of the New York City Writing Project. We are deeply grateful to them for opening up to us the whole range of possibilities that has evolved from this activity. The lesson starts off in a very traditional way, with students reading Hemingway's much-taught short story, "Hills Like White Elephants" (reprinted below). What follows the story is a schematic, step-by-step outline of the activity, which could be used with any poem or short story appropriate for a particular grade level. The complete version takes about five class periods, plus revision time outside class.

HILLS LIKE WHITE ELEPHANTS/ERNEST HEMINGWAY

The hills across the valley of the Ebro were long and white. On this side there was no shade and no trees and the station was between two lines of rails in the sun. Close against the side of the station there was the warm shadow of the building and a curtain, made of strings of bamboo beads, hung across the open door into the bar, to keep out flies. The American and the girl with him sat at a table in the shade, outside the building. It was very hot and the express from Barcelona would come in forty minutes. It stopped at this junction for two minutes and went on to Madrid.

"What should we drink?" the girl asked. She had taken off her hat and put it on the table.

"It's pretty hot," the man said.

"Let's drink beer."

"Dos cervezas," the man said into the curtain.

"Big ones?" a woman asked from the doorway.

"Yes. Two big ones."

The woman brought two glasses of beer and two felt pads. She put the felt pads and the beer glasses on the table and looked at the man and the girl. The girl was looking off at the line of hills. They were white in the sun and the country was brown and dry.

"They look like white elephants," she said.

"I've never seen one," the man drank his beer.

"No, you wouldn't have."

"I might have," the man said. "Just because you say I wouldn't have doesn't prove anything."

The girl looked at the bead curtain. "They've painted something on it," she said. "What does it say?"

"Anis del Toro. It's a drink."

"Could we try it?"

The man called "Listen" through the curtain. The woman came out from the bar.

"Four reales."

"We want two Anis del Toro."

"With water?"

"Do you want it with water?"

"I don't know," the girl said. "Is it good with water?"

"It's all right."

"You want them with water?" asked the woman.

"Yes, with water."

"It tastes like licorice," the girl said and put the glass down.

"That's the way with everything."

"Yes," said the girl. "Everything tastes of licorice. Especially all the things you've waited so long for, like absinthe."

"Oh, cut it out."

"You started it," the girl said. "I was being amused. I was having a fine time."

"Well, let's try to have a fine time."

"All right. I was trying. I said the mountains looked like white elephants. Wasn't that bright?"

"That was bright."

"I wanted to try this new drink. That's all we do, isn't it—look at things and try new drinks."

"I guess so."

The girl looked across at the hills.

"They're lovely hills," she said. "They don't really look like white elephants. I just meant the coloring of their skin through the trees."

"Should we have another drink?"

"All right."

The warm wind blew the bead curtain against the table.

"The beer's nice and cool," the man said.

"It's lovely," the girl said.

"It's really an awfully simple operation, Jig," the man said. "It's not really an operation at all."

The girl looked at the ground the table legs rested on.

"I know you wouldn't mind it, Jig. It's really not anything. It's just to let the air in."

The girl did not say anything.

"I'll go with you and I'll stay with you all the time. They just let the air in and then it's all perfectly natural."

"Then what will we do afterward?"

"We'll be fine afterward. Just like we were before."

"What makes you think so?"

"That's the only thing that bothers us. It's the only thing that's made us unhappy."

The girl looked at the bead curtain, put her hand out and took hold of two of the strings of beads.

"And you think then we'll be all right and be happy."

"I know we will. You don't have to be afraid. I've known lots of people that have done it."

"So have I," said the girl. "And afterward they were all so happy."

"Well," the man said, "if you don't want to you don't have to. I wouldn't have you do it if you didn't want to. But I know it's perfectly simple."

"And you really want to?"

"I think it's the best thing to do. But I don't want you to do it if you don't really want to."

"And if I do it you'll be happy and things will be like they were and you'll love me?"

"I love you now. You know I love you."

"I know. But if I do it, then it will be nice again if I say things are like white elephants, and you'll like it?"

"I'll love it. I love it now but I just can't think about it. You know how I get when I worry."

"If I do it you won't ever worry."

"I won't worry about that because it's perfectly simple."

"Then I'll do it. Because I don't care about me."

"What do you mean?"

"I don't care about me."

"Well, I care about you."

"Oh, yes. But I don't care about me. And I'll do it and then everything will be fine."

"I don't want you to do it if you feel that way."

The girl stood up and walked to the end of the station. Across, on the other side, were fields of grain and trees along the banks of the Ebro. Far away, beyond the river, were mountains. The shadow of a cloud moved across the field of grain and she saw the river through the trees.

"And we could have all this," she said. "And we could have everything and every day we make it more impossible."

"What did you say?"

"I said we could have everything."

"We can have everything."

"No, we can't."

"We can have the whole world."

"No, we can't."

"We can go everywhere."

"No, we can't. It isn't ours any more."

"It's ours."

"No, it isn't. And once they take it away, you never get it back."

"But they haven't taken it away."

"We'll wait and see."

"Come on back in the shade," he said. "You mustn't feel that way."

"I don't feel any way," the girl said. "I just know things."

"I don't want you to do anything that you don't want to do—"

"Nor that isn't good for me," she said. "I know. Could we have another beer."

"All right. But you've got to realize—"

"I realize," the girl said. "Can't we stop talking?"

They sat down at the table and the girl looked across at the hills on the dry side of the valley and the man looked at her and at the table.

"You've got to realize," he said, "that I don't want you to do it if you don't want to. I'm perfectly willing to go through with it if it means anything to you."

"Doesn't it mean anything to you? We could get along."

"Of course it does. But I don't want anybody but you. I don't want any one else. And I know it's perfectly simple."

"Yes, you know it's perfectly simple."

"It's all right for you to say that, but I do know it."

"Would you do something for me now?"

"I'd do anything for you."

"Would you please please please please please please please stop talking?"

He did not say anything but looked at the bags against the wall of the station. There were labels on them from all the hotels where they had spent nights.

"But I don't want you to," he said. "I don't care anything about it."

"I'll scream," said the girl.

The woman came out through the curtains with two glasses of beer and put them down on the damp felt pads. "The train comes in five minutes," she said.

"What did she say?" asked the girl.

"That the train is coming in five minutes."

The girl smiled brightly at the woman, to thank her.

"I'd better take the bags over to the other side of the station," the man said. She smiled at him.

"All right. Then come back and we'll finish the beer."

He picked up the two heavy bags and carried them around the station to the other tracks. He looked up the tracks but could not see the train. Coming back, he walked through the barroom, where people waiting for the train were drinking. He drank an Anis at the bar and looked at the people. They were all waiting reasonably for the train. He went out through the bead curtain. She was sitting at the table and smiled at him.

"Do you feel better?" he asked.

"I feel fine," she said. "There's nothing wrong with me. I feel fine."

1. *Reading.* Students read the story silently, in class.

2. *Writing.* Students write a free, speculative reaction for three or four minutes—a true stream-of-consciousness "free write," in which each writer tries to make a direct connection between the thoughts going through her mind and the surface of the page. Comments are invited on all kinds of reactions to the story: feelings, distractions, awareness of one's own reading process, reminders of real-life events, prior related experience, whatever comes to mind.

3. *Oral reading.* A very few students (two or three) are asked to read from their papers just to show the diversity and range of responses to the story. The accuracy or correctness of people's reactions is not to be debated now.

4. *Small-group discussion.* Students gather in groups of four or five to discuss the story for fifteen minutes or so. They are free to talk about any aspects of the story or issues it raised for them. The only instructions are that everyone in each group should have a turn and that one representative from each group will later report briefly on the group's discussion.

5. *Reports to the large group.* Students regather and listen as spokespersons for each small group report. The teacher may wish to point out the wide variety of approaches taken, particular polarities or controversies emerging, and perhaps the fact that students are becoming invested in the story.

6. *Writing an assertion.* Students are now asked to reread and study the story with this task in mind: "Write a one-sentence assertion—a statement of one thing you believe to be true about this story. This may be an assertion about one of the characters, about the author's intention as you understand it, about the times represented in the story, about your own emotional reaction to the story, about the overall value or quality of the story, or about any other idea this story brings to mind for you. The key point here is for you to find something you're sure about, something you feel you could prove to someone else or convince someone to think about this story."

7. *Oral reading.* Read around the whole class, giving everyone a chance to state their single-sentence assertion aloud. No debating or evaluating of people's ideas is allowed now. Notice and enjoy how finely polished many of these statements are. In fact, the students have inadvertently been led to create some real thesis statements.

8. *Guided imagery.* Note: This next step, which was not a part of the original N.Y.C.W.P. design, purposely loops off in a somewhat different direction, asking students to put aside their discursive analysis of the story and turn to a more intuitive approach. The goal is to provide a second thesis statement, one that's derived more from personal experience and connection than from academic analysis of the story. By the end of step 12, each student will have developed two starts: one for an expository/analytical piece and one for a more personal/expressive piece. Teachers who wish to steer this assignment in only one of these directions may naturally omit the other strand of activities. However, if there's time for both, each of the two directions is likely to influence the other in valuable ways. For more explanation of guided imagery, see Chapter 11.

The teacher can use words like the following to conduct the guided imagery:

Let's put aside our assertions for a while, go back, and think about the story in another way. For this activity, all we need is our minds, and so you can put down your pencils and clear off the table in front of you. What we want to do now is use our mind's eye to look back to the

---

time and place of the story, recreate that scene in our minds, and walk around in it. And so, as a way to begin, I would invite you to relax, take a couple of deep breaths, and close your eyes . . . and settle back in your chair . . . as much as you are able . . . and let your arms drop and hang loose at your sides . . . and take a deep breath . . . and let it out . . . and as you relax you may become aware . . . of the sound of students outside in the hall . . . or the sounds of people getting comfortable in the room . . . and you can notice the feeling in your hands where they are resting . . . and as you relax you may notice the gentle movement of air moving through your nose as you breathe . . . a slight coolness as you inhale . . . a gentle warmth as you breathe out. . . .

And as you continue to relax . . . you can create in your mind's eye . . . a vivid picture of the scene in Hemingway's story . . . the parched, brown valley in Spain . . . and you can place yourself in that time and place . . . and you can now walk through the scene . . . toward the train station up ahead . . . and you may become aware of the sand crunching under your feet as you walk . . . and you can feel the hot desert air against your cheek . . . and as you look up across the dry valley . . . you can notice, on the far horizon . . . rolling, whitish hills . . . that slightly resemble the backs of elephants . . . and as you continue walking . . . you become aware of the glint of the midday sun from the steel track rail beside you. . . . And as you come to the station . . . you step up onto the old wooden platform . . . and as you walk along it you notice the creaking of the boards under your feet . . . and looking down toward the other end of the station . . . you see a small restaurant . . . a cantina, with a few round tables sitting outside its door . . . and sitting at the only occupied table are a man and a woman . . . and you stop and watch them from a distance . . . and you are aware of tension in their faces as they talk . . . and discomfort in the movements of their bodies. . . .

The woman's face is pained . . . and the man is leaning toward her, talking rapidly . . . and you realize that they are having a misunderstanding or disagreement . . . a disagreement that is profound and life-changing . . . and you find that you can connect with the feeling of their conversation. . . .

And as you connect with that feeling . . . you may find that you are reminded . . . of a particular misunderstanding or disagreement in your own life . . . perhaps a disagreement very different from the one in the story . . . but with some of the same feelings . . . a time when you and someone you loved came into conflict . . . a time when the two of you had an important conversation . . . that comes back to your mind now . . . a conversation that occurred in a particular time and place . . .

that you can now begin to recreate in detail . . . using your mind's eye . . . and now you can recreate that other time and place . . . where you and another person have had a disagreement . . . and you can return to that scene . . . and join with that moment . . . and now, for a few moments . . . you may relive that important experience from your own life. . . .

And now, taking all the time you need . . . prior to leaving this time and place . . . you may gather up the details of what you are seeing and hearing and experiencing there . . . and you can bring these details with you . . . as you leave that experience behind . . . and begin to return to this time and place . . . and to our work together.

9. *Listing.* "Now you can pick up your pencils again and make some notes about what you have just been seeing and feeling and hearing—just a list of words, for now—feelings, images, colors, sounds, whatever you have just been experiencing. No need to write prose now, just list."

10. *Writing.* Students have now experienced this story in a number of ways and should be well prepared to write about it. The teacher may suggest that students "review your varied responses to the story, including your assertion and your more personal reflection, and pick whatever topic or idea seems most urgent, most interesting, or most valuable to you. Anything is appropriate: an essay, a poem, another story, a missing scene from this story, a reminiscence about a similar experience in your own life, a character sketch that comes to mind, a related piece of your own autobiography, whatever. We'll work on some rough drafts now, taking thirty minutes of class time to get something started." (Note: In this version of the activity, the aim of the assignment is to open up the range of possible student writings as widely as possible. But if the teacher wishes to focus students' work onto a narrower topic, she could easily do so by shifting the instructions at this stage.)

11. *Share in small groups.* Students read their first drafts aloud to one another in groups of three, offering each other comments on the general direction and feel of each piece.

12. *Share in large group.* A few volunteers share their drafts in the whole group. The teacher tries to tease out volunteers who will represent the widest possible range of approaches to the topic. Comments at this stage center on the meaning and content of the writing.

13. *Revision.* Students now create a full second draft outside of class. (A week may be involved, with some in-class and some out-of-class work, for the remaining steps of the activity. However, not all classes during the week need to be used for the work.)

14. *Return to peer groups.* Students read aloud or submit their second draft in writing and receive detailed feedback from their peer group on both the content and form of the piece, as directed by a response guide-sheet provided by the teacher. One of the rules for this stage is that every-one must suggest improvements to others and receive some for themselves: the assumption is that everyone's draft can somehow get better, and so it is not OK for group members to simply say, "Oh, this one is perfect the way it is."

15. *Publishing.* The final, polished pieces resulting from this project are bound into a class booklet called "White Elephants," and copies are shared with other classes reading the story.

16. *Debriefing the lesson.* The group discusses the whole lesson, each of its steps and stages. Students can use this as an opportunity to sum-marize their understanding of the story and the issues it has raised for them as well as to review procedural matters and talk about any changes they'd like to make in the use of peer groups, sharing, and the rest in future projects of this type.

We think that this activity is a good example of Hillocks' environmental mode, the kind of instruction associated with the highest degree of student growth in writing. In it, the teacher organizes, structures, and facilitates so that students engage the content of the lesson (in this case, a short story and the issues it treats) at a deep level. The activity consists of a series of steps that students take to become further and further immersed in the story and the active process of exploring its meanings for them. And notice, just as our comments earlier suggested—and as Hillocks' research recommends—the teacher "teaches" nothing in this lesson: instead, she is facilitating students' learning, structuring an environment in which that exploration can proceed efficiently.

Indeed, whenever we've taught this lesson or observed others using it, we have been impressed by the depth of the engagement it engenders, regardless of whether the students are high-school kids or adults. There is passionate, eloquent involvement, expression, and exchange over im-portant issues: abortion, the domination and manipulation of women by men, the nature of love, the need for trust, the problem of loneliness, the need to stand up for one's beliefs, dependency—not to mention a whole range of more literary questions, including the unique nature of Heming-way's art, key internal features of the story itself, the accuracy of Hem-ingway's depiction of certain times, places, and people.

We also hope it is clear that the underlying structure of this activity—the rhythmic alternation between speaking, listening, writing, and read-ing; the variation between solitary, small-group, and whole-group activity; the focus both within and outside the text; the act of looking both inside and outside the classroom in which the story is being studied—is applicable to any story or poem, any article, and almost any piece of written content. And there is nothing sacred at all about the *order* of the shifts and rhythms in this plan; depending upon the material at hand, it may work just as well to completely rearrange the steps and stages. As you look at other integrated activities in the book, you'll see our own ways of varying the selection and sequence of ingredients.

Part II

Creating
a Community of
Writers

Chapter 4

Climate in the Classroom

After ten years of working with teachers of writing at all grade levels from kindergarten through college, we now realize that one particular set of understandings and skills comes first. And this most crucial family of concepts has nothing to do with NAEP reports, or Hillocks' environmental mode, or Graves' studio-conference methods, or the doctrines of the National Writing Project. No, the field that writing teachers need to understand first, before anything else, is group dynamics. Our strong sense of this priority reflects two insights. One is that we are all teachers of *students* first, before we are teachers of any subject. And second, writing, real writing, requires that teachers create a special kind of group climate in their classrooms.

LITERACY AS A SOCIAL PHENOMENON

Recent research on the ways people learn to read and write has strongly shown that *literacy is socially constructed*. Both educators and the general public have suffered for too long under the delusion that reading and writing are essentially solitary skills that develop best through isolated, individualistic practice. This mistaken view is understandable only if we focus narrowly on those brief, isolated segments of the reading and writing processes when a person is actually decoding a text or penning a draft. However, the research has reminded us, among other things, that most linguistic learning is not solitary at all, but profoundly social, arising out of a rich and complex web of immediate, living needs, purposes, meanings, relationships.

Young children learn how to speak, for example, not to prove their mastery of the abstract rules of grammar but to get real things done in their here-and-now world: to get talked to, fed, picked up, and loved—

that is, to communicate in increasingly detailed and satisfying ways with the people in their lives. By the same token, when we read, we don't do it to prove that we can decode a certain chunk of print, but to serve some real, usually socially constructed need that we have: to keep up on current events, to understand what a lease says, to enjoy a salacious anecdote about a celebrity, to learn how to operate a new appliance, to see what Grandma's letter says, and so forth. Similarly, almost any piece of real writing originates in some real social purpose and, after being composed, is sent to some audience in the real social world to accomplish its purpose.

The large body of research on emergent literacy developed over the past several years has demonstrated the deep sociolinguistic roots of growth in language ability by looking at the development of three-, four-, and five-year-old children. How is it, linguists like Bissex, Halliday, and Brice Heath have asked, that some children come to school already reading and writing at a dazzling level of skill? It turns out that these children have had effective, deeply embedded language-learning experiences in the interpersonal contexts of their lives; in other words, many of their early social experiences have helped them learn how to get meaning from print and put meaning into print of their own.

Of course, children don't join in such experiences with the hope of acquiring linguistic skill; they join in them because they are meaningful, useful, and fun. One child creates a neighborhood newspaper; another posts a sign on his bedroom-hideout door ("SKULS GANG—KEEPOUT"); another writes a "story" completely with pretend letters that he can later use as a cue for storytelling; a two-and-a-half-year-old inquiring reporter interviews her father on the topic "What you want from Santa, Dad?", carefully listing the responses in imitation cursive writing. In each of these events, the children involved stretch their linguistic capacities.

These kinds of social contexts that teach literacy—the talk that goes on in families, children's games and play activities, sibling bickering and negotiating, storytelling events, sharing and discussing books, playing with drawing and writing—*these are not just backdrops of language learning but their driving force.* In other words, the social context is not just the setting for language growth, but its cause and its means.

THE SOCIAL CONTEXT FOR WRITING
IN JUNIOR AND SENIOR HIGH

Why is classroom climate just as influential in teaching writing to secondary students as it is for the younger children in emergent literacy studies? One reason lies in the profoundly social nature of writing itself. Just as with small children, the writing of teenagers inevitably puts them in relation to others in a community, a family, or a social group—registering a complaint, taking a stance on an issue, asking for help, sharing a piece of one's autobiography, or even revealing a vulnerability. Writing does this in a different way than speech, for it is not evanescent but permanent and forms a record, something with *legal* standing. To "put it in writing" means to make a commitment. Secrets can end up in the wrong hands. Writing can mean defining a history, keeping a log, producing a dissertation, apologizing to a friend—all social acts. In school, writing may reveal your weaknesses in a way that a spoken answer or a multiple-choice test doesn't show. If your essay is read aloud in class and heard by your enemies, you may be in for unmerciful razzing or worse, so it often seems wise to play it safe.

As a consequence of these social issues, most older students feel personally vulnerable about their writing. Teachers often tell their students, "I'm not judging you as a *person* when I grade your writing," but that ignores a large piece of reality. Other people, often the students' parents and friends, *do* connect grades and performance with the student's essential being. The student herself may do so. And if the writing is any good, it involves an engagement and a voice that *does* reflect the writer's deeper self. Many of the same teachers who say they aren't judging the student personally find it extremely difficult to risk their own egos by submitting their writing to the scrutiny of their students or professional colleagues, not to mention editors and more distant audiences. Asking for engaged, thoughtful, inventive writing in any classroom is thus asking students to take risks, to contribute their own initiative, and to take responsibility—all difficult enough for teenagers ordinarily, and especially challenging when the prevailing social setting makes one feel so vulnerable.

Along with risks, junior high and high school students sense deep-seated contradictions in the expectations surrounding their writing. Consider the traditional teacher expectation that students are supposed to take initiative in their work, particularly work such as writing. Since teachers give the assignments, determine grades, and set the rules, *they* are the ones with the real responsibility and initiative. Highly structured formulae for essays and the intensive marking of grammar errors show that the teacher is the one with the most responsibility. These practices implicitly contradict any assertions the teacher might make about students taking more responsibility for their work and imply that students aren't really able or allowed to make any of the *important* decisions. Indeed, the way writing is usually taught is a sad but undeniable reminder that most classrooms are thoroughly authoritarian social structures where the first priority is for students to be passive and orderly, to follow directions, and to accept the rules and values dictated by the teacher.

Students looking ahead to grinding out ETS writing samples or state writing competency exams may well feel that their own initiative is quite irrelevant to writing: "Just show me what to do so I can pass the test and get into a good college." The trend toward measurement, accountability, and teacher specification of every criterion of performance all contradict any sense that writing involves exploration of ideas, questioning, or developing individual points of view. Complex scoring rubrics and preset criteria imply instead that there's one "right" answer to every question, and that writing means coming as close as possible to concocting that right answer.

At the same time, our culture places special value on originality, creativity, and newness in expression. Most teachers—and other readers—want to be surprised in some way, to discover something, and to get a sense of the *writer's* discovery as well. In still another way, then, writing in school presents students with a set of contradictions about which they usually have little conscious awareness but plenty of unconscious conflict.

Students experience these contradictions so extensively that they usually need clear, repeated signals to convince them that a teacher sincerely wants them to control their own work. For example, a teacher may say to students, "Now I want you to express your own ideas," but if many other conditions (like underlying, unchallenged school norms and expectations) tell them that this is not really wanted, then kids rarely believe the spoken instructions. When positive encouragement is repeatedly contradicted by implicit discouragements, it becomes harder and harder for students to listen to the spoken words. Only if the teacher builds into the classroom context clear and congruent encouragement for putting down honest ideas and questions rather than set formulae for producing "acceptable" products will the message become believable.

So here's our hypothesis: what students learn about writing depends more than anything else on the context in which they write—that is, on the ways in which writing is used in the classroom group; the attitudes of the teacher toward the students and toward writing itself; relationships among the students; the students' sense of what their teacher thinks about them; why they are writing; how people treat the ideas and beliefs expressed in their writing; the tone of the room, the school, and community; and the purposes for learning implicitly expressed by that community.

Whether you are conscious of it or not, your classroom is a fertile social context for literacy learning. And if the linguists are right that the social context is the driving force behind literacy acquisition, then *the social context of your English/language-arts classroom is the most pow-erful and important variable you can experiment with.* More important than what textbook or speller or dictionary to use; more important than what kinds of assignments to give; more important than how to set up cumulative writing folders; more important than the criteria by which you assign kids to peer response groups; more important than ''teaching Graves'' versus teaching Calkins or Hillocks. More important than any-thing.

WHAT EVERY WRITING TEACHER SHOULD KNOW ABOUT GROUP DYNAMICS

Most teachers know that climate has a tremendous influence on student learning, and we all use a wide range of conscious and unconscious means to create a classroom that reflects our own personality and our assumptions about how kids learn. Now, recognizing that social context is our most powerful available tool in literacy development, it seems important to go beyond our everyday, seat-of-the-pants climate-setting behaviors and be-come much more conscious and analytical about the social atmosphere that we create as teachers. For teachers who want to understand and steer the climate of their classrooms more actively, there is a large body of both theoretical and practical literature about nurturing the development of learning groups. This literature on group processes offers specific guidance that can be translated quite easily to the special concerns of English/language-arts instruction.

Indeed, if you have already been experimenting with some elements of the process model of writing instruction in your classroom, chances are you have already been implicitly reinventing a wheel called group dy-namics. Implementing peer editing groups, establishing a writing work-shop, encouraging individual students to read their work aloud to the whole class, and trying to understand the outcomes of these methods—all these things implicitly engage you in the study, or at least the firsthand experience, of some complex group processes.

So it seems wise and natural to look at the field of group dynamics to see what it can offer writing teachers. The only limitation we can think of to studying this new field is that delving into it cold is not the same as searching out this special literature in the heat of a pressing professional puzzle—when you are already grappling with some specific group issue in your daily teaching life. We ourselves began to directly study group dynamics after we kept bumping into certain recurrent problems and patterns in our own teaching. Finally, we got tired of recreating the most elementary concepts, solutions, and practices that others had long since devised and tested with a variety of learners and we started reading about them in the literature of group dynamics.

But we have never regretted our own redundancy and seeming inefficiency, because we really owned our reinvented concepts about group behavior, even though there turned out to be little that was original about them. Like us, you may need to invent and monitor your own ideas about group process as you go about the business of teaching writing, rather than just reading someone else's summary of his own hard-earned thoughts.

Obviously, this book is no place for a complete review of group dynamics, and our bibliography lists a number of delightful resources for those who wish to study the field more thoroughly. Here, we want to concentrate on four elements that have been very helpful to us as writing teachers, and that are accordingly woven into the structure of many of the ideas and activities in this book:

1. Task and maintenance activity.
2. Functional roles of students and teachers.
3. Stages of group development.
4. Ingredients of group development.

Task and Maintenance Activity

One of the simplest and most fundamental constructs in the study of groups is the distinction between task and maintenance activity. "Task" work is defined as anything people do that is directly connected to the formal and official purpose of the group itself. This is hardly alien language to educators, of course. In schools we commonly refer to "time-on-task" behavior, when student directly engage in reading, writing, discussing, or doing dittos about official subject matter in the curriculum guide, and we tend to worry quite a bit about students' "off-task" behavior. Indeed, if some of today's time-on-task gurus could somehow observe Shakespeare composing Macbeth, they would undoubtedly mark it down as "off-task behavior" each time the Bard lifted his quill off the page and stared at the ceiling.

In the field of group dynamics, however, off-task behavior is called "maintenance," in the sense of its being socioemotional or interpersonal activity that maintains people's ability to work together. This includes everything people in a group can do that's not task work: eating, gossiping, moving furniture, borrowing pencils from each other, discussing rules of behavior, dividing up tasks to be done, facilitating people's opportunities to participate in various activities, expressing and responding to feelings, and so forth. Maintenance activities might be described as all the complex support behavior necessary to make task behavior work.

Obviously, some groups can get bogged down or sidetracked in certain maintenance behavior, like eating or gossiping, to the degree that no task work gets done (or people just gain weight). But in group dynamics the category of maintenance isn't viewed as something bad, something to be curtailed or eliminated (as we often classify many alleged "off-task" behaviors in schools). On the contrary, maintenance is normal and necessary whenever humans try to work in groups; it not only meets the creature needs but provides the social lubrication that makes collaborative effort possible.

Think of any effective group you have been in and you will recollect a mixture of task and maintenance behavior from any session or meeting that comes to mind. At some points there may have been donuts, chit-chat, hugging, thermostat adjusting, pep talking, haggling over the agenda, joking—and during the same session, you may also recall a lot of cold, hard work that got done. Indeed, group dynamics theory says that if there isn't *enough* maintenance activity or if it's not the right kind, the task outcomes of any group will be compromised.

This all may seem pretty obvious, but in classrooms we rarely honor this reality of human life—in fact, we too often try to quash it. We put kids into groups of four to read their writing aloud, for example, and then act surprised and rebuke them when they use the first few minutes in the group for some transitional chit-chat ("off-task behavior"). Such a response violates our knowledge of how human beings work in groups. Indeed, peer editing is one of the most tried and most abandoned methods associated with the process approach, and the key reason for its "failure" in many classrooms is the failure of the teacher to comprehend and steer the natural group processes that arise in this kind of social structure.

Balancing task and maintenance activities supports the teaching of writing. Students need trusting classroom relationships so they can serve as an audience for one another, and so they will want to write for each other. Teachers of students from sixth grade up often observe that their kids hesitate to share work in class and want only the teacher to read what they have written, thereby cutting themselves off from the larger community, a vital source of ideas, support, and feedback. But the special sort of trust necessary for sharing serious writing is developed in important ways through maintenance activity—personal talk, laughter, learning about one another's backgrounds and experiences. The practical activities described in Chapters 6 and 7 offer ways to harness this force (using writing along the way) rather than repress it.

Functional Roles of Students and Teachers

In our pre-service teacher training, most of us probably remember some instruction in the various roles, both constructive and obstructive, that students and teachers play in groups. We may even have done a little bit of role playing, with some of us acting as gatekeepers, others as encouragers, and still others as harmonizers or saboteurs. In our workaday school lives, we all have some tacit awareness of the roles individual students take in groups. After all, we may talk insightfully about the ways in which a single kid—often a problem student—affects the flow of events and behavior in a class. But beyond this kind of occasional insight, most of us do not consciously study or take very seriously the patterned roles that people assume in groups. As a result, we may misunderstand what's going on in our classes or miss opportunities to exert more influence on how a class develops.

Experts have categorized the ways people participate in all sorts of groups—whether they be corporate committees, social organizations, or school classrooms—and while their lists may vary somewhat, a typical one, from Philip Hanson's *Learning Through Groups*, is shown in Figure 4–1. As you can see, the list highlights the importance of maintenance activity.

The force of most of these roles is obviously exerted not through lectures, drills, or quizzes, but in participatory activities (if a class includes no such activities, the roles are enacted through disruptive behavior or are relegated to social interactions outside the classroom). What the list reminds us is that, in our culture, such behaviors are rarely taught directly or even talked about. Therefore, in addition to simply *using* participatory activities, we need to teach students the constructive roles that make them work well through guided practice and self-evaluation. Fortunately, it is altogether natural and appropriate to gain such practice through group work on writing. In Chapter 14, we'll explore in detail the steps in training students to take responsible and active roles as they learn to use revising and peer editing groups.

The teacher's role is equally crucial in teaching writing. Plenty of classroom inquiry examines student behavior. We need also to look at several particular *teacher* roles that contribute most to make writing classes into mature and effective working groups. If you read the research on teaching writing (the sort of principles outlined in Chapter 2), you must conclude that the traditional authoritarian/presentational teacher role is not of much use. Hillocks' and others' research has shown convincingly that the presentational approach, when the teacher acts as a dispenser of information and precepts about writing, is profoundly ineffective.

Figure 4–1 *Categorizing Participation in Groups (from Hanson,* Learning Through Groups)

TASK ROLES*

FUNCTION	DESCRIPTION
1. Stating or clarifying the problem or task	Proposing goals and deciding what needs to be accomplished; defining a group problem; agreeing on a specific task.
2. Establishing procedures	Asking for and offering suggestions about the best way to proceed; organizing the group to work on tasks more effectively; agreeing on rules to be followed.
3. Asking for and giving information	Requesting and giving facts, opinions, feelings, and feedback; searching for ideas and alternatives. This may involve going out of the group for resource material or inviting experts into the group to provide information—not for answers to the group's problems.
4. Summarizing	Listing the various things that have been done or said; restating in a clear and brief form the ideas that have been expressed in the group. Summarizing may clarify the status of the group and provide some direction.
5. Keeping the group on topic	Helping the group to remain focused on a particular topic or task; directing the group's attention to the problem at hand.
6. Integrating	Pulling together different pieces of information (ideas, opinions, suggestions) to form meaningful wholes; helping members to build on one another's work.
7. Evaluating	Helping the group to critique its progress, the quality of its decisions, and the effectiveness of its feedback.

*See Benne & Sheets (1948) for original conceptualization of group-member roles.

(Continued)

Figure 4–1 (Continued)

MAINTENANCE ROLES

FUNCTION	DESCRIPTION
1. Gatekeeping	Bringing silent members into group action; aiding in keeping communication channels open and facilitating the participation of others. (One also can *close* the gate of a talkative member to allow others a chance to speak.)
2. Checking for understanding	Helping people to communicate more clearly, particularly when they are not understanding each other; finding out if everyone is clear on what has been said; clearing up confusion.
3. Giving support and encouragement to others	Accepting or not accepting other people's opinions in a manner that causes them to think about the disagreement and not in terms of personal rejection; encouraging others to express ideas and opinions; being responsive to others; giving empathy and emotional support to others.
4. Helping others to test their assumptions	Checking to see if decisions are made on the basis of irrelevant data or false assumptions and determining whether these ideas or prejudices influence members' behaviors toward one another; testing the feasibility of ideas ("will it work?").
5. Participating-observing	Observing one's own behavior while participating actively in the group and observing the behavior of others in order to provide feedback.
6. Checking for feelings	Facilitating the expression of feelings; asking others how they feel when appropriate and volunteering one's own feelings.
7. Mediating	Attempting to settle disagreements or differences between group members in a constructive way; trying to bring about a compromise if actual differences cannot be resolved.

Instead, what the research clearly calls for is environmental-mode instruction—that is, for the teacher to act as a *facilitator* of inquiry. Working in the facilitator role, the teacher tries to systematically arrange materials, activities, and people in such a way that students are immersed in powerful inductive experiences. The facilitator recognizes that teaching is not learning, that learning is something that occurs inside of learners when conditions are right; and she sees the art of her work not in her own personal display, but in arranging those conditions for students. She recognizes that an informational performance in front of a large group sitting in straight rows is rarely related to learning of any sort, and especially not to an activity like writing. Again, this is exactly what Hillocks' comparison of presentational to other modes of instruction confirms.

The only missing link in Hillocks' description of environmental-mode instruction is the word "facilitator" itself. Perhaps the reason why writing experts don't openly use this term is because it smacks of the supposedly "touchy-feely" era of the 1960s, a period that many people now mistakenly believe to have been suffused with radical, permissive innovation in schools. But "facilitator" is no dirty word, nor do we think the Rogerian branch of humanistic psychology from which it derives can ever go out of style, though it is much misunderstood. In fact, Carl Rogers was one of the great experts on group dynamics, and his work explains clearly that a facilitator is not a mere permissivist. In a writing class, the facilitator-teacher must design assignments that preserve meaningful choices and a sense of authorship for students, create prewriting activities that help students gather and organize material for writing, set up classroom conditions for drafting, provide audiences to give feedback to writers, find channels for the publishing of student work, be an audience herself, and many other things. These are challenging, creative tasks for an educator, requiring professional expertise that reaches far beyond the recitation of rhetorical rules and grammatical precepts.

Yet a writing teacher is not just a facilitator. Indeed, one crucial aspect of a writing teacher's role is flexibility: a teacher should be able to play a variety of different roles in the classroom, to adjust his behavior to a wide range of thinking and feeling events that may occur with individual students and the group, rather than being locked into a single way of responding or behaving. Just the self-evident fact that a big part of a writing teacher's job involves reading a wide variety of written work by students tells us that flexibility is vital; the teacher has to be able to respond appropriately to every different sort of person and work. We have written elsewhere about some of the other roles that we think teachers need to be aware of and use, and we will examine uses for some of them in later chapters of this book as well. Among these are the observer role, the presenter role (yes, there is a time and place for information-giving, and when we use it we should be as effective as possible), and especially the role of model, about which we want to say a few words here.

Earlier in this chapter, we talked about the double-binds, mixed messages, and schizophrenic signals students experience in schools. The most important insight we've ever gained into this problem comes from Richard Bandler and John Grinder, who have written extensively about the language used by people in the helping professions. They put it quite flatly: if a person offers you two contradictory messages, one verbal and the other one nonverbal, the one that will be believed and acted upon at the deepest levels is the nonverbal one. This means that as a teacher what you do is immeasurably more important than what you say. This challenges you to become aware of the fit between what you say and what you do—to see yourself as a model. If you tell students that writing is fun, you should write with them and have fun; if you tell them that writing is a tool of thinking, you should let them see how you use the tool to think, yourself. If you want students to learn to edit their own papers, you shouldn't always locate their errors for them, but rather show them how you find your own. If you believe that content is more important than form, then you should spend most of your teacherly time and ink on responding to content. Think much more of what you are modeling in the classroom, and worry much less about what you tell.

Stages of Group Development

An important insight from group dynamics is that groups, like individual people, develop through a series of identifiable stages from the beginning to the end of their life. Teachers have long been sensitive to some rhythms of group development, and even the sad old maxim "Don't smile until Christmas" reflects an implicit, if defeatist, developmental theory of groups. But the formal models from group dynamics have more constructive insights to offer. Most of the models currently in use have four or five stages, and we reproduce three of the better-known versions side by side on page 59. (The Jones and Charrier models are discussed in Philip Hanson's book, *Learning Through Groups*.)

Of course no classroom group of junior or senior high school kids ever develops through the neat, linear, nonrecursive steps suggested by these models. Indeed, we know that any scheme of fixed developmental stages, whatever its focus, can only be a crude generalization; such models are really more like metaphors that help us understand learning a bit better. But given this caveat, the developmental models point to several important

THREE MODELS FOR GROUP DEVELOPMENT		
RICHARD AND PATRICIA SCHMUCK	JOHN JONES	GEORGE CHARRIER
1. Psychological membership	1. Dependence	1. Polite 2. Why we're here
2. Establishing shared influence	2. Conflict	3. Bid for power
3. Pursuing goals	3. Cohesion	4. Constructive
4. Self-renewal	4. Interdependence	5. Esprit

conditions or activities necessary for creating a supportive group in which risks can be taken, real ideas and criticisms shared, and writing thus learned effectively.

Each of the three models, despite differences in terminology, says that in the early days of a group, individual members need to express their presence and make their needs known, to find an active, meaningful role in the constellation of the group. This vital, basic, developmental task simply cannot be accomplished if the teacher dominates all the time and talk, and no one else has a chance to show herself. Using the various steps of these models, we can notice how a teacher may inadvertently work against the early stages of group development when he:

- Punishes all forms of socializing that arise in the group.
- Refuses to share responsibility with the students.
- Has to dominate and "win" in every encounter with students' expressed needs.
- Quashes any student bid for power that might arise.
- Sees conflict as negative and tries to suppress it.

Indeed, looking at these models, it is not hard to see why few classroom groups ever grow very far, even though most teachers sincerely wish their classes would reach the higher stages of self-renewal, interdependence, esprit.

The task-maintenance dichotomy connects in an interesting way with developmental stages. Consider the following relationships:

DEVELOPMENTAL STAGE	LEVEL OF ACTIVITIES
1. Psychological membership	High maintenance Low task
2. Establishing shared influence	High maintenance High task
3. Pursuing goals	Low maintenance High task
4. Self-renewal (end of group life span)	High maintenance Low task

This construct offers a number of interesting and practical implications for the growth of a group from initial into later stages. In general, it suggests that there is a predictable and natural pattern, a kind of productivity curve correlating the amount of task work done with the achievement of socioemotional or maintenance functions of the group. By implication, if maintenance doesn't occur as needed, the task work will be stunted.

These models suggest actions that teachers can take to move into and through the early stages of group development. If we agree with Richard and Patricia Schmuck, two of the outstanding authorities in this field, that the core issue of Stage 1 groups indeed is psychological membership, then we can devise classroom activities (with writing, of course) that help students develop strong feelings of membership, of being recognized, known, and valued in the group. Many of the activities and assignments described in the coming chapters are directly applicable to this sort of membership building. In turn, if we agree that sharing power and authority is the next issue in a developing group, then we need to implement activities and structures that genuinely diffuse leadership and responsibility throughout the classroom community. And so on.

A bit more challenging is the assertion of many group theorists that conflict is an inevitable stage of development without which a group can never become fully mature or genuinely cohesive. This does not mean that teachers should provoke or welcome conflict, but that when conflict does inevitably occur—in the form of disputes between students, challenges to the teacher's authority, breakdowns in morale, failure to follow agreed-upon rules—the way these events are handled can advance the development of the group. Yes, we are saying that conflict is an opportunity. We have come to agree with Bandler and Grinder that *nothing that can happen in a group is bad*, once you understand how every event can enrich the history of a group and move it toward a higher level of development. The only "wrong" thing a teacher can do is try to smother, suppress, or gloss over conflict—which, of course, is exactly what most teachers are trained to do.

Nurturing group development helps to teach writing. Be aware that brand-new groups don't usually get much task work done until they work out interpersonal issues. It will take time for small groups to reach the stage at which they can help each other effectively revise their writing, so don't expect too much too soon or shuffle groups too often. It will also take time before individual students feel safe enough to share deeply felt, highly personal writing with the whole class in oral reading. This recognition of the gradual process of group development goes against some of our most usual teacher behavior, of course: in fact, we often struggle valiantly trying to overcome such natural group development patterns in school. But we must accept that the fundamental task of the first stage in group work is socioemotional growth and so we must concentrate on devising structured activites—including writing—that will allow students to accomplish the developmental tasks of this stage promptly and fully, so that they will soon be ready to move on to the next.

As a group moves into the second stage of its development, conflict may develop, either about the content of students' writing or about the procedures being used in the classroom. Help students learn how to speak up rather than passively drop out if something is bothering them, how to disagree respectfully, how to listen to varying opinions, and how to solve their own procedural problems without always depending upon a teacher. Help student writers understand that they don't need to accept all advice and criticism, but that they do need to decide whom they wish to convince and attempt to communicate with that audience.

Class groups can be helped to reach more advanced stages and settle conflicts in growth-inducing ways by encouraging self-awareness about the group's particular behavior patterns and modes of operating. It's difficult to solve a problem if people aren't fully conscious of it and can't really address it. Conversely, a group gains a feeling of power and pleasure if it can talk—and write—about the way it gets work done. Students get to know each other's work styles, who is good at spotting comma errors, and who has a knack for arbitrating disagreements. At this stage, all can learn about writing from one another.

Ingredients of Group Development

The concepts we have discussed so far concern several of the ways to nurture the development of a mature, interdependent working group. However, the functioning of a group involves not just one or two elements, but a whole constellation of interrelated forces. To help a group reach the more advanced stages of development, we need to examine what these forces are. Richard and Patricia Schmuck, in their very helpful book *Group Processes in the Classroom*, offer a formula for the combination of elements—the ingredients, if you will—of a productive, fully formed group. They posit six key elements, issues that need to be effectively attended to if a group is to develop to its full potential. These are:

- Expectations.
- Norms.
- Leadership.
- Friendship.
- Conflict resolution.
- Communication.

Each of the key chapters in *Group Processes in the Classroom* explains one of these elements and suggests ways for teachers to make sure each attribute will develop fully. For our purposes as writing teachers, we can make quick translations and applications of this formula to the special kind of groups we are working with—junior and senior high school language-arts classes.

EXPECTATIONS

Healthy groups have positive expectations for their own work and for the relationships among the people in the group. In group dynamics, expectations are defined as the working predictions that people use to negotiate their experience. As research cited in Chapter 2 indicates, a teacher who appreciates students and their powers with language brings important positive expectations to the climate she will create in the classroom. She has made a working prediction that students will in many ways succeed, and the prediction itself helps to structure the situation to enhance the likelihood of kids succeeding. Similarly, if students make a working prediction that a class will be a special, positive experience, their expectations can add momentum to the creation of a mature, interdependent group.

Unfortunately, in a school writing class, students often arrive with the wrong expectations about the subject, the class, and the group: they have already learned to dislike writing and predict failure and bad feelings for themselves; they expect the class to be like any other, where they play the passive student game, serving as a compliant audience to a teacher-centered performance; and they certainly don't expect to work with other students in an intimately collaborative and respectful way.

The sort of teaching and learning we are talking about in this book obviously calls for students to do something different from what they may expect upon entering the class. And as Schmuck and Schmuck and other experts point out, students can shape a classroom to fit their own prior expectations even when doing so degrades the quality of their own experience. *Students are always uncomfortable when their expectations are not met,* and they will act to redirect the class experience back into familiar channels and patterns. They'll try to make you teach writing in a way that's familiar to them, that meets their expectations, even when what you are offering them instead seems like it ought to be much more appealing.

Expectations are most powerful and volatile at the very start of a new group. This is when the teacher has the best opportunity to change students' expectations, if she will stick with her plans and live through the adjustment. To show students they will have more responsibility and authority over their own work, the teacher must begin transferring these responsibilities to kids right away. If the teacher wants a class where students do most of the talking, students should be doing the talking right from the start; otherwise, contrary expectations are being confirmed and solidified. The teacher must back up her intentions with actions, or else the students will continue to believe (and rightfully so) that nothing has really changed and their old-style school-game expectations are still valid.

Indeed, there are very few ideas in this book that are familiar and comfortable to most students, that will meet their expectations of standard schooling or traditional writing classes. Expect some adjustment and some testing of wills while the students are suffering this disorientation. During this period, the teacher must maintain her *own* expectations that kids can really learn in a better way and can let them know it. Then she must have lots of patience and hang on tight while the new expectations gradually take hold.

NORMS

Norms are formal and informal rules that govern the appropriateness of behavior in particular social groups, like writing classes. Some norms arise and operate implicitly (like the norm against making eye contact with strangers in elevators), while others may be announced and enforced by someone in authority. Norms are what expectations solidify into. Many of the expectations discussed above, which students bring into the classroom, are predictions about what norms will prevail: who will do most of the talking, what kinds of conversation or feedback is appropriate, what sorts of responsibility students will be given, even whether one can get up and walk around the room during writing time, and so on. Unless the teacher changes the norms in the classroom—either by directly announcing changes, or by devising activities that implement the changes, or simply by modeling the changes himself, the students will continue to operate on the standard set of student-school norms.

Schmuck and Schmuck remind us that the basic set of classroom norms is quite rigid and inflexible and generally stresses competitiveness, pitting individual students against each other. Further, it goes without saying that the traditional norms of the classroom usually conflict directly with the students' peer-group norms. In a writing classroom, it's vital to have norms that validate cooperative and collaborative activity and that overlap the students' peer norms. By this we mean that the class should provide a forum for students to relate to their peers both in official task-oriented capacities and in genuine personal interchange, centered on the activity of writing and learning to write.

Often, changes in seemingly minor nonverbal norms can signal and encourage changes in the more substantive task-related practices. Arranging chairs in a circle or in small groups before students enter the room can signal a change. A teacher who writes while students write enacts an astonishing change in normative behavior in many schools. Establishing a pattern of five minutes' journal writing every day as the period begins, while people are getting settled and attendance is being taken, signals a change from the standard lecture or discussion. And there are many more ways teachers can begin to change expectations, to create a new set of norms more supportive of growth in writing. The following elements point the way.

LEADERSHIP

Leadership in effective groups is not vested in one authority figure but is shared and diffuse. Schmuck and Schmuck cite research showing that students' achievement is higher in classrooms where influence is widely dispersed among all the people in the group and where the authority of the teacher derives not from her position or from coercion, but from her personal relationships with the students and from her role as an expert in the task work of the group.

These ideas have rich implications for teaching writing. The words "authority" and "authorship" obviously contain the same root; and, as we explore more fully in Chapters 9 and 17, the question of what authority authors will have in school is a deep one. An essential way for the writing teacher to alter expectations and norms is to actively, consciously disperse leadership and authority and to assume the role of facilitator more of the time.

The first step is simply granting students the same degree of authority and responsibility that any author needs to have. This means that we must not always police their choice of topics; monitor their collection of material; demand that they organize their plans according to a set format; dictate the length, the tone, and the structure; and then, when a draft is done, locate all their mechanical errors for them. All these steps in writing are important, but we can help *students* initiate, self-monitor, and self-evaluate, which is really what writing is all about. Students need to be the leaders of their own writing if they are ever to learn how to write. All of the specific methods we discuss later in the book are based on this assumption.

But dispersed leadership is not just a matter of the teacher becoming a facilitator to individuals. Leadership can and should be distributed to the class as a whole and to various subgroups within the class. Indeed, the writing class is a wonderful, natural opportunity to establish much-needed collaborative forms of learning in school. Collaborative activity works powerfully because it breaks old norms and sets new ones using the same group forces that tend to sustain the old. The teacher who introduces group work enacts a change in classroom relationships, rather than just talking about it.

One of the principal reasons why so many kids do poorly in school, as William Glasser reiterates in his fine book, *Control Theory in the Classroom*, is that they have no feeling of control or power over anything that happens to them. A writing classroom offers many ways to change that powerlessness, replacing it with opportunities for students to rotate through a number of significant leadership roles: identifying topics and questions they'd like to learn and write about, devising and debating criteria for good writing of particular kinds, sharing writing with the whole class, being responsible for writing or publishing activities, serving as editors who offer constructive feedback to other writers, and so on.

FRIENDSHIP

Friendship, or what Schmuck and Schmuck also call attraction, is vital to the development of group energy and high morale. And since friendship depends upon people knowing each other, having opportunities to share personal ideas and feelings, engaging in a gradual process of sharing and self-disclosure, it is hardly surprising that real friendship hardly ever develops in most school classrooms. Indeed, many of the official structures and norms of classrooms seem designed to prevent outcroppings of true friendship, to stifle the affinities and attractions between people. Certainly one commonality in most schools is that the teacher is not a friend to students in the usual sense of the term; at best, the teacher tries to be "friendly but firm," an oxymoronic way of relating. Ask yourself this: how many people you call friends treat you *firmly*?

In writing classrooms, however, many of our key activities can nurture friendships and invite students to enjoy their affinities and attractions for each other, as a very comfortable and natural by-product of the work going on. Maintenance activity, as indicated earlier, can encourage friendship, but task work builds it as well. By jointly authoring pieces of writing, by sharing autobiographical writing, by working in peer editing groups, by reading aloud to the larger group, students participate in a deepening process of sharing with other individuals and with the group as a whole.

This is one area in which the role of teacher as model is essential for changing norms in the classroom. The teacher shares his writing, his feelings, his honest reactions to others' work (within the bounds of his official role), and by doing so enters into a relation with his students that few teachers ever enjoy: a kind of intimacy based upon a joint exploration of writing and the subjects we write about. Indeed, one of the most common outcomes in writing-process classrooms is a rich affective climate, a great and conscious affection of all the students and the teacher for each other as individuals and the group as an entity. As students begin to follow the teacher's modeling, relationships extend through the classroom and lay down the basis for real growth in writing—safety, willingness, a reason for communicating, and grounds for receiving constructive criticism from the teacher and from one another.

CONFLICT RESOLUTION

Mature groups develop effective ways for dealing with the conflicts that arise as people go about complex tasks over long periods of time. As Judith Viorst explains compassionately in her book, *Necessary Losses*, no human being can be an absolutely perfect companion to another. Needs, styles, backgrounds simply don't match totally. Misunderstandings will occur because people differ. Every teacher, and especially every teacher of writing, is aware of the conflicts that weave in and out of the everyday affairs of even the most harmonious classroom: "Ms. Smith, do I *have* to take my group's advice on my paper?" "This assignment just isn't working for me. I wish she'd let us write about . . ." Or the opposite: "Tell us what you want on this paper!" and the teacher answers, or would like to answer, "But I want *you* to learn to make some of these decisions!"

The danger, if the teacher avoids or suppresses every conflict within the group or insists on winning in every conflict that does arise, is that students will conclude that they must censor their comments and their writing so it is "safe." Kids may cut themselves off from sharing with the group or worry that they had better not disagree with the teacher. Writing is likely to become formal, stiff, or worse, empty of real engagement; peer response to writing may become tame, timid, and false. As usual, the teacher is a model, and students will watch to see how she handles conflict.

Though adolescents have many reasons to perceive difficulties in their relationships with peers and adults, a student-centered writing classroom has excellent resources for expressing and working on these conflicts. The students in such a classroom will have learned, as one of their most fundamental skills, how to give and receive constructive feedback on writing, a superb kind of training for honestly discussing differences that may not always be resolved. The teacher who has been trying to implement the ideas described here has in fact been giving a large-scale demonstration of democratic problem solving all along the way, and her students will be well equipped with procedures and attitudes needed to deal with conflict as it arises. (The group training described in Chapter 14 under peer critiquing particularly embodies these procedures.)

Good teachers have many other skills and strategies for making conflict the occasion for students' growth. They promote listening skills, so that students get a real hearing from one another, something embattled individuals often want more than to "win" their point. They help students learn how to recapitulate discussions and arguments, in order to analyze just what their disagreement is. They hold back from intervening in every conflict and gently urge the small group or individuals to work on a solution or a compromise, so that students aren't always dependent on an authority to get along. And they use humor, a strategy people have always used to handle conflict—not to dismiss or make fun of a problem, but to see it in a larger perspective. As people discover, months later, that both sides in the last disagreement have now changed their minds, even the conflict becomes part of the valued history of the group.

In fact, there is likely to be little process-related conflict in this kind of classroom once the group has achieved some cohesiveness, because peoples' needs are so well met. There may be disputes over substantive aspects of the task work at hand, and students can always import their own problems from outside the group. But the fact remains, as literature of the field of group dynamics explains, the teacher who accommodates all of these factors is going to create a mature, productive group with a very high level of personal investment and very little taste for nonsubstantive conflict. And there will certainly be no need for the kind of conflict that occurs as kids' way of expressing their suppressed anger over being ignored or belittled in school (which we believe is actually the main source of conflict in classrooms) because the aim is to treat everyone, and treasure everyone, as a valuable and responsible person.

COMMUNICATION

Perhaps one of the reasons why the language-arts classroom offers such an extraordinary opportunity to develop a mature, cohesive group is that its main purpose is the same as one of the key attributes of any effective group: to study and improve communication. It is the explicit aim of English teachers to help students focus their attention on the nature of language and writing, to explore the different modes of communicating, to demonstrate means for effectiveness in communication, and to instill a love and respect for this marvelous human power. Therefore, it is quite natural to attend to the quality of communication in a writing class; we don't have to specially order up this ingredient of positive group dynamics à la carte, because it is already on the menu. In a writing class, we already know that we want to create experiences that help students stretch their capacities, to use language in the broadest possible array of uses; our writing activities should naturally reflect this aim.

But in addition, in a writing class teachers and students seek improvement by talking about, and writing about, writing—we communicate about communication. So we need to pay attention to how language functions in the class itself, to encourage reflexiveness, to explicitly study how our language works in the here-and-now classroom. This means that we monitor and try to improve communication within the classroom group. We aim for a situation where everybody can communicate with everyone else smoothly and openly; where patterns of communicating within the group are diffuse and shifting, rather than being tied to certain fixed subgroups or dominant students; and where everyone can address everyone else, in writing or aloud, with communication and feedback that's open, caring, and undefensive. We regularly take time out to talk about whether these opportunities really exist, and how to provide them if they are being blocked.

Our aim, both for writing and for group development, is a rich flow of language. Students should have extensive opportunities to express themselves on topics that matter, with plenty of response from a variety of people who bring different perspectives to these topics. And then students must regularly get the chance to reflect in words on how the process goes, thus providing both the practice they need and the basis to analyze and improve their ability to communicate.

Chapter 5

Planning for a Writing-Centered Class

WHAT DO YOU TEACH?

We realize that readers of this book have a wide variety of teaching assignments and, accordingly, widely differing amounts of time available to work on writing. A few of you teach expository or creative writing courses and so obviously make writing the focus of most of your time and activities. But most teachers have other content to teach: periods or genres of literature, novels, poems, plays, essays, nonfiction prose, grammar, usage, spelling, vocabulary, library skills, speech, and all the rest. Some teach a selection of these items in generic courses called "Junior English" or "seventh-grade language arts," while others must integrate them in courses like "Science Fiction" or "Women's Literature."

For the purposes of this book, we're going to assume the latter case: that you have some chunks of English curriculum to teach, and that the writing activities we'll be describing must fit in with the rest of your curricular obligations. Of course, those with all-writing courses will be able to do more activities more often than the rest. But in the end there may not really be such a split between the two main kinds of teaching assignments. For, as you'll see, we believe that people teaching the traditional mixed-content English courses should give a lot of class time to writing. This is because we trust, and the research confirms, that kids will effectively learn many of the required "subskills" of English if they get lots of actual writing practice in the course of thinking and learning about other things. If kids are writing, sharing, revising, and talking about writing constantly, there will be little need for the separate teaching of spelling, usage, grammar, library skills, or many of the other items in the typical language-arts curriculum.

WHO ARE YOUR STUDENTS?

By now the process model has taken strong hold in some elementary schools, so some of your students arrive with a solid background in writing; they are fluent, confident writers who know how to attack a writing task, approach the work in appropriate steps, know how to seek help, know how to think about an audience, are skilled at editing their own pieces for publication, and generally like to write. They may even use some of the new process terminology, talking about "drafts," "rewrites," "reader response," and the like.

But it's much more likely that your students *won't* come to you as active "process writers." According to data from the National Assessment of Educational Progress, only about 7 percent of American schoolchildren are receiving intensive, process-oriented instruction. The rest get something less powerful, less coherent, and less effective. Most of your students probably will have had sparse and sporadic writing experience in elementary school. They will have written mostly in response to teacher-made assignments in a single draft with little time or guidance for planning or revision, and certainly few opportunities for collaboration with other students. Much of this writing has been harnessed to testing, making kids prove that they read some assignment or studied some material.

Students will not have shaped their work for many audiences other than their teacher and will not have shared or "published" often. They will not have learned to take a staged, craftsmanlike approach to the work. They will be unfamiliar with the classroom workshop atmosphere, where students direct their own efforts or use small-group collaboration to provide help for writers at work. Your students' past papers have probably been heavily corrected by many of their teachers, with a particular focus on spelling and mechanical errors. As a result of all this, students will bring to your class either mixed or negative attitudes toward writing. Many of them have been convinced by their experience that writing is a painful, impractical activity at which they usually fail. They have come to see writing not as meaning making, but as a correctness-testing game.

Even those few students who have enjoyed an exemplary, process-model background are likely to have gaps and weaknesses as well. It is very unlikely that any of your students, whatever their elementary-school writing experience, will have had much experience in expository forms of writing: in writing about materials or subjects outside of their own immediate experience, writing for purposes other than personal expressive ones, and writing to audiences other than close and familiar ones. They will have little or no useful experience in gathering and organizing information for writing, except for material from their own experience and memory.

WHAT KINDS OF WRITING SHOULD YOUR STUDENTS DO?

Teachers need to find a balance between three main sorts of classroom writing activities:

1. *Self-sponsored writing.* Every secondary English classroom should have regularly scheduled times when students can work on writing projects of their own choice. This means that students must have predictable, continuous opportunities to develop pieces of writing for which they have selected their own topics, determined their own purposes, chosen their own audiences, and are working on their own timetable toward a finished product. They get help from the teacher and from classmates as they need and request it. In Chapter 7, we talk about how to provide the time, space, atmosphere, materials, norms, and record keeping necessary for this kind of writing.

2. *Formal assignments.* When designed to offer students real choices and true ownership of the work, formal assignments guided by the teacher are another source of growth for young writers. Some composition experts assert that students should *always* select their own topics, and it will require some detailed explanation, in Chapter 9, to clarify how we think teacher-made assignments can become equally meaningful. For now, we'll simply assert that teacher-directed assignments can provide the sort of inquiry-based, environmental-mode writing practice that is associated with strong growth in writing performance. Chapters 9 through 15 cover various aspects of teacher-initiated writing activities, as well as issues that overlap with the two other types of writing mentioned here.

3. *Writing to learn.* Students also need frequent opportunities to use writing as a tool of thinking: to use short, spontaneous, unedited, exploratory, personal pieces of writing to help them engage and think about ideas. This kind of writing has enjoyed increasing recognition as an aid to learning across the curriculum; we must not forget that English courses have plenty of content to be taught and learned, too. Chapter 18 offers a variety of examples of writing-to-learn activities that can be applied in English or any other content class.

To glibly assert the need to "find a balance" among these three kinds of writing activities, as we just did, makes things sound simpler than they are. Everything depends upon what "balance" means to you. To the traditional English teacher, a good balance may be 100 percent formal, teacher-made assignments. To many of the "natural process" writing advocates like Graves and Nancie Atwell, balance means 100 percent students' self-sponsored writing. We think that all three kinds of writing are genuinely important to growing writers, provided that each is done in an appropriate and thoughtful way.

So what balance do *we* prescribe? The need to provide student-sponsored writing makes us ask: how much time each week do kids need for their own writing? We think one full day a week—the equivalent of 20 percent of your total instructional time—is a minimum in any course. It is important to devote time in sizable chunks so that kids can get warmed up and draft, revise, share, edit, and publish their works.

Teacher-given writing activities should not invade students' scheduled writing time; instead, these assignments should happen during other parts of the instructional week. How much of the rest of class time should be given to teacher-initiated writing activities? Obviously, this is a matter of individual judgment, curriculum concerns, and other circumstances. Some assignments will be short, contained within a few minutes or a single period. Others, like the complex, integrated activities we describe further in Chapter 18, might last for several days and might be the main means of instruction for a whole unit or even a course.

Similarly, there's no need to specify a percentage of class time that might be allocated to writing-to-learn activities, since these will naturally arise in connection with the content being studied in any given course. From the teacher's point of view, writing to learn is not so much additional writing practice, but an alternative teaching method, a way of helping students grasp particular course content.

Now, obviously, these three categories only tell us about who's structuring the time and activities and not much about what *kind* of writing is done. For example, a student might self-sponsor writing of anything from political editorials to fairy tales; in writing-to-learn activities, students might be expressing feelings, classifying, evaluating, or synthesizing. Similarly, formal assignments may point students toward poetry or scientific explanations or parodies of journal keeping or just about anything else. We need to think, in other words, not just about who's initiating the activity, but what kind of writing is going on.

We recognize five types of writing that happen in school, the categories being defined by the *purposes* for writing.

1. *Writing to show learning:* filling in blanks on ditto sheets and in workbooks, answering study questions at the end of textbook chapters, writing essay examination questions, and the like. All of these represent writing used primarily as testing, as a concrete way of checking to see if students have done certain kinds of assigned work.

2. *Writing to learn writing:* asking kids to produce a specimen of their writing so that its correctness can be assessed. The focus here is not learning to think or communicate, but reproducing formulae, tallying errors, and generating scores that represent degrees of "mastery" of the conventions of written language.

3. *Writing to communicate:* what we used to call expository writing. This is writing that's focused upon affecting an audience somehow: informing, instructing, persuading, analyzing.

4. *Writing to express the self:* writing done in comfortable, familiar, everyday language that expresses our feelings and savors our experience. The audience for such writing is often the writer as much as it is an outside reader. Along with feelings, this writing also involves processing ideas and beliefs in a very personal way before turning them into public, communicative language.

5. *Writing to create:* writing that goes beyond communication into the realm of aesthetic creation, bringing a beautiful artifact of words into being. Finely crafted poems, stories, and plays fit this category. However, there's plenty of overlap; a very clever persuasive piece may be valued as much for its beauty as its point.

Purposes 1 and 2 are not of much significance to this book. While writing as testing is a handy way to extract an imperfect sample of students' learning, it is already the predominant purpose for which students write in today's schools (Applebee 1981), and as such may explain the fearful attitude toward writing that most students acquire. Teachers do not need to assign more of this kind of writing. On the contrary, we should use it better (by making better assignments) and less often (to leave time and energy for more important and promising purposes for writing). The second purpose listed above, writing to generate a text only so it can be marked up and scored, is counterproductive and degrading to the teaching of writing and has no place in school when kids have so much to say that's real.

This leaves us with the three other purposes for writing: to create, to express, and to communicate. Some readers will already recognize that these three categories overlap with the model created by James Britton (1970), who has posited a continuum of language (both speech and writing) that many of us find tremendously useful in our work with students. Instead of the old dichotomy between creative and expository forms (which

---

undergirds most English curricula and commercial language-arts text-books), Britton offers a much more generative model, based upon *purposes* for using language.

POETIC ◄————————— EXPRESSIVE ——————————► TRANSACTIONAL

Britton argues that we begin as children (and begin each day, as adults) with *expressive* language, the close, comfortable, familiar, homey language in which we can most freely talk about our experiences, feelings, beliefs, and understandings. This is our linguistic home base, the core of our language use. Then, says Britton, our language can move out from the base in two different directions. One is toward the *transactional*, when we want our language to get some real work, some transaction, accomplished in the world. This takes in the audience-centered modes of discourse: persuasion, description, information, analysis, and the like. Alternately, our language can move out toward the *poetic* pole, when we create language or writing that is an object of contemplation, polished and shaped in texture and sound—whether a work of art or a jump-rope chant.

Britton's theory has developmental and curricular implications as well. In this model, growth means extending your range from the expressive base. If all children start with the comfortable, expressive core of language, development means becoming able to move farther out toward the transactional and poetic ends of the continuum.

POETIC ◄——◄——◄——◄— EXPRESSIVE —►——►——►——► TRANSACTIONAL

But notice that development doesn't mean relocating from one point to another, but increasing one's *range*—becoming more elastic or flexible. The expressive is always the base, and even the most mature and developed adult speaker or writer returns to the expressive base a dozen times each day: gossiping with neighbors and friends, jotting down notes, chatting on the phone, talking across the dinner table.

In school, the model gives us insight as well. If we accept Britton's view of development, the literacy curriculum should help kids to extend their linguistic range in both directions. It would start by accepting and celebrating their expressive language and then provide occasions that invite students to grow toward the transactional and the poetic, to extend their language range. But school would always respect the expressive base and recognize the importance of kids' being able to touch that base every day. In reality, however, what schools mostly do is push kids toward the transactional end, neglecting everything else. And too often, we expect kids to grow toward the transactional without maintaining any connection to the expressive base.

POETIC   EXPRESSIVE – – – – – – – – → TRANSACTIONAL

Notice that writing to learn, which earlier emerged as one of the main *structures* for writing activity in the classroom, can also be thought of as one of the important varieties of expressive-mode language. When kids use short, spontaneous, unedited, exploratory, personal writings to channel, crystallize, record, direct, or guide their thinking, they are in effect using expressive language in a special and important way. (We talk about writing to learn in detail in Chapter 8.)

SUMMARY

There are three main ways of structuring writing activity in the classroom, and we think teachers should give some classroom time to each:

1. Students' self-sponsored writing.
2. Formal, structured assignments.
3. Writing-to-learn activities.

How a teacher divides class time among these different kinds of writing activities will depend upon the students and their needs, the course and the curriculum, and the teacher's own philosophy and style.

We can also think of three main modes of writing that students might want and need to develop:

1. Poetic.
2. Expressive.
3. Transactional.

Again, the modes stressed in any given class will be governed by the interacting needs of the students, the curriculum, and the teacher.

Putting these concepts together in a matrix, as shown in Figure 5–1, offers a kind of guide to the possible combinations. A teacher could use this matrix to think about alternative ways of structuring time and activities in a given course. In using it, we of course recognize that in most real-life writing tasks our purposes are complex and overlapping; these conveniently categorized modes of writing will actually intersect in many ways.

Figure 5–1 *Matrix for Class Time Spent on Varieties of Writing*

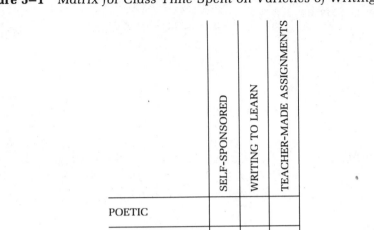

	SELF-SPONSORED	WRITING TO LEARN	TEACHER-MADE ASSIGNMENTS
POETIC			
EXPRESSIVE			
TRANSACTIONAL			

Chapter 6

Day One,
Week One

SOME BASIC PRINCIPLES

The key is to begin right away, using writing to create community and to transfer authority from the teacher to the students. There are three key things that ought to happen on the first day, or within the first few sessions, of a writing course:

1. *Everyone writes.* If a class is going to stress writing, it should start off with writing—teacher and students writing together. This is congruent with everything else that will follow in the course: it demonstrates the simple value of class time used for writing, it begins the workshop atmosphere, it enacts doing instead of telling as the starting point of learning, and more.

2. *Writing is shared.* To the extent that they feel comfortable doing so, volunteers should share their writing. Everyone needs and wants a response to most of what they write. The teacher models an empathic, human reception for all writing that is offered to the group; and while she's careful not to overpower the group with her own adult abilities, she takes the risk of sharing her own writing too. The class begins to establish itself as a safe and trustworthy and active audience.

3. *Everyone helps define the group.* Either implicitly or explicitly, in the early days of a class the teacher and students should be building consensus about the aims, possibilities, and procedures of the course. Teachers will naturally vary in how they enact this; some will be glad to let students plan the entire course; others will want to balance kids' ideas with their own aims; still others will give students advisory input and plan most of the class themselves. The vital point is that students must have a genuine, not just window-dressing, chance to direct the class, to buy in, to invest in the process and the group that is about to begin.

In terms of the group dynamics principles we reviewed in Chapter 4, we are reiterating the idea that a mature and fully effective group will develop only if students have a chance to help create the expectations, norms, friendships, leadership patterns, communication channels, and conflict-resolution mechanisms of the class. Teachers who skip these steps, or try to dictate all these factors themselves, are squandering the main resource they have in helping adolescents grow: students' sense of control, ownership, authority over their own learning.

A VARIETY OF APPROACHES

How can you get all this done in the first days of a class? Here are some approaches that we and other teachers have found successful. As you'll see, these activities accomplish the three purposes above in lots of different ways; some take several entire class periods, while others can be completed in a single day's meeting. You'll also notice that some are teacher guided while others are much more open and student centered. In any case, you'll undoubtedly want to adapt what you use to your own situation.

Interviewing Activity

This first activity has gotten to be a bit of a cliché, and for good reason: it works. It starts a writing class with participatory, student-centered, high-energy activity, low-stress writing, and enjoyable sharing.

1. *Introduction.* Tell students that everyone will shortly be doing some interviewing in pairs to get acquainted with one other person in the class.
2. *Brainstorming.* List with the group some questions that you could ask your partner, questions that would help you find out what makes this person special, unique, different, and distinctive. Jot the suggested questions on the board. Encourage kids to use creative, off-the-wall questions, as well as the usual "name, rank, and serial number" items. If the group omits any questions you feel would be especially helpful or appropriate, add your own suggestions to the list. Eight to ten questions on the board should be enough.
3. *Interviewing.* Instruct students to pair up with someone they don't already know well. (If the number of students is odd, the teacher joins a pair; if it's even, he'll have to write a self-portrait or submit to a gang

interview after the others have finished.) Tell students that the aim of this exercise is to get to know more information about the person, using their own questions as well as any helpful items from the brainstormed list. If the questions and answers lead pairs into more general conversation, that's just fine. People will be allowed seven to eight minutes each and must be reminded to switch roles halfway through the fifteen-minute period allowed for this work. Remind everyone to take notes during the interviews, for use afterward.

4. *Writing.* When the pairs return, give the writing assignment: "Using any parts of your notes however they help you, along with your impressions and any prior knowledge of the person, write a single paragraph about the person you interviewed. In ten minutes or so we'll read these drafts aloud to the whole group, so that's your audience. You could think of this as a chance for the group to re-meet each individual in the class, learning a bit more about what makes everyone special and unique. Take any approach you like to this paragraph, and remember, this is not for a grade, just for sharing out loud. Papers don't have to be neat or spelling correct; all you have to be able to do is read it aloud." Allow ten minutes' work time for the writing.

5. *Read aloud.* Share around the circle, having pairs read theirs together. (You might elect to have pairs volunteer instead if you think that going around the whole group would put too much pressure on some authors or take up too much time.) Enjoy, and notice the delightful variety of approaches to the assignment. When everyone has read, help students discuss how they felt about doing each step in the assignment: hearing the task, doing the interview, writing the paragraph, sharing, being an audience. Try to get at both the cognitive and affective processes they can notice.

VARIATION ONE: WHAT IS A PARAGRAPH?

This activity lends itself to many variations. For example, halfway through the sharing, ask students to stop and, based upon just having heard ten or twelve examples, define a paragraph. Kids will have a very tough time giving any useful definition at all (teachers do too, in the same situation). The point of this activity is not to berate students for forgetting the paragraph recipes in the textbook but rather to show them that writing taps into a great deal of unconscious, implicit knowledge derived from a life's experience of talking, reading, and experimenting with writing. In other words, knowing how to do something does not necessarily mean knowing how to talk about how you do it. Now you can suggest that as the remainder of the paragraphs are read, people should try to listen at two levels: first, of course, to continue enjoying the content that is being offered in each piece; but second, to pay some attention to the structure, pattern, or underlying organization of each paragraph.

After more paragraphs have been read, ask students to describe the patterns in some of the paragraphs. They'll probably notice the use of chronology (the subject's past–present–future) or a focus on a single key trait, or comparisons to the interviewer, and other strategies. Probably there will be very few paragraphs that follow the textbook pattern of a topic sentence, three supporting sentences, and a concluding sentence—and the students will learn something about paragraphs that they'd never get from memorizing characteristics of paragraph types.

VARIATION TWO: REVISION

Ask each pair to meet again and spend five minutes exchanging feedback on the subject "One thing I'd like you to change in your paragraph about me." That is, every writer will be asked to change, delete, substitute, soften, sharpen, add, or otherwise revise one element of his written text, according to the wishes of the responder-subject. The responder has to provide reasons for the change; and, just for this exercise, it isn't fair to dodge the task by saying, "It's perfect." Authors make the changes, and then everyone gathers once again in the whole group to talk about (1) what sort of changes were asked for; (2) how the responder phrased or delivered the request; (3) how the writer felt about the request; (4) how hard or easy it was to work the change into the text; (5) what implications this has for working on other pieces of writing.

VARIATION THREE: PUBLISHING

Have students take all their notes and each other's home phone numbers, and in the following day's class session have them create one camera-ready page about their interviewee for inclusion in a class booklet to be photocopied and distributed under a title like "Profiles of People in Room 105." These one-page profiles may simply be polished and expanded versions of the rough drafts written in class, or new pieces based upon further interviews, or illustrated texts or collages—this assignment can be kept wide open. It's fun to leave an empty box somewhere on the page to be filled with a Polaroid picture of the subject, and this also makes the resulting class booklet even more helpful in getting people acquainted with each other.

VARIATION FOUR: CONNECTING WITH LITERATURE

Read aloud or distribute some paragraphs from literature in which characters are introduced or described. Invite students to compare and contrast the strategies used by the published authors and themselves. The description of Pap in *Huckleberry Finn* is a fine place to begin.

VARIATION FIVE: TOPIC INTERVIEWS

A favorite with some classes is for students to interview each other about their names and all the implications these have had in their lives. The class can create its own list of questions to help the interviewers get started, or the teacher can provide questions such as the following:

- What is the history, origin, or definition of your name?
- How and why did your parents choose the first name they gave you?
- What nicknames have you had?
- What attitudes do people display toward your name?
- What influences has your name had on your life—advantages or disadvantages?
- Would you prefer another name? If you were forced to adopt another name, what would you call yourself?

PLANNING TO USE AN INTERVIEWING ACTIVITY

We've had so much fun and so much success with all these variants of the interviewing-and-writing activity that we want to offer a detailed inventory of its ingredients. Below we list all of the options and considerations that a teacher might wish to consider as she plans.

THE TEACHER'S INSTRUCTIONAL GOALS

Why use this activity? To build friendship and acquaintances in the class at the start of the year? To give writing practice to build fluency? To have kids experience the complete, step-by-step model of the writing process, from initial assignment all the way to publication? As the beginning of a research unit? To teach characterization?

INTRODUCING THE ACTIVITY TO STUDENTS

Why are we doing this? Will interviews be wide open or focused on a particular aspect of person (names, travels, hopes)?

BRAINSTORMING OF INTERVIEW QUESTIONS

To help kids generate a list of sample questions that fit the focus. Call out ideas and list on board? Individually on paper before interview? How many questions should the teacher add or dictate?

INTERVIEWS

Grouping: *Pairs, or threes, fours? Self-selected or teacher-chosen?*

Room setup: *Arranging seats for efficient interviewing. Should kids just interview the student in next seat, or to their left, or move their chairs? Everyone needs to be knee to knee to be heard.*

Note-taking: *Should kids keep their own notes or fill in a teacher-made handout or chart containing prepared questions? Will the brainstormed question list on the board provide enough guidance? Too much?*

Time: *How long per pair for first round—five to fifteen minutes? How to signal that time is half over?*

INSTRUCTIONS FOR WRITING

Quantity/Time: *a paragraph, page, ten minutes?*

Focus: *Alternate approaches that might be suggested as kids set out to write. Examples: Discuss the one key trait of your person, talk about two or three items, the most surprising or unique thing you discovered, how the two of you are alike and different, or write as a riddle without naming the person, etc. Alternately, leave the focus open for students to find their own.*

Audience: *Read aloud to partner when done, or share with whole group? (No need to tell kids now what ultimate audiences might be— just the one for the next stage.)*

Correctness: *What level of proofreading are you seeking in this first, rough draft? Discourage worry about perfection.*

INITIAL SHARING

Aloud or by exchanging papers? In pairs, whole group, groups of four, half the class? Who shares—volunteers, everyone, those chosen by teacher, one from each group, kids nominated by other students?

DEBRIEFING

Discuss how people got the work done, how they felt as they worked, what different approaches to the assignment were taken, etc.

REVISION/EDITING

Will there be any further polishing or editing? If so, will there be whole-class time and activities for revision? What focus will the editing stage have? Content or mechanics or both?

Examples: *Meet with your partner to exchange suggestions about the accuracy of the information and the correctness of the writing and then* rewrite. Or use your draft and your notes to change modes and write a poem about the person you interviewed, perhaps using a teacher-supplied frame ("maker of . . . lover of . . . believer in . . ." etc).

PUBLISHING

How will the final versions be shared? Hang on walls, make display, read aloud, put in writing folders, exchange with another class, create a publication?

Example: Kids take their first drafts and (inside or outside of classroom) develop them into camera-ready one-page introductions of each student for a class "Who's Who" booklet or display. Each page can follow any format: wanted poster, profile, simple paragraph, collage. A photograph of the person can enhance this.

TEACHER ROLES

Participant or spectator? Model or monitor? If numbers don't come out right you can either use yourself to fill in or form nonstandard-sized groups instead.

EVALUATION

When and how will these different stages of student work be responded to, evaluated, and/or graded?

ANOTHER VARIATION

Self-interviews. Kids can write about themselves instead of another student, using many of the above activities. The interviewing still works the same way, but the interviewer hands over the notes to the subject when done. The outcome of this version might be a paper, booklet, or classroom display by each student introducing her/himself to the class. Another especially valuable topic for student interviews is their previous experience with writing, or with reading novels—or, in fact, with any subject they are about to begin studying (especially if this is not an English class).

Surveying Classmates

Another activity, which we've adapted from Judy Johnstone, a teacher at Carl Sandburg High School,* is not only useful for getting acquainted at

---

*Anyone wishing to correspond directly with Judy or any of the other teachers whose ideas are outlined in the book will find a complete list of names and school addresses in the appendix.

the beginning of the semester, but also encourages respect for differing beliefs and demonstrates that it usually takes revising to make oneself understood. Students identify topics on which they'd like to learn the opinions of some of their classmates. Then they create their own individual lists of questions for eliciting such information. In groups of three, students exchange their lists, and each student provides written answers to the others' questions. Then the members of the group talk over the questions as well as their answers. Many students will find that they need to revise their questions in order to get the information they want.

After this "field test," they use their revised questions to conduct surveys in groups of four or five. Again, each student provides written answers to the questions from the others in the group. Each student then writes an analysis of the information gathered, and a few volunteers give a brief report to the class. It is important that the analysis include not just what people answered, but an interpretation, what the writer thinks this information means. The goals of this activity are several: (1) to help students become better acquainted with one another, (2) to encourage students to listen to one another's opinions and take them seriously, and (3) to illustrate that making oneself understood is a complicated task.

Many variations of this activity are possible. Questions can be designed by groups instead of individuals. The groups then survey others in the class and prepare a collaborative report. Or each group designs questions and surveys itself. The whole class might determine the questions, with groups surveying themselves, discussing their answers, and reporting results to the class.

Free Writing

Peter Elbow has formalized and explicated two of the most helpful writing activities we have at our disposal: free writing and focused free writing. Either could provide an excellent first-day activity for a new class, especially if the teacher wants the students to have a wide-open, self-chosen topic.

Free writing is connecting, as perfectly and completely as possible, with your own stream of consciousness—writing down whatever is going on in your mind at a particular time. To do this, you simply pick up a pencil and write continuously, without allowing yourself to stop for any reason. You write whatever you are thinking of, feeling, or experiencing here and now; what appears on the page may be words, phrases, or even doodles, jumping from topic to topic without much discernible order. If you cannot think of anything to write, then you write over and over, "I can't think of anything to write. I can't think of anything to write." Or to restart the flow you can doodle or darken a line—sometimes the graphic activity unleashes more words than empty writing does.

In any case, free writing takes advantage of one of the unique and delightful traits of human beings: our brains are always making meaning, seeking connections, creating stories and metaphors. We can't seem to stop doing this; even when we go to sleep, our brains are busy making up dreams. Free writing taps into this inherent meaning-making genius of our species beautifully: if you tap your own stream of consciousness for even a few minutes, the seemingly chaotic flow of jabber you write down almost always contains a seed, a sprout, a start of something valuable to explore and write about further.

So a brief period of free writing makes a fine and especially open way to start off a writing class:

1. Explain the concept of free writing, and invite students to join you in a set period (three to five minutes) of pure free writing, perhaps working on a 4-by-6-inch card to emphasize the shortness and informality of the assignment.

2. Have students look over their writing and circle one idea, a word, or a topic that gives them an idea for some further writing.

3. Have kids write for ten minutes on this topic, letting it take them wherever it goes. Stress that this is just exploratory; it is not for a grade, and it is not to be turned in.

4. Ask students to get into groups of three or four and share something with each other, as they are comfortable. Each person can either read a bit of her original free-write or the second piece, or tell about (instead of reading verbatim) the topic she discovered and explored, or simply talk about what she noticed about her own thinking and feeling processes while writing.

5. After groups have had ten to fifteen minutes to discuss, regather in the large group. Invite volunteers to read some or all of their writing aloud. The teacher models the receiving of writing, giving a friendlike, content-centered response to each piece shared.

6. A member of each of the small groups then reports briefly on what sorts of things were shared and what direction the small-group discussion took.

7. The teacher might raise the question "How was this activity like or unlike writing you're done in school before?" A discussion about past experiences and attitudes toward writing might be a good way to end this activity.

VARIATION: FOCUSED FREE WRITING

Focused free writing is pretty much the same thing as the free writing we've just described, except that instead of trying to connect with one's unstructured thought-flow, the writer gives himself a focus or a topic beforehand and then writes whatever comes into his mind about that central focus or idea. As he writes continuously, letting ideas flood in, he may occasionally drift far off the original focus. When this happens, the writer should gently pull himself back to the center and then continue. The seven steps described above can be used for focused free writing as well as for the completely open version. The teacher could suggest a topic ("My development as a writer" works well) or could help students brainstorm a list of possibilities from which to choose.

Considering Classroom Roles and Responsibilities

Here is an activity to help students become more conscious of the roles they adopt in the classroom, to encourage them to communicate with one another as well as with the teacher in their academic work, and to take more responsibility, both as individuals and as a group. Thus, it helps establish a climate in which writing has a more meaningful social purpose and a real audience, and in which suggestions about how to improve writing can be taken positively.

1. The teacher begins by posing the following question: "Imagine that Martians are being briefed before a trip to Earth. Their mission is to study the strange institution Earthlings call 'school.' The Martian instructor wants to give the explorers very concrete explanations so they will be able to tell the difference between teachers and students when they arrive here. What actions—what very specific behaviors—should he tell them to watch for, so that even if they don't understand the language, they will be able to recognize "a teacher" or "a student"? What would they see each one *doing*?"

The teacher lists items on the board in two columns, "Teacher" and "Student," as students contribute them. A typical list would look like this:

TEACHER	STUDENT
Sits at large desk.	Sits at small desk.
Sits, stands, or moves around.	Usually remains seated.

TEACHER	STUDENT
Adjusts windows, shades, lights.	Leaves room as she finds it (even if it's dark).
Usually speaks to whole class.	Usually speaks to teacher during class (but whispers to other students).
Speaks without raising hand.	Must raise hand before speaking.
Does most of the talking.	Mostly listens.
Asks questions.	Answers when teacher asks questions.
Gives directions.	Acts after teacher gives directions.
May hold chalk, write on board.	Usually writes on paper at desk.
Is older.	Is younger.

2. In discussion after completing this list, it isn't hard for students to notice that most of the teacher behaviors are *active*, involve responsibility, and are directed toward the whole group, while most of the student behaviors are *passive* and involve responding to some initiative the teacher takes. This applies both to the things each one says and to the nonverbal signals each uses. Students can discuss whether they wouldn't like to alter the balance a bit. But what does this mean they should *do*?

3. It's time to do a little focused free writing. Ask students to think for a minute of a really good—or very bad—teacher they've had, and to recall things that teacher did and ways the teacher acted. What qualities and actions stood out? (See Steve Pearse's chapter in Anne Ruggles Gere's *Roots in the Sawdust* for a nice variation on this activity.) Then, after sharing some of the writings, ask students to help make a list of the characteristics of a good teacher. Their list might run as follows:

- Assigns really interesting reading.
- Conducts good discussions.
- Cares whether we do well or not.
- Is interested in what we have to say.
- Explains why we are studying a particular topic.
- Treats students fairly.
- Returns papers promptly, with helpful comments on them.
- Encourages individuals who are having trouble.
- Listens when kids come to her with problems.
- Keeps things moving, doesn't let us get bored.

- Tells some personal stories, but also makes sure things get done and doesn't let us wander too far off the track.
- Helps us choose our own writing topics, or include our own ideas when writing about a topic.

Discussing this composite description, students can see that a good teacher has a lot to do, and that maybe it's just about impossible for one person to do it all. Many (though not necessarily all) the items on the list are things that students can also do for each other, and they should consider which roles they believe are appropriate for them to begin sharing with the teacher. For example, students can give comments and encouragement to one another. In small-group work, someone in each group can be given the role of guiding the discussion back to the topic when it wanders. As the semester progresses, student groups can take responsibility for conducting discussions (perhaps using a structure provided by the teacher) about particular material or chapters being read. Thus, students receive specific, guided practice in the skills needed for becoming more active in the classroom. (See the section on the training of peer critiquing groups in Chapter 14 for more on preparing students for such roles.)

4. Students can now write for ten to twenty minutes (or as homework for tomorrow's class) on specific suggestions for dividing up the work and responsibilities in this new class. These papers can be shared aloud, in teams or in the whole group, or can be exchanged and read silently. The teacher may wish to formally draw upon these written suggestions in structuring later class activities.

Chapter 7

Time to Write:
Workshops and
Journals

Of all the instructional strategies developed during the first wave of writing-process pedagogy, the writing workshop is probably the best developed, most fully tested, and widely proven method. Because others have written so well on this subject, we will keep our description here brief and schematic. If you wish more detailed background on the operation of a writing workshop, we strongly recommend the books of Donald Graves, Lucy Calkins, and Nancie Atwell. Along with this recommendation, we'll assert again that, for us, the writing workshop is just one of the kinds of writing activities that you might want to initiate in your classroom. The authors we have named will tell you, with varying degrees of vehemence, that the writing workshop should be the *only* kind of writing activity going on in your class. We disagree.

THE WRITING WORKSHOP

A writing workshop is a regularly scheduled, substantial chunk of class time when students work on self-chosen pieces of writing. The term "workshop" is full of rich implications about what such a place looks and feels like. In a workshop, craftspeople gradually, patiently create finely wrought products over time, working through a series of steps and stages. They use various tools associated with their product, they collaborate with their fellow craftspeople, and they take pride in the refinement of a product to its finished stage. One of the interesting things about crafts workshops is that historically they have been educational institutions as well, training the next generation of practitioners, whatever the craft. So in many crafts shops, there is a master craftsman who doesn't just work but also spends time observing, assisting, helping, and teaching the apprentices.

In a writing workshop, everyone is engaged at the craft of writing, creating and refining pieces of their own writing, working at various stages of the process of composition. Writers are surrounded by the tools and resources of their craft and freely use them. Writers consult with and assist each other. Writers in a workshop take time to share and celebrate each others' finished products. The teacher, as master craftsman, serves as a model for the student apprentices, demonstrating the practice of the veteran and reflecting the values, the pride of the trade. He observes the work of the beginners in the shop, responds, coaches, gives hints, and occasionally evaluates. The fundamental assumption of the workshop as educational institution is clear: this is learning by doing, learning through practice, aided by modeling and feedback from a master practitioner.

To implement a writing workshop in junior or senior high school, you'll need certain kinds of structure and organization. Obviously, if your students are not used to working in this way, you will have to train them, to develop the norms, expectations, leadership behaviors, and communication patterns necessary for a productive workshop to operate. How much structure you need, and what kind, will depend upon you and your kids. In order to give you some choices, we'll describe one writing workshop we know of—one that uses little overt structure. And then we'll outline another, more structured version for those who need more order.

A Loosely Structured Workshop

When Steve Ogilvie's juniors come to class on Friday at Elmwood Park High School, they know it's writing-workshop day. Steve doesn't have to give any orders or instructions; the twenty-five students go directly to the file cabinet at the side of the room and get their writing folders. They take their folders to their desks, and by the time the bell rings most of them are already at work. The students sift through their folders, deciding what to do. Some will elect to start a new piece, while others will pull out an old draft and continue revising it. A few may exchange drafts with a neighbor and talk very quietly. These kids are starting on a full period of writing time.

Throughout the workshop, Steve is running five-minute individual conferences. He has two chairs pulled knee to knee far in the back of the room, and he quietly calls students to meet with him one at a time. These conferences are held on a regular schedule, so the seven or eight kids scheduled for each Friday workshop day know it's their turn. (This means that each kid gets seen in a conference once every three weeks, or twelve times a year.) Steve doesn't call kids in a preordained order; he scans the room sensitively to avoid calling a student who's deeply engaged in work and to find people who are at a good stopping point for a conference.

The conferences vary in content and process, according to what the student is working on. Most of the time, Steve has not read the draft or paper in advance. He is there as a sounding board for a writer in the process of writing. He lets students decide what kind of help or feedback will be most useful to them at whatever stage they've reached. If students don't have an agenda of their own, Steve may follow the Gravesian model, asking questions like "What's the piece about?" "Where are you in the work?" "What do you need to help you move on from here?" At some conferences, students read a key passage aloud to Steve and get his (and their own) reaction. As the student leaves, Steve makes a quick note in a spiral notebook, recording what was discussed—for example, "3/24— Lead for zoo story" or "Support for hypothesis in Nazi piece."

Sometimes, toward the end of the period, the class stops writing five or ten minutes early, so that one or two students can read a piece or a passage aloud, or to attend to some logistics of the workshop. But mostly, for each kid in Steve's room, workshop day is pure, solid writing time, with a conference every third week.

A Workshop with More Structure

Steve's workshop looks very loose; there's little overt structure, few official procedures, and hardly any direct teaching. But this workshop works because Steve has the calm, patient personality to create the climate and sustain its purpose. Some teachers or students might be more comfortable with a bit more structure and documentation. Nancie Atwell has described such a workshop in her book *In the Middle: Writing, Reading, and Learning with Adolescents*. Based on Atwell's version—which itself draws heavily on the work of Graves, Calkins, and Giacobbe—we can describe a day in the life of a workshop that's a bit more structured than Steve's, but has the same aims at heart. Figure 7–1 gives an overview. Assuming a 50-minute period, here's a little more detail about how time and activities might be apportioned on an average workshop day:

• 5 minutes: *Focus lesson*. The teacher presents a mini-lesson on some concept or technique for writing. These topics are chosen on the basis of what the students in the workshop have recently been trying to do, problems they have been struggling with. For example, if the teacher notices many people are having trouble punctuating dialogue, she'll offer a focus lesson on quotation marks and dialogue writing at the start of the work-

Figure 7–1 *Typical Schedule for a One-Period Writing Workshop*

5 Minutes (optional): Mini-Lesson

A short lesson on some aspect of writing that one or more members of the class have been trying to use in their current writing (e.g., quotations, descriptions, supporting arguments, footnotes, etc.).

5 Minutes: State-of-the-Class Conference

A quick round in which individual students tell in a few words what they will be working on today.

30 to 40 Minutes: Writing Time

THE STUDENTS: Go to their folders and get out current work. They may either start a new piece, work further on a continuing piece, proofread and edit, or work quietly with other students.

THE TEACHER: 1. Writes herself to model.
2. Monitors to give momentum to the workshop.
3. Conferences one to one with varying purposes:

Process conference—responding to meaning, content.
Editing conference—done at final draft stage.
Evaluation conference—done occasionally, to grade.

10 Minutes: Sharing

Time to pull things together at the end of the workshop. Options:

1. A few individuals share their writing aloud.
2. The class debriefs the activities of the workshop.
3. Planning for publishing or other related activities.

TOTAL: 50–60 Minutes

(One to five days per week, depending upon grade level, the focus of the course and curriculum.)

shop time. Obviously, if there's only one workshop session per week, these focus lessons might also be transplanted to some other day, to leave more real writing time.

• 5 minutes: *State-of-the-class round.* Everyone says in a few words what they will be working on that day, such as "Second draft of my photosynthesis paper" or "Starting a new sonnet." The teacher makes a note of each in her log. This creates an implicit contract between student and teacher for the day's work, and it also lets everyone know what others are working on, so they can later connect for sharing or for getting help.

• 30 minutes: *Writing time.* Working from their folders, students draft, revise, polish, collaborate, as they choose. The teacher's role during this time is more complex. She needs to divide her time between several possibilities:

Writing: Especially early in the course, it is vital for the teacher to be a writer in the workshop, working on her own pieces. The teacher should have and keep a folder, demonstrating (and experiencing) her own process. In general, the teacher should do everything she asks the students to do, at least some of the time. As important as modeling is, though, its greatest impact will be early in the course when students are surprised and impressed by the novelty of a teacher who writes. Once the teacher is an established fellow writer, she can spend less class time modeling her own writing and turn to some more powerful teaching activities.

Monitoring: Some teachers like to spend the first few minutes of the workshop moving around the room, taking a quick peek over people's shoulders, providing information or answering questions for kids who are stuck, getting a sense of what's being written and how the work is going—and, obviously, serving as a physical, implicit stimulus to work.

Conferencing: Conferences can be structured around many purposes. As we saw above, Steve Ogilvie likes to let students provide the direction for each conference. Other teachers prefer to have a focus or theme for given conferences, and there are many ways to do this. Graves, Calkins, Atwell, and others have long chapters on all the various types of teacher–student conferences, ranging from conferences in which teachers simply offer a feeling, human response to a kid's ideas, all the way to evaluation conferences in which a whole portfolio of work is reviewed to yield a letter grade. Helping students without taking over the writing is a complex, sensitive task, and we review some specific techniques for doing this in Chapters 12 and 13.

• 10 minutes: *Sharing/Debriefing/Logistics.* The last few minutes of the day can be saved for students who have something to share aloud, for making decisions and plans about group publishing projects, and for debriefing the group process of the workshop itself.

How Topics Are Generated

The writing workshop technique has been pioneered mostly at the elementary level, and this raises some questions about its applicability to older students. Junior and senior high school teachers often wonder: "What about assignments? Some of my students will freeze up and not be able to think of anything to write about. They'll sit there and stare into space and waste the whole workshop. Can't I at least give assignments to these kids?"

The fact that some students don't immediately thrive in a writing workshop reminds us of why the workshop is so important. Remember, one of the main purposes of having a writing workshop is to give kids time when their writing is completely their own, when *they* make all the choices—sometimes tough and painful choices—real writers have to make. This means that students make their own decisions from the very start ("What shall I write?") to the very end of the process ("Goodbye, my little piece of writing, going off to your audience!").

Clearly, in a writing workshop we are not giving kids some kind of permissive, do-your-own-thing, fun-and-free day off work. On the contrary, we are handing them a lot of responsibility, a challenge. We are asking them to run their own learning, to make their own meaning, to generate their own ideas and set their own work schedule. We're treating them like responsible people and giving them a chance to grow in this responsible role. Of course, this way of working violates almost all their training in school, which tells them to do what the teachers says when they're told to do it. The key thing we teachers must do to make the workshop function is to stick with our plan. We must give kids time to adjust and refuse to back down and return to the old ways, when we made all the decisions. We have to have the courage to live through the uncomfortable, uncertain transition period, which is almost always very short.

Back to the question of where topics will come from for the kids who are stuck. Mainly, they will come with time. For some students, there may be a few dry minutes or even days at the start, but as soon as they realize that the choices are truly open and that others are taking advantage of the invitation, they will join in. You can help these kids through those tough first days. Use your conference time to meet with kids who are stuck. Talk to them about their interests, families, enthusiasms, problems, travels, pets, friends, teams, cars, whatever. In other words, do a topic search with them. Look for strong responses or interests, and reflect those back as possible writing topics.

Or get them started doing some Elbow-style free writing. Show them how to do it. Do it with them, right there: both of you write for two minutes straight and then talk about what popped up. Or suggest some reading: have the student bring a book, or *you* bring in some articles or magazines that might grab the kid's interest. Encourage him to spend writing workshop time reading until an idea strikes him or until he feels ready to try free writing as described above. Nancie Atwell implicitly goes about halfway toward assignments by suggesting not topics, but *genres*, encouraging kids who are between pieces to try a new genre. Her helpful list of possibilities appears as Figure 7–2.

Figure 7–2   Modes and Genres of Writing *(from Nancie Atwell, In The Middle)*

Personal experience narratives

Fictional narratives:
  Short stories and novellas (tall tales, sci-fi, historical, romance, fairy tales, contemporary realism, etc.)

Autobiographies

Biographies

Essays

Research reports

Textbooks

Reviews of books, records, plays, movies, and TV shows

News stories

Reports of current events and features

Children's books

Jokes and riddles

Games and Puzzles

Captions and labels

Coloring books with text

Cartoons

Annotated calendars

Advertisements

Poetry:
  Ballads
  Limericks
  Rhymed couplets
  Acrostics
  Counted-syllable formats
  Free verse
  Other formats

Correspondence:
  Friendly letters (to pen pals, teachers, friends, and relatives)
  Invitations
  To the editor
  Celebrating holidays
  Marking special occasions
  Requesting permission
  Letters of thanks, complaint, love, application, sympathy, inquiry, farewell, protest, advice, apology, congratulation

Editorials and opinions

Parodies

(Continued)

Figure 7–2 (Continued)

Song lyrics

Diaries and journals

Field journals and learning logs

Petitions

Scripts:

  Skits

  Plays

  Radio plays

  Puppet shows

  TV commercials

  Speeches

Public notices:

  Posters

  Dittoed announcements

  Intercom announcements

Last will and testaments

Eulogies

Recipes

Memoranda and messages

Interviews

Oral histories

Instructions and advice

Rules and regulations

Lists and notes

Mottoes and slogans

Scrapbooks (and accompanying
  texts)

Yearbook blurbs

Contest entries

Time capsule lists

Awards and inscriptions

Forms (for others to complete)

Computer programs

Resumés and cover letters

Finally, if a kid is totally blank and utterly teacher dependent, don't force him to go cold turkey and sit, as if punished, with nothing to write as the workshop hour drags on. It's not his fault he's learned what school teaches about who runs his work. Give him a suggestion or two, but do it privately in conference after you have exhausted *all* the other alternatives. Such topics should arise from whatever you've learned in conversation with the kid. "Why don't you write about how you got interested in drag racing?" "Could you write up some instructions for someone who's never gone snorkeling before?" "What's it like working at Taco Bell?" But remember, this is a last resort: workshop time is for kids' own writing, from start to finish.

One way to work on the topic problem proactively is to have students spend part of their first workshop day developing an agenda or list of topics they want to write about during the coming year or course. There are several ways to do this; one is simply to start with a group brainstorm about all the topics a person could write about, or some of the different genres of writing people in the group would like to try out. The teacher can list ideas on the board for a while, as kids call them out, and then, once sufficient energy is built up, shift to an individual activity where kids extend the list privately, with their own ideas. Each kid can end up with a list of topics to write about and a list of genres, or types of writing, they'd like to attempt during the year. Then, later in the year when dry spells strike, the student's stimulus of first resort will be her own agenda of writing possibilities for the year, which has been stapled right inside the cover of her writing folder since the first week of class.

Another way of generating an agenda of topics (at least autobiographical ones) is to have students make a road map of their life, a historical graphic representation of the key events, twists, turns, and bumps along the road of their own life to date. Kids can use little graphic symbols for some of these events on the map. This too can be stapled inside the cover of the folder as another list of topics. (See Carl Koch and James Brazil, *Strategies for Teaching the Composition Process*, for more on this idea.)

Record Keeping

What about record keeping? How can I prove that I'm using my instructional time well if students are all doing something completely different? How can I show what I've taught through this individualized activity? How can I prove that I am teaching some of the subskills in the curriculum guide?

If you share these concerns, then Nancie Atwell has lots to offer you. In her workshop there are several kinds of records. She reassures us that once you've got the system set up, the record keeping is not onerous and actually facilitates the process. Among the documents kept in Atwell's workshop:

1. *Permanent writing folders.* Each student has one, in which are stored, clipped in sets, the drafts and final copies of all pieces of work completed during the year.

2. *Temporary writing folders.* Here, kids keep pieces currently in progress, including notes, drafts, and a couple of forms (see below). Some teachers operate folders on a regular schedule, cleaning out the temporary folder and transferring some items to the permanent one once a month.

3. *Student's topic list.* This is generated as described above (it may be a roadmap or other graphic model) and consists of topics and/or genres of writing the student plans to try during the year. These can be checked off as they are attempted and completed.

4. *Status-of-the-class record.* This is a class list used by the teacher at the start of each workshop session to note what each student will be working on during the class. Atwell uses codes to keep it short (D1 = first draft, R = rewrite, etc.).

5. *Focus lesson plans.* The teacher keeps track of what mini-lessons he has taught over the course of the term.

6. *Content conference notes.* When kids are at the early stages of working on a piece, the teacher conducts process or content conferences with kids, in which she helps them focus their ideas. Brief notes on the subject and direction of these conferences provide an important record.

7. *Editing conference notes.* When students have finished writing a piece in Atwell's classroom and have edited it to their own satisfaction, they put it into a special in-basket. Then, Atwell assumes the role of copyeditor—a true copyeditor, just like one at a publishing house, rather than a "gotcha"-type teacher-corrector. She marks up the text for publication and makes notes in her "Editing Conference Journal" in three columns: the name of the piece, notes on some skills that the student has begun to use correctly, and notes on no more than two skills that need further work. Then, in the editing conference at the next workshop session, Atwell teaches the student the one or two target skills.

8. *Student's skills list.* Just as Atwell has made a record of each student's skills to be worked on, so too do students record each of these areas on a record sheet of their own. Over time, this gradually accumulates into a long list of "Things I can do as a writer." This document stays in the folder and becomes a reminder to students during self-editing of things they are supposed to be able to do.

9. *Evaluation conference notes.* For the last several workshops of each quarter or term, Atwell conducts evaluation conferences, in which she and the student writer look over the polished pieces that are in the permanent folder. Atwell devises some questions to guide their discussion and puts these on a form that she fills out as the conference proceeds. "What's your best piece of writing this term? Why? I notice ——— about one of your pieces from last quarter. Can you explain how you made that decision about the piece?" This conference yields the cumulative grade for the course or for the writing segment of the course.

Looking at all this paperwork, you may react in a couple of ways. If you run a workshop like Atwell, you're certainly not embarking upon some informal ad hoc innovation. You're running a very tight ship, collecting a mass of rich and valuable data about what is being taught and learned and about the performance of each student. Indeed, it would be hard to imagine a junior-high or high-school course with more complete documentation than Atwell's: compare her writing workshop records to the typical science or math class, where the only evidence of work accomplished is a few numbers written in a grade book, numbers derived from point totals on Scantron-scored tests long since thrown away.

Indeed, we think that this much record keeping begins to raise questions in the other direction: it may be too much, too ponderous, too preoccupying, potentially an end in itself. For many kids and teachers, this degree of documentation is simply unnecessary. We think most teachers will want to pick a few key elements to track, rather than risk becoming a slave to record keeping. The purpose of all this, after all, is simply to monitor, review, and guide students in the workshop—and to be able to clearly show what you are doing to any curious outsiders.

JOURNAL WRITING

The keeping of personal journals is an old and wonderful idea, and it's a strategy almost all English teachers have tried at one time or another. For some of us, journals have become an integral, treasured part of all our teaching, while for others they are an abandoned innovation that didn't seem to fit or to work. Because journals are a main mechanism by which students can get regularly scheduled in-class writing practice on topics of their own choice, whether they're part of a workshop setting or a more traditionally organized classroom, it's important to review their use here. If you already use journals, we hope this discussion will help you extend your repertoire; if you don't, we hope you'll consider giving journals another try, perhaps structuring their use a bit differently.

Ideally, we think kids ought to have some daily journal writing time except when they've focused on specific pieces in their regular writing workshop. However, in some classrooms or curricula, where whole periods of writing workshop time are not possible, daily journal-writing time of ten or fifteen minutes can fulfill *some* of the same functions that the writing workshop does: providing writing practice, keeping the choice of topics with the students, allowing students to divide their own time between new and old topics, and perhaps even giving kids some response to their work as well.

Many teachers save a regular part of each day or week for journal-writing time. The very first seven or ten or fifteen minutes of the period each day is a natural time, and so is a longer chunk of time less often, such as twenty minutes each Tuesday and Thursday. While this kind of time cannot be of as much value as the sustained longer workshop, it's a step in the right direction. Kids are likely to become quite enthusiastic and possessive about their journals and may begin to pressure the teacher for more time.

What can kids write about in journals, and what guidance should the teacher provide? The quick answer is: the topics and sources should be the same as in the writing workshop. After all, we're trying to use journal writing here for self-sponsored writing, as a kind of shorter version of the workshop itself. This means any and all of the topics and genres we talked about above should be possible for journals. But there's a problem. Too often, neither teachers nor students see journals so openly; instead, we mistakenly (and unconsciously) define journals too much in terms of personal *diaries*.

Obviously, there is great value in students using their journal as a personal diary; indeed, during the adolescent years, we want to affirm anything that kids can do to become self-reflective, to openly express their feelings and concerns. When a student uses a journal in this way, to sort through personal issues, and then shares it with a teacher, this is a gift of rare intimacy and trust. Needless to say, sensitive and caring teachers respond with empathy and encouragement.

But this is not all that journals are for, and believing so can choke off other topics, subjects that don't seem sufficiently self-revelatory or diary-like. If we're not very careful, this embedded misconception can not only narrow the range of seemingly appropriate topics, but also reduce students' general comfort level and sense of success with their journals. However, the problem is easily solved: we simply have to actively define, perhaps redefine, journals. We have to explicitly review for the kids and ourselves the limitless range of possibilities. One way to start students off with journals is to explain that there are ten general categories of things they might want to write about.

1. Reflections on your own personal life and feelings (the journal as diary).

2. Reflections on outside, real-world events that come to your attention through the newspapers, radio or television, or direct experience.

3. List of things to do, remember, think about, work on.

4. Reflections on your schoolwork, reactions to your reading assignments, notes or jottings about assignments or projects.

5. Reflections on the interpersonal processes developing in your writing class, in your peer editing group, etc.

6. Reflections on your development as a writer (or as a speaker, or user of language in general).

7. Reflections on your own thinking and reasoning processes.

8. Free writing: whatever is going through your mind here and now.

9. Doodles: any mixtures of pictures and/or words that reflect a state of mind; reflections on these doodles.

10. Direct comments, questions, or notes to the teacher.

This list covers just the broadest and most obvious categories of journal writing. In classes where the teacher is using a lot of writing-to-learn activities, the journal is also likely to be a natural place for these activities (see Chapter 8 for more on this). A number of writers have expanded our understanding of what can be done with journals. Ira Progoff, in his book, *At a Journal Workshop*, lists many more possibilities and thought-provoking ways to organize ideas in a journal. In *The Journal Book*, Toby Fulwiler and dozens of other journal enthusiasts share a delightful array of alternatives that bring to life the practical use of journals for learning in many subject areas and grade levels. Jana Staton has written extensively about the last type on our list, the kind of journal in which there's a real, ongoing written conversation between student and teacher.

Logistics of Journals

There are many effective ways to keep journals, and both writers and teachers tend to be emotionally attached to their own special formats. We'll just mention what works for us. We ask our students to keep their journals on loose-leaf paper in a three-ring notebook, so that they can take individual entries out and share them without having to part with the whole journal, as you must with spirals or bound books. This format also works well when you're away from your journal and write an entry on a single sheet; if it's the right size, you can just punch holes in it for the notebook, and if it's not, you can paste or staple it to a standard-size page and slip it in.

As far as the journal *as writing practice* is concerned, there's no need for anyone to review or even read what kids have written. And, of course, because of the nature of the content, some of what appears in a journal may not be meant to have any outside audience. However, with both these provisos, we think it is very important for teachers to read *most* of what kids write in journals. Students do like to get a response to some or all of their journal writing on a regular basis. So we ask that they turn in one entry (or whatever more they wish to share) once a week. While we're reading this piece or pieces, students can keep writing in their journal as usual. It's wise to have journal entries submitted on a staggered schedule by classes (first period on Monday, second period on Tuesday, etc.), so you don't get 150 of them on one day.

When we respond to journals, all we do is read them as another human being, perhaps in the role that James Britton called "trusted adult," receiving the writing and the ideas and reacting naturally. Post-it notes are a great way to offer short responses, comments, and questions without writing directly on the face of someone's journal, which should be avoided.

Teachers often worry that students will use their journals to write about sex, pregnancy, grave family problems, the use of drugs, the contemplation of suicide, or other issues that test the confidentiality of the journal relationship and may impel the teacher to act. There's no use pretending this can't happen; indeed, every teacher who uses journals has had times when her judgment and wisdom were tested. These very rare events, though, are no reason to abandon journals, to give up this priceless way to know all your students closely and individually, in a fashion that would never evolve from knowing them in a group.

There are a number of steps a teacher can take to protect himself against a situation that would be uncomfortable or would pose a painful conflict. The first and most direct way is for the teacher to state and set limits: if you don't want to hear about, think about, deal with drugs or sex or some other topic, you can simply ask students not to include these topics in the journal entries they select to submit to you. The cost of this approach, of course, is that you are saying that you want to hear about some of their lives, but not everything. It may put some limits on the potential trustfulness of the relationship. Another approach is to tell students, "Write about anything you like in your journal, but be aware that if I read something that indicates that you or someone else is in serious danger, I cannot promise to keep it a secret. I may talk to you about it and I may also decide that it's my responsibility to inform other people who could help." With this warning, you reserve your right to act, and you'll know that students who do report serious problems are very likely asking you to be the intermediary in getting help.

On these rare occasions when a student's journal (or other piece of writing) communicates urgent personal problems, it's undeniably tough. We English teachers are forever complaining, "I'm not a psychiatrist—I have no training—I don't know how to deal with this." The fact is, of course, that we *are* psychiatrists in our classrooms every day: we observe, analyze, and draw conclusions about the mental state of our students and groups. We may not have very good training, but we do know a few things about the care of psyches—and perhaps all that background in literature doesn't hurt our judgment either.

The journal entry that drags a teacher briefly into a student's serious personal problem is too often recalled as a teacher's horror story, a cautionary example of a good activity gone wrong. Some people even use these stories as a reason to not try journals at all. But instead, we should recognize these occasional events as times when something happened *just right*. It may not be comfortable, but how can anything be wrong when a troubled student uses an established, private channel to enlist the help of a responsible adult—an adult who has proven, by the way she teaches and by who she is in the classroom, that she is a person who cares?

Chapter 8

Writing to Learn Every Day

We have provided plenty of time for students' self-sponsored writing through the writing workshop and journal keeping. Next we need to consider the possibilities for writing that is more guided and focused, writing that brings students more fully together as a learning community. One way to do this, obviously, will be through formal, structured writing assignments that teachers can make for a whole class. These kinds of activities are the main subject of Chapter 9, and such assignments can be deepened and strengthened through the approaches described in Chapters 10–15.

But there is another kind of writing activity that's in between: writing to learn. Writing to learn is not about crafting your own narratives or poems, not about conducting a transaction with the real world, not about creating beautiful objects with words; it's about using writing—usually expressive-mode writing—as *a tool for thinking.*

Writing to learn may be defined as short, spontaneous, unedited, exploratory, personal writing that's used not to affect an audience but to channel, crystallize, record, direct, or guide a person's thinking. A handy, familiar example of writing to learn is the homely grocery list. Before you go shopping for food, chances are you make out a list of all the things you need. While you are writing your list, some entries will probably remind you of other things you need but had forgotten. Some people even find themselves subconsciously clustering items by the aisle in the store where they are located. In other words, your emerging grocery list not only records your thought process but may stimulate and channel it as well.

Then you take your list to the store and buy the pickles, ham hocks, rye bread, cauliflower, and other things you need (and probably a few unlisted, impulse purchases too). Once you've paid for your cartful of groceries, what do you do with your list? You throw it away. You do not revise the list, polish or edit it. You do not send it off to the *New Yorker* in fond hopes of getting it published. Chances are (if you shopped alone) that no other audience would ever read your list at all. The list is—was—writing as a tool of thinking, a crescent wrench of the mind. You used it to organize a little bit of your behavior, and now you're done with it. There are lots of powerful ways students can use such tools in school, many of which are outlined in this chapter. And writing-to-learn activities always make us language-arts people happy because they are another way of sneaking more writing practice into school, giving kids more ways to succeed at writing, more opportunities to use writing to get important work done.

In fact, we don't even think of writing to learn primarily as a language-arts activity, but instead as *a teaching method*. Whenever you as a teacher have a particular piece of content to teach to your students, you always must select from a range of instructional options: you can give a lecture, show a videotape, organize some small-group work, coordinate independent projects, or do any other of dozens of things. Or you can have students *write*. They can write about what they *know* about the subject at hand, what they *feel* about the topic, what they *wonder, predict, judge*, and so on.

Clearly, this is not writing as a language art, but as a thinking tool. Writing to learn offers teachers a very efficient way to help kids learn content, whatever content you have to teach. As a teacher, you can use these writings to organize time and groupings and activity and talk in the classroom. They can help students generate ideas for discussion, discover what they know about a topic before they begin studying it, recognize the questions they have as they proceed, figure out how elements of a topic are related, and more. Indeed, as a tool of teaching and learning, writing to learn is an asset to teachers of all subjects, not just those of us in English or language arts.

So what do these activities look like in a little more detail? As we've already noted, most writing-to-learn pieces are:

- Short—usually just a few sentences, notes, phrases, or listed items.
- Spontaneous—by definition, writing to learn is spur-of-the-moment, unplanned, one-draft, rough-draft writing.
- Exploratory—the aim is to think, to speculate, to turn over ideas.
- Personal—usually written in informal, expressive-mode discourse.
- Reflexive—primarily intended for the self as audience, rather than an outside reader, though writing-to-learn pieces may be shared.
- Unedited—not polished or revised.

Writing to learn fits between formal assignments and self-sponsored writings of the workshop in a particular sense. As with formal assignments, the teacher usually provides the material, the interaction, or the idea that stimulates the writing. But as in the writing workshop, the author retains complete control over what she writes: there are no "musts" or requirements. Instead, this is a genuine opportunity for the learner to explore ideas on her own terms. This means that writing-to-learn activities almost always use expressive-mode language and are written with the student herself as the primary audience. Though writing may be shared, summarized, or referred to, it is never handed in, graded, or formally evaluated. Writing-to-learn pieces belong to the student as tools belong to a mechanic or craftsman: when a craftsperson is through with a job, no one is interested in the state of his Phillips screwdriver—they want to see the results of the work. With writing to learn, the product is the learning, and writing—the screwdriver—is put quietly back in the toolbox.

A TOOL FOR THINKING

In a moment, we will offer a list of specific writing-to-learn activities that can be adapted to the content and the moment of almost any course. Before introducing the list, though, we'd like to clarify what we mean when we say that writing to learn is a "tool for thinking." These days, the "thinking skills" fad is every bit as popular as the notion of a writing crisis and just about as susceptible to scams and dogmas. We'd like to offer a brief mechanism for sorting things out. The issue is: if you're going to use writing as a tool to help students think about a given piece of content, exactly how do you want them to think about that content? To answer that question, you need to answer some others:

1. What specifically is the *content*? What are the key ideas or concepts for students to engage with?
2. What *kind of thinking* might students to do in relation to this particular content? There are many different ways for students to connect intellectually with a given piece of content, and you must consider what some of the most appropriate, challenging ones are.
3. What kind of *writing-to-learn activities* will help kids think about this content in those ways?

The missing link is a scheme for *thinking* about using writing for thinking skills—not to make this scheme into a partisan doctrine, but to provide a descriptive system for checking whether we are considering all the alternative writing possibilities. We'd like to recommend the thinking categories of Louis Raths as outlined in his book *Teaching for Thinking*. Raths' book originally appeared in 1976, long before the Thinking Boom, and it evades some of the traps that more recent theorists have fallen into.

Eschewing any battles over what are the higher- and lower-order thinking skills, Raths essentially says: Here are thirteen ways of thinking that human beings seem to find important and useful. In school, we teachers ought to check frequently to make sure kids are getting a fairly balanced opportunity to develop each of the types. Here are Raths' thirteen thinking skills, with a very brief sketch of each, as originally developed in a workshop handout by our colleague, Linda Tafel, of the National College of Education:

1. *Comparing:* Students have the chance to observe differences and similarities in fact or in contemplation. They examine two or more objects, ideas, or processes with the idea of seeing what relationships one has to another.

2. *Summarizing:* The idea of a summary is to state in brief or condensed form the substance of what has been presented, read, or observed. It is restating the gist of the matter, of the big idea or ideas, concisely but without omitting important points.

3. *Observing:* Behind the assignment to observe, there is the idea of watching, of noting, of perceiving. Usually we are paying strict attention; we are watching closely, and for a purpose; we are involved in something, and we have good reason for noting carefully. On some occasions we concentrate on details; at other times on substance or on procedures; and sometimes on both. Sometimes we are concerned with great accuracy of observation, and sometimes only with approximations.

4. *Classifying:* When we classify or sort things, we put them into groups according to some principle that we have in mind. If we are asked to classify a collection of objects or ideas, we begin to examine them (observe); and when we see certain things in common (compare), we start by putting those objects or ideas together. We keep at it until we have a number of groupings.

5. *Interpreting:* When we interpret an experience we explain the meaning it has for us; interpreting is a process of putting meaning into and taking meaning out of our experiences. We check our inferences against the facts to see if the data support the interpretations. There is a tendency to generalize on the basis of insufficient evidence.

6. *Criticizing:* When we criticize we make judgments; we analyze and make evaluations. We do this in terms of some standards that are implicit in our statements. Criticizing is not a matter of finding fault or censuring.

It asks: What is the evidence in support of the idea? What standard is being used? What value or worth is present?

7. *Looking for assumptions:* An assumption is something that is taken for granted—an underlying, implicit element of thinking or valuing. When we search for the assumptions in a piece of reading, in human interactions, or in real-world artifacts, we are consciously comparing our own thinking/ valuing system against others.

8. *Imagining:* To imagine is to form some kind of idea about what is not actually present; it is to perceive in the mind what has not been wholly experienced. It is a form of creativeness. We make mental pictures, feelings, sounds, experiences, or possibilities.

9. *Collecting and organizing:* The beginning of any thinking process is the material or content at hand. Often the material is not already within ourselves but must be sought out, collected, and organized. We start with the student's own curiosity, his own question, his own seeking. How to collect the data should be part of the planning process.

10. *Hypothesizing:* A hypothesis is a statement proposed as a possible solution to a problem. It suggests a way of "going at" something. Very often it also represents an effort to explain why something will work, and it operates as a guide in going ahead with the solution of a problem. It is tentative and provisional. It represents a guess. Sometimes we restrict the term by calling it "a working hypothesis." When we are faced with a puzzling situation, an obstacle, a block of some kind, it is almost automatic for us to conceive some way out of the dilemma. These hunches or ideas constitute hypotheses.

11. *Applying facts and principles in new situations:* This is one of the most common ways of emphasizing thinking. A student is supposed to have learned certain principles, rules, and generalizations. A new situation is presented to the student to see if the principles can be tested or applied.

12. *Decision making:* This skill is similar to applying principles to new situations, stressing the moments at which choices between alternatives are made. The student is asked to give reasons for choices made.

13. *Designing projects and investigations:* If students are working on projects of their own, for their own purposes, they are apt to work hard and long at the task. Almost always a significant project involves many or all of the other operations of thinking described above.

WRITING-TO-LEARN ASSIGNMENTS

Steps one and two, then, involve looking at particular chunks of curriculum you need to teach and considering which thinking skills seem most relevant, or most likely to help enrich students' understanding of and engagement with the material. Then, as step three, you can select from among many kinds of writing-to-learn activities, some that will allow students to enact and share the thinking you'd like them to engage in. Below are a number of such writing-to-learn activities. This group of possibilities is long and varied, and some activities intersect, overlap, or (as much as we have tried to make it otherwise) simply repeat things said earlier in the book.

Admit Slips

Upon entering class, students turn in short pieces of writing on a previously assigned topic, such as a summary of the previous night's reading. To begin the class, the teacher reads some or all of them aloud, with or without names. This activity can be used to focus on the day's topic or upcoming activity. It also provides an audience for students' work.

Exit Slips

Exit slips are similar to admit slips, only at the end of the session. Students do a short piece of writing, giving their response, summary, or questions about the day's class. The teacher may collect and read them, or save them for reading aloud at the next class.

Short Writes in Class

Short writes can be done on index cards, on paper, or in journals, and there are many varieties:

• *First five minutes of class each day.* Students may write on the topic of the upcoming lesson. This can be the same question each day (reflections on the reading, questions I have this morning, etc.) or may be in response to a specific question or quote put on the board each day by the teacher. Short writes work especially well to begin a class, since they cause students to stop socializing, look down at their writing, tune in to the lesson, gather their thoughts, and get centered.

• *Focusing write.* As the class shifts to a new activity or discussion, students may write for two to three minutes to refocus on what they know about the topic at hand. This helps students clear their minds of previous issues and prepare to join in a discussion of the new topic.

• *Mid-activity/discussion write.* Too often in presentations, teachers feel a need to plunge on and "cover the material" when in fact students would benefit greatly from an occasional pause for them to write and reflect on their thoughts. Some possible focusing questions: What am I thinking or wondering right now? What do I grasp up to this moment? Having a short write in the middle of an activity or discussion gives students a chance to consolidate what's been learned so far and helps them prepare to go on.

• *End of activity/discussion write.* To help conclude or reflect on a completed topic, students may sum up, list what has been learned, and note what questions remain.

• *New topic previews.* Writing just before embarking on a new area of study can also be useful. Students can focus on what they know beforehand, their expectations, their questions going into the new area. Notice the strong connection between this idea and research that shows the value of prediction and prior knowledge in reading comprehension.

• *Focused free writing on key words or key terms.* Students may also write definitions of, elaborations on, or questions about the central vocabulary of a topic. This helps to consolidate their knowledge of concepts.

Learning Log or Journal

Some teachers who have become committed to writing to learn have formalized this approach by asking each student to keep a continuous learning log throughout the class. While some individual topics may be set by the teacher, the essential idea is for students to make regular journal entries on a number of general and recurrent topics—three, four, or five entries per week, in class or at home. This document becomes a special place where the learning in the course is both accomplished and reflected. As some of the possible entries below indicate, a beneficial side effect is that students become more consciously aware of, and reflect upon, their own learning process—a formal cognitive operation, according to Piaget.

• *Reflections on homework.* Students can use their learning log to reflect on homework—summarizing key points, noting questions or puzzles remaining, or responding to the teacher's skillfully posed higher-order thinking questions (not the standard end-of-the-chapter factual recall kinds of questions).

• *Dialectics.* The log may serve to relate information and thinking processes. Each log page may be divided in half. The left side is used for note taking during reading or a class lecture or activity, and the right half is used for the student's reactions and questions. In math, one side could be used for the student to do problems, and the other to explain in words how she approached them, where difficulties arose, and what she wants to ask the teacher.

- *Dialogues.* Students can use their learning logs or journals to create dramatic dialogues between opposing characters, historical figures, points of view, intellectual traditions, and so forth.
- *Response to reading, homework, problems.* Students may write a summary, or translation of an assignment after it's been completed, giving an account of their experience with the work. Figure 8–1 shows how Lisa Zissionopoulos, a student at Hinsdale Central High School, uses her writing for math homework assigned by teacher Kathy Stambaugh.
- *Paraphrases.* The log may be used for summaries of key ideas, quotations, and/or scenes.
- *Thinking analysis.* A student may write an explanation of his thinking process in a given subject, up to the point where any difficulties are encountered. He could, for example, show how a math problem is tackled and worked through up to the point where he becomes stumped.
- *Independent study.* The log may become an appropriate mechanism for monitoring a student's progress in independent projects. Along with learning-in-process reports, a student can keep an account of how her time was spent.
- *Collected works.* Since it may reflect much of a student's learning over time, the learning log may appropriately be used as a basis for a part of a student's grade. Students resubmit the log toward the end of the course for a summative review.
- *A note on teacher response to logs.* The more central the learning log becomes to the conduct of a course, the more important (and seemingly problematic) it becomes for the teacher to evaluate the log. Though the teacher will of course see some individual entries along the way, there needs to be a procedure for him to look at the larger collection, especially if the logs are also being used as a channel for private communication between teacher and students (see below). One system for review is for classes or groups of students to turn in logs on a staggered schedule: group 1 on Mondays, group 2 on Tuesday, and so forth. The teacher's examination of the logs should be quick and impressionistic; these are not meant to be edited, published pieces. Use Post-it notes for response, so the logs won't be permanently altered or defaced by your markings.

Collaborative Writing

One of the best ways for students to externalize, verbalize, and further organize their thinking is to work with one or two peers to actually draft a piece of writing together. This may be done by pairs or small teams. It works well on a paragraph or short research/observation report.

Figure 8–1   Learning Log Used for Math

Honors Geometry : Finding the Distance Between Parallel Lines

Directions: <u>READ</u> the following mathematical procedure carefully <u>THINK</u> about what each step accomplishes, then <u>WRITE</u>, in your own words what you think each step accomplishes.

Problem: Given $\mathcal{L}_1 = \{y = 2x + 3\}$ and $\mathcal{L}_2 = \{y = 2x + 6\}$, find the distance between these parallel lines.

<u>Procedure</u>

Explanation

1) Assume x=1 then $y=2x+3$
   $y=2(1)+3$
   $y=5$

1) Substituting x for 1 to find what y equals.

2) If $m_{\mathcal{L}_1} = 2$ then $m_{\mathcal{L}_1 \perp} = -\frac{1}{2}$

2) Finding the slope of the line $\perp$ to the first equation by taking the neg. reciprocal.

3) $y = mx + b$
   $5 = -\frac{1}{2}(1) + b$
   $5\frac{1}{2} = b$
   $\frac{11}{2} = b$

3) Finding what the y-intercept is by substituting in x, y, & m into the equation of a line.

4) $\mathcal{L}_3 = \{y = -\frac{1}{2}x + \frac{11}{2}\}$

4) Substituting in the information you previously got, to make an equation for the line $\perp$ to $\mathcal{L}_1$.

5) $\left. \begin{array}{l} y = -\frac{1}{2}x + \frac{11}{2} \\ y = 2x + 6 \end{array} \right\} \rightarrow$ $-\frac{1}{2}x + \frac{11}{2} = 2x + 6$
   $-x + 11 = 4x + 12$
   $-1 = 5x$
   $-\frac{1}{5} = x$

   $y = 2x + 6$
   $y = 2(-\frac{1}{5}) + 6$
   $y = 5\frac{3}{5}$
   $y = \frac{28}{5}$

5) Solving the equation of $\mathcal{L}_3$ by substituting what y equals in $\mathcal{L}_2$. Then substituting what you found x to be into the equation of $\mathcal{L}_3$ to find y.

6) $(x_1, y_1) = (1, 5)$ and $(x_2, y_2) = (-\frac{1}{5}, \frac{28}{5})$
   $d = \sqrt{(x_2 - x_1)^2 + (y_2 - y_1)^2}$
   $d = \sqrt{(-\frac{1}{5} - 1)^2 + (\frac{28}{5} - 5)^2}$
   $d = \sqrt{(-\frac{6}{5})^2 + (\frac{3}{5})^2}$
   $\therefore d = \sqrt{\frac{45}{25}}$ or $\frac{3\sqrt{5}}{5}$

6) By using the distance formula find the distance of $\mathcal{L}_3$ which is the distance between $\mathcal{L}_1$ & $\mathcal{L}_2$.

Observation Reports

Science labs have always provided a special and valuable kind of composing: gathering data from the close observation of physical objects, processes, phenomena, and events. This sort of writing can be extended to data gathering and observational reports in a number of other subject areas and formats. For example, social observation (ethnography) and interviewing are subtypes that can be useful in social studies classes.

Instructions/Directions

The "how-to" is one of the most primitive and inherently engaging forms of writing. Classroom possibilities include how to conduct a science experiment, how to build a piece of equipment, how to plan a political strategy, how to solve a quadratic equation. Notice the natural audience possibilities, if the purpose is real inquiry in the class and not just writing practice. Notice also that evaluation can occur naturally: can the reader do the task, based upon the instructions?

Faction

Students can create fiction that depends upon a solid understanding of facts studied in a course. Examples: imaginary scenes from history or from novels; roving reporters interview Pythagoras, Madam Curie, Hitler, or whomever. You can't write a "missing chapter" of *Huckleberry Finn* or corridor gossip from the Constitutional Convention unless you know the context.

Correspondence Between Students and Teachers

Learning logs or journals can be a private channel of communication between teachers and students, which typically develops into an exchange of information about both academic and interpersonal issues. For this to succeed, however, the teacher must make significant efforts to institutionalize the practice, perhaps by initiating the first notes, by installing a mailbox, by doing much modeling, and by responding promptly. Here's a variation from Toby Fulwiler: explain in advance that questions may be made public unless otherwise requested; then copy selected questions for projection on an overhead, and discuss the issues in class.

Class Minutes

Each student may serve (on a rotating schedule) as minute taker for one daily class session and must produce a set of official class minutes by the following class. Minutes are either posted in a regular spot or copied for distribution to the group. Reading and correcting these minutes provides an excellent focusing activity for the start of each day's class; having everyone's attention gives each student author a chance to shine. Authors often try to infuse the minutes with as much personality as accuracy will permit. The teacher should do the first day's minutes to set the tone.

Problems, Questions, Exercises

Students can write their own study/writing questions on the material being covered: essay questions, mathematics word problems, science experiments, and so forth. Doing these early in a unit can provide an agenda for the work.

Upgrades: Formal Writing from Writing-to-Learn Pieces

Any piece begun in one of the above writing activities can be pushed toward a more formal, more edited paper. In fact, this program of frequent, exploratory, natural, daily writing-to-learn efforts is almost guaranteed to produce ideas that students will be eager to follow up and develop further. Some instructors have students search for a fixed number of promising starts, developing one or more into formal essays for evaluation.

Part III

*Designing
and Conducting
Writing
Activities*

Chapter 9

Designing Writing Activities and Assignments

We've talked a lot about self-sponsored writing and writing to learn. But what about writing assigned by the teacher? There's no doubt that as teacher-made assignments are traditionally given, they often deprive students of more opportunities for learning than they provide.

On the one hand, teacher-directed assignments often include far too little teacher involvement: typically, the teacher does nothing to help students with the work between the time she announces the topic and the time the papers are due. This kind of instruction, when measured against the newer process paradigm, doesn't look like instruction at all. It utterly fails to enact any steps or stages in the creation of the work, and it reinforces the common and crippling student misconception that writing is supposed to be a single, spontaneous act.

On the other hand, many assignments stipulate *too much* teacher involvement. Donald Graves points out that choosing a topic is one of the most important steps in the writing process, and yet students get to practice it least. In addition, it is all too easy for us as teachers to provide such extensive guidelines and formulae that we take out of students' hands most of the authoring decisions they need to make in order to become practiced writers.

We don't think it's safe to generalize about whether teacher-made assignments and structures *always* confine or *always* liberate student writers. Indeed, unless you can witness firsthand the live human interaction, it's hard to know whether *any* particular intervention or words have freed kids to think and grow, or whether they have restricted them and made them more dependent. We've observed teachers provide writing stimuli that encourage students to look for more possibilities, that help them discover how much they have to say, or that engage them in dialogue and

117

exchange of ideas. Conversely, we've observed teacher–student conferences in a "process writing workshop" where supposedly nondirective "help" from the teacher actually limited students and signaled to their well-tuned antennae just what the teacher "really wanted."

We believe it is possible to unravel this knot by redefining the term "writing assignment" so that it includes *everything* a teacher can do in the course of students' writing a particular piece—rather than referring only to the teacher's statement of a topic. By doing this, we can expand our picture of what such strategies might include, so that the concept of a stimulus or "assignment" refers to a much broader list of possibilities.

Many helpful teacher actions are possible at all stages of writing assignments, including conducting prewriting activities, helping with drafts in individual conferences, teaching focus lessons on particular writing methods or structures, providing models, organizing oral sharing sessions, suggesting revision strategies, and scores of other possibilities. Suggesting a topic is just a beginning, just one of many activities a teacher can use to help students develop a given piece of writing. But even if it is just a beginning, there is an art to designing these first steps, topics, and activities. Needless to say, the best ones are far more complex than the kind of truncated "compare and contrast" commands that far too many of us remember from our own high-school days.

In this chapter, then, we'll apply the concepts discussed in Parts I and II of this book to redefine "writing assignment" so that it includes all the actions, decisions, and interventions a teacher may carry out as students write. In the process of doing this, we also want to demonstrate that a writing assignment needn't be given in isolation just to teach skills, but instead can be thoroughly interwoven with reading, discussion, listening, thinking, and anything else that might go on in a supportive and intellectually stimulating classroom.

Our expanded definition of the term "assignment" results in an outline of the many elements involved in planning a particular writing activity—not a neat formula, but rather a series of questions a teacher might consider. For any given assignment, the teacher may give instructions in some areas, and leave others to student initiative; he may structure activity directly through explicit statements or indirectly through a series of activities; he may encourage choice through explicit option-generating methods with the class, or let choices emerge gradually as students read, hear, and think of more alternatives; but he can at least consciously decide what's appropriate and what his students need, rather than act merely out of habit. In the process of taking this larger view, we can also begin to unravel the question of *more versus less* for teacher-structured assignments and make some sense of the question of whether teachers should be giving assignments at all—and, if so, how much of the time.

HOW A WRITING ASSIGNMENT CAN FAIL

One way to help us think about what makes a good writing assignment is to begin by considering a bad one. What follows is a question used on the ETS Advanced Placement English Composition test:*

Directions: *You will have 20 minutes to plan and write the essay assigned below. First, consider carefully the following statement. Then, read and follow the directions that are given in the assignment that follows the statement.*

> *Wastefulness is part of the American way of life. We use three packages or wrappings when one would do, build machines to be obsolete in five years, and generally waste time, energy, and natural resources. Yet we consider thrift a virtue and we consider ourselves efficient.*

Assignment: *Are these statements justified? Do they tell us anything about ourselves? Explain and defend your answer, using illustrations from your reading, study, or observation.*

You are expected to express your thoughts carefully, naturally, and effectively. Be specific. Remember that how well you write is much more important than how much you write. DO NOT WRITE ON A TOPIC OTHER THAN THE ONE ASSIGNED ABOVE. AN ESSAY ON A TOPIC OF YOUR OWN CHOICE WILL RECEIVE NO CREDIT.

You must fit your essay on one special answer sheet. You will receive no other paper on which to write. You will find that the space provided is enough if you write on every line, avoid wide margins, and keep your handwriting to a reasonable size.

TURN YOUR ANSWER SHEET OVER *and begin writing your essay on the lines provided.* DO NOT WRITE IN YOUR TEST BOOK. *You will receive credit only for what you write on your answer sheet.*

---

*We're not ignoring the fact of life that students often are compelled to write on bad assignments like this one, sometimes in very high-stakes circumstances. Certainly, part of our role as writing teachers is to prepare kids to cope with such occasions. But for our day-to-day instruction, we do not take our cues from test items devised by prompt-writers. We want to give students the best writing assignments and activities we can, to build their fluency and flexibility and confidence. Then, even on those few occasions when they must write to an ill-designed prompt, they will have wide and deep resources to carry them through.

You probably already have a mental list of the problems such an assignment presents. Here's ours:

• The directions are laced with threats and warnings, setting a tone that's hardly conducive to expressing oneself "naturally."

• There is no specified audience. To ask "Do they [these statements] tell us anything about ourselves?" begs the question: who are we? One would write very differently to be "effective" with a corporate executive, a packaging salesperson, a conservationist, or an auto mechanic.

• The assignment discourages prewriting and revising by stating that "the space provided is enough if you write on every line. . . ." This sounds as if every inch had better be filled, and not with plans or outlines. The final paragraph of the assignment commands the student to simply "begin writing."

• It asks students to "be specific," even though the statements themselves are flaccid generalizations, and it invites further unfocused generalizing by asking, "Are these statements justified?" High-school students are likely to know little that's specific about this topic, except in a personalized way. In fact, the request for specificity is something of a trap, for the essays receiving the highest scores tend to straddle both sides of the argument.

• By providing just twenty minutes to deal with an astoundingly complex issue, it rewards quick and facile "BS" writing, rather than encouraging any real thought on the subject. In a very real sense, it encourages students to fake and pretend, rather than really write. But perhaps these are valuable traits in the endeavors that many "successful" students elect to follow.

HOW A WRITING ASSIGNMENT CAN BE STRENGTHENED

What could be done to improve such an assignment, particularly if we wanted to turn it into one that *encourages* good writing, rather than trying to reward superficiality or to trick students into doing badly? We might answer this question by drawing on as many of the principles outlined in Chapter 2 as seem relevant. We'll use them in an order that makes sense as we think through the assignment, rather than in their original numerical order.

• *Principle 15: Writing for learning across the curriculum.* The topic of environment and waste actually holds promise, and is never far from the top of the American political agenda. It's worth keeping in some form.
• *Principle 1: Have positive expectations for students' achievements.*

This means that the tone of the instructions must be changed. Students should be addressed as responsible citizens: "Perhaps you'd like to do something about environmental problems and industrial waste here in our own community. . . ." This also helps address Principle 4: Writing for real, personally significant purposes.

• *Principle 5: Writing for a wide range of audiences.* Given the above shift in approach, one could go on either to specify a single audience, such as the owner of a local bottling company fighting a new deposit ordinance, or to have students first take on the roles of various people in the community—corporate executives, environmental activists, town aldermen, Federal EPA representatives, and so forth—and write position papers to be given a trial run at a class "town meeting." To move beyond role playing, real representatives of business and environmental groups could be invited into the class to respond to students' questions and ideas.

• *Principle 10: Use of inquiry-oriented activities.* This means the assignment must provide data to work with, an intellectual environment, not just a few vague generalizations. For one example, data from Barry Commoner's helpful book on environmental issues, *The Closing Circle*, indicate that people don't buy more clothes, use more cans, etc., per capita, than they did thirty years ago. But more goods are now made from synthetic materials that are processed from petroleum (plastics, synthetic fibers), or refined by using large amounts of electricity (aluminum), and these materials do not break down when discarded into the natural environment.

• *Principle 3: Instruction in the process of writing.* The data and the purposes outlined above could readily lead to prewriting activities— focused free writing for students to quickly inventory what they know about the issue, small groups working over data to infer implications (this would also address Principle 8, collaborative activities for promoting writing), or role-playing discussions to get the debate started. Revising could come after the "town meeting," using the discussion to reveal which arguments need strengthening.

• *Principle 6: Rich and continuous reading experience.* Much has been passionately written on environmental problems. During the writing activity, it would certainly make sense to assign short readings from works by Commoner, Rachel Carson, or current newspapers, and to obtain fresh information from industries, advocacy groups, the EPA, and the like.

Obviously, we've moved this writing assignment in the direction of an integrated activity like the extended Hemingway lesson described in Chapter 3. It's important to stress, however, that every writing task need not turn into a long-term project. Each of the strategies suggested above is elastic

—expandable or compressible as necessary—and not every step need be covered thoroughly with every topic. Early in the semester, a teacher may stress prewriting and spend several days using it for just one assignment, to give students a good start and an understanding of how different strategies can help them. As students learn to work effectively in large and small groups, and to do more of their own prewriting, the emphasis may shift to group- and self-critiquing, revision strategies, and public sharing.

This range of options can now help us think about whether a teacher should introduce an assignment on environment and waste at all—whether, as Donald Graves suggests, teachers should instead let students discover their own topics and issues of concern. In fact, we'd like to state right here our belief that the more freedom and initiative students can assume in the classroom, the more they will learn about writing, and the more writing will serve as a liberating and growth-producing activity. The problem is that we—and Graves—are proposing this freedom and student-centeredness in a social context that remains highly authoritarian. At the present time in this culture, schools are not models of democracy. In fact, democracy is still an experiment, something we've had only a few hundred years to begin growing into. Older students particularly, who are not accustomed to choosing their own topics or making their own decisions about when they are ready to have something evaluated, may find it hard to take advantage of such freedom or may misinterpret it as weakness on the teacher's part and not make good use of their time. Both students and teachers become addicted to the security of directions.

The question, then, is how to move students toward greater freedom and responsibility. We've been searching for bridges, ways to help students make this move, and we believe that when teachers work on this task their role in the classroom is not lessened but truly revitalized. As a first step, teachers can look for assignment activities that don't just announce topics, but help students become engaged, so that they discover more of their own inner resources and motivations. Even if it's the teacher who initiates the topic—say, by bringing in a newspaper article on an environmental battle like acid rain—the students can be helped to examine their own responses and realize they have much to say and more they'd like to learn. (We'll describe some of these activities in the next chapter.)

Second, many assignments are actually very open rubrics that offer a wide variety of choices for writing, if only these are teased out a bit. An effective prewriting activity not only introduces the topic but helps students brainstorm the many options they have. When we introduce a topic like "an accident you had or witnessed," we always suggest a long list of possibilities—falling as a small child, breaking a toy, dropping your mother's favorite vase, breaking a bone, accidentally hurting someone else, having or seeing an auto accident, making mistakes, and having close calls—as well as happy accidents, like meeting someone by chance and so forth. According to some world views, there's almost nothing in life that couldn't be written about in response to our accident assignment.

Third, conceiving of an assignment as a full range of teacher interventions rather than simply the announcement of a topic reminds us that a writing activity has many aspects, any of which may be structured by the teacher or wholly, partly, or totally left to the students' initiative. Personal topics often call for much less specification by the teacher than the more transactional subjects studied by the whole class. Insecure students may need more support than confident ones.

There are plenty of intermediate steps and options between teacher specifying and student choosing. For the environmental topic we described above, students can generate a list of questions and/or related issues they wonder about as a result of an initial news article, and each student can go to work on an item from the list: if none of those satisfy, you and they can keep brainstorming until meaningful connections do evolve. Is this a teacher "assignment" or a student "choice"—or perhaps a bit of both? In fact, it divides the notion of assigning a topic into several steps and allows the teacher and students to share the responsibility.

This sequencing of the work in explicit, manageable steps is the fourth of our bridges between teacher direction and student initiative. It not only allows shared responsibility, but also helps teachers to actively encourage this sharing—showing students how they can identify their own topics, consider alternatives, generate details, evaluate, and improve—without telling them what they must write. Many teachers find that as students become more involved with their writing during the semester and discover the value of journal writing, revising, and seeking peer responses, they begin to use these methods more on their own.

CONSIDERATIONS IN DESIGNING WRITING ACTIVITIES

Designing an effective writing activity, then, needn't require that you forage for unusual topics or tricky new methods. You can use subjects already included in your courses, topics you've tried before, and materials close at hand: and you can revise and deepen them, break the work into manageable steps, create strategies to help students become involved, to extend their knowledge so that they have more to say, to help them generate arguments and then compare, refine, and polish them. The following list of considerations for designing writing activities is meant to help teachers do this. It is really nothing more than a recasting of the fifteen principles of the process paradigm into an order and form useful for planning writing activities.

Contextual Issues

1. *The students.* What do students need at this point? What is their developmental level? Their working style? The class climate? At what point in the year, and in the group's development, will this activity be used?

2. *The extent of student initiative.* Many items below may be determined by either the teacher or the students. What decisions are students ready to handle? (Don't underestimate your kids.) What is appropriate for this topic? For which items will students need guidance? Which instructions should come early? Which ones later?

3. *The extent of the project.* How much class time is available? What is the desired length of the writing? How important is this activity?

Basic Direction of the Writing

4. *The topic.* What, specifically, is meant to be the subject matter of this writing? Is wide choice by students welcome? Will there be a specific question, text, or material? Does the topic open up further choices? If so, what?—a combination of teacher specification and student choice? Is this part of a larger sequence or unit? If so, how does it contribute?

5. *The purpose.* What is the *real* reason for the assignment—to help students learn subject material? to increase trust in the classroom? to communicate with a particular audience? to develop self-awareness? to create pleasurable language? to teach a particular writing skill? What purposes will *students* have as they write—to convince an audience of something? to understand their own ideas about a subject? to get a grade? What motivational activities, explanations, introductions to issues will be needed?

6. *The audience.* Who, besides the teacher, is this writing intended for—the student herself, classmates, other classes or grades, parents, the community, a particular outside group? What data about this audience will students need? How can students be helped to anticipate the needs and attitudes of their audience?

7. *Mode of writing.* What genre (or range of possibilities) will be appropriate—letter, story, editorial, poem, research report, dramatic script, something other than these?

Classroom Process

8. *Structure of the class.* Should this be an individual project? What help can students give each other? Should there be collaboration by small or large groups? Should there be a combination of methods (e.g., groups for brainstorming, but individual writing)? Should students respond to data separately and then combine or compare results? What sequence of dialogue and peer interactions will occur as the activity proceeds?

9. *Getting started.* What prewriting—journal keeping, listing, talking, clustering, brainstorming, or other initial help—will be needed to select a more specific topic, choose sides on an issue, marshal arguments, and so forth?

10. *Data gathering.* How should information be obtained—by internal research using journals? interviews? exploring or observing? films? questionnaires? reading in a text or library? Will you need to provide materials—articles, examples or pieces of data, people to interview? What help do students need (for example, will they need to learn how to conduct an interview)? Will data be needed before or after prewriting?

11. *Support during the process.* What problems are students likely to encounter? How will you monitor needs and give help—through one-on-one conferences, over the shoulder in the computer lab, by responding to early drafts? When is the best time for various explanations—at the start, or as the need arises? Should there be focus lessons on how to handle the various steps? Should organizing come first or wait until students have material to organize?

12. *Revising.* Should revising be optional or required? Should the focus be on content, clarity, correctness—just one, a combination, or all three? How will students gain perspective—by rereading their own paper, peer critiquing, comments from the teacher, response from an outside audience? What guidance or instruction will be needed? How should it be handled—through class lesson or guidesheets?

13. *Publishing.* How will the writing be transmitted to its audience (besides the teacher)? Will it be presented aloud in class? read silently by selected peers? Will pieces be bound together as a magazine and placed in the library, sent to relevant community organizations, or displayed or circulated elsewhere?

14. *Evaluation.* What are your expectations? Are certain elements essential? What is the range of ways a student can succeed—are any unusual but valuable outcomes possible? What is the purpose of the evaluation—to be diagnostic, to improve on the next paper in a sequence, to generate a final grade for the year? What aspects of the writing will be evaluated, and what is their relation to the original purpose of the assignment? How and when will expectations be communicated to students? What comments will be provided—suggestions, questions, encouragement? Will self- or peer evaluation be involved?

This is a long and complex list, so we'd like to suggest some ways to keep it from becoming overwhelming. First of all, you must see it as a menu, not a checklist. A checklist is an instrument that reminds you to do *everything*; a menu offers you many choices, from which you pick a few. You wouldn't order everything on a menu; instead, you pick one dish from each section. And you don't devour everything you've ordered all at once, but rather in stages we call courses. Writing assignments are like that. The teacher needs to select *some* elements of the task to specify, but not everything—far from everything. A good assignment leaves many meaningful choices and decisions for students to make, though it may provide help in the process of finding and making these choices. And the teacher doesn't give all the parts of the assignment at once, but spins them out one or two at a time, letting the work unfold in small steps as the students' engagement deepens.

We are talking about two principles that make this list really useful: *selection* and *sequencing*. You need to pick a few items to specify and then present them in a sequence that helps writers. Good assignments do not consist of a teacher delivering a carefully picked group of specifications all at once. Try to imagine how students would react to our tried-and-true interviewing assignment from Chapter 6 if, instead of announcing the steps one at a time, the teacher presented the whole series of activities right at the start. Read the following aloud, without pause, to get the effect:

In a minute, we're going to do some interviewing on the subject of names. But first we're going to brainstorm a list of some of the questions that you could ask someone if you wanted to find out about them by interviewing them about their name. I will write these suggested questions on the board. After that, we'll get into pairs and take turns interviewing each other for about seven or eight minutes each. You'll make some notes during these interviews. Then we'll each write a single paragraph that introduces the person to the group. To do this, we'll draw upon our notes, however they help us. Then we will take turns reading our paragraphs to the whole group. About halfway through the sharing, I'll ask what a paragraph is, and we will discuss that for a while. Then, as we listen to the rest of the paragraphs of introduction, we will try to "hear" the underlying structure of each paragraph. Then, when everyone has read, we'll try again to define paragraphs. Then we'll talk about what it felt like to be forced to write, to interview an-other person, to share our piece in the large group, and to be an audi-ence for others. Next, we'll all go home with the phone number of the person we interviewed and try to come up with a longer and more pol-ished version of our introduction that fits on an 8½-by-11-inch page, leaving a 3½-by-4½-inch blank spot for a photo. When we return here, we'll paste the pictures into the appropriate places on the pages and then photocopy and bind the set, making a booklet about the members of the group. Someone will make a cover, and we'll circulate the final product to an audience of our peers.

Imagine a teacher telling students all these steps at the start of the assignment. To do so would make many writers feel overwhelmed and discouraged. It doesn't generate energy for the work, but instead makes people nervous. Yet notice that this is exactly what many content-area (and sometimes even English) teachers do when they introduce their big Term Paper assignment: they hand students an imposing, multipage, typed sequence of specifications that, in its completeness, in its failure to *select* and *sequence* the instructions, actually becomes immobilizing and disen-abling.

So the art of lesson design involves not just selecting elements to specify, but figuring out the order and pace with which to present them to students. You can use the above list as you design activities. Obviously, the number of possible combinations, like any other artistic choice, is just about in-finite. But this huge range of choices reminds us that there are many different ways we can influence our students' writing, rather than being confined to the drills and paper grading that have always taken up so much time and have returned so little result. And it suggests ways in which writing can be integrated with other activities—reading, discus-sion, research, thinking, debating—so that even if the curriculum leaves limited time, teachers can find creative ways to incorporate the writing process into their everyday teaching.

Here's an example of how Elaine Taylor, a teacher of seventh-grade English at Wauconda Junior High School, used some of the many elements of a good assignment to get her kids writing and using writing to learn something important. Elaine explains that she designed the activity out of desperation. Interestingly, her students did fine when she let them choose their own topics, but on more arbitrary teacher-assigned tasks, even the prolific writers clammed up. Yet she felt they'd need ways to respond better when external needs *did* set out the subject matter. This activity represented her effort to make the act of assigning more mean-ingful.

Elaine first gave out the following questionnaire, and asked her students to fill it out with a thorough explanation for each "Why" question.

AGREE/DISAGREE STATEMENTS

Circle A if you agree with the statement and D if you disagree with the statement. On a separate sheet of paper, discuss, for each statement, why you answered as you did.

1. *Children who have AIDS should not be allowed in school.*

    A   D   Why?

2. *AIDS victims should be quarantined.*

    A   D   Why?

3. *More money should be spent on AIDS research.*

    A   D   Why?

4. *Parents should not allow their children to play with children who have contracted AIDS.*

    A   D   Why?

5. *The rights of all children are more important than the rights of children with AIDS.*

    A   D   Why?

Elaine was surprised at the amount of time her students demanded for writing out their justifications.

Her next step was to put the kids in small groups to compare and discuss their answers with one another. Then they read, silently, the following article by Mike Royko from the *Chicago Tribune*.

FEAR OF AIDS BOY SHOWS A SICK HEART

A 13-year-old girl who lives in the suburb of Wilmette has sent me a letter that shows that kids can sometimes have more sense than their elders.

"In one of our elementary schools," she writes, "there is a . . . boy . . . who has AIDS.

"A lot of my friends, their brothers and sisters and their parents are against his being in school.

"There was a meeting for parents the other night, and there were a lot of parents who want him out of the school.

"So far, 23 parents have pulled their children out of school until this matter is settled.

"I know that AIDS is a terrible disease and that the boy might not have many years to live.

"The thing that's really bugging me is what all the parents and their families are putting the boy and his parents through.

"No one will let their child play with the boy, and there are even some bad rumors about him going around.

"I know that these people are concerned. But for heaven's sake, why can't they try to make the boy's life happy?

"How would they feel if their own children, suddenly, through a blood transfusion, got AIDS and then, with all the trauma, when they needed friends the most, they all became afraid and wouldn't come near them?

"I don't know how you feel about this, but if you feel the same way I do, you could write about this and tell those people what pain they are causing for the boy and his family."

Unfortunately, there isn't much that I could say to those parents that would change their thinking.

By now, medical people have explained to them that they don't have to worry about their children catching AIDS from that unfortunate boy. It's not transmitted by being in the same classroom or the same schoolyard. Their children are not in any danger if they play with the boy.

Nor is there much point in telling them that what they're doing is cruel and unfair. If they don't recognize that themselves, your telling them or my telling them isn't going to change their thinking.

So the best thing to do is let them indulge in their own fears. If they want to pull their kids out of school, they should be allowed to.

Remember, the majority of the parents at that school aren't becoming hysterical or irrational.

And what you can do is to learn something from it.

In your letter, you questioned how someone's "friends" could desert them when they're needed most.

The key to your question is the word "friends." It's one of the most misused words in the language.

The people who take a walk when someone has problems aren't friends. Oh, they might have given the impression that they were. Dinner together? So good to see you again. Golf next Sunday? Oh, thanks for the anniversary gift, it was beautiful.

But friend? A long time ago, a very smart guy told me that if by the time you are getting gray you can count your real friends on the fingers *of both hands, you're fortunate. He may have been exaggerating. One hand might do it.*

So the people fleeing from that boy and his family aren't friends. At best, they're acquaintances, and not worth bothering to know.

And their fear, disgust, or whatever emotions motivate them should tell you that someday they'll suffer even more than that boy and his family.

Eventually, they'll have to face the same thing that boy and his family are facing. Not necessarily AIDS. But it will be something. We're all just passing through, and eventually something jumps up and grabs us, whether it's disease, accident, or the vital parts just wearing out.

Some can handle it better than others. Others start to collapse at the thought of the end.

I have a feeling that people who are that repelled or terrified by the non-threatening presence of one sick child in their midst are going to spend their last moments kicking and screaming.

After reading this, the students wrote paragraphs to state their reactions, and shared the paragraphs aloud. Finally, Elaine asked how many had changed their minds about their responses to one or more of the questionnaire statements. Obviously, many who had reacted with the fear that children all too readily pick up from their parents had rethought the problem with much more care.

It's worth noting that Elaine certainly did define the topic for her students, but it wasn't an arbitrary one. We don't think her assignment was authoritarian or limiting, but in fact opened up more possibilities for them. She had several purposes, of different kinds, in setting up this activity. She wanted to help her students respond to teacher requests for writing. But she also wanted them to think seriously about a real topic that was swirling all around them at the time. She didn't lecture, or tell them what to think, or insist that they change their values. But she did include some reading on the subject and allowed the process of talking, reading, writing, reacting, and talking some more do its work in moving them toward responsible evaluation of an issue.

The activity took just two class periods. It did not require much help from her, and did not need to include, at least at that point, a revising stage. Kids did the most important revising in their minds. Formal evaluation, too, seems optional. The most important evaluation, self-evaluation, had already occurred, as students reached important realizations, whether they changed their views or not. Next time they'll probably gather more data and consider more perspectives before drawing conclusions about unsettling public issues.

Elaine Taylor skillfully designed an assignment for the particular needs of her students at a given time, using material that was available and current. By understanding as many elements of students' writing processes as possible, teachers can create their own fresh assignments for their own kids' immediate needs, incorporating as much freedom as the students will use. Teachers can acquire the tools to troubleshoot and refine their materials as well, rather than jump arbitrarily from one fad or classroom trick to another when things don't go perfectly the first time.

Anyone who uses an assignment such as Taylor's needs to nurture and influence many elements in the classroom—the overall climate, the balance of initiative between teacher and students, the sequence of steps in the students' writing activity. We've already discussed classroom climate and considered the main kinds of writing activity available—self-sponsored writing, writing to learn, and assigned writing. In the following chapters, we'll examine the teaching of key aspects of the writing process, one at a time. Later, in Part V, we'll explore more extended integrated activities and research projects.

Chapter 10

Prewriting

If engaging with topics of real significance and breaking the work into steps are two of the most important elements in students' learning to write, then solid, extended prewriting is the most effective activity to be found in the writing teacher's tool kit. It offers high return for the time invested. And if you're just beginning to rethink your teaching methods and are feeling overwhelmed by all there is to deal with, prewriting is the place to begin.

Before we offer specific suggestions, it's important to consider some of the characteristics of good prewriting activities, so you can more easily create your own and evaluate others you come across.

1. Prewriting involves using structured activities to help students gather and organize material for writing and become engaged with specific topics. This may include internal activities such as thinking, memory search, and contemplating personal values; but it can also include such things as dialogue, research, data gathering, experiments, class discussion, or debate. One advantage of a shared subject for the class—*if* it's developed in a meaningful way—is that it creates a community of inquiry, an experience that can be far more satisfying, for many students, than sitting alone searching arbitrarily for topics to write about.

2. Teacher-guided prewriting doesn't necessarily mean dictating the content of students' writing, or even indicating the form or structure of what the student will write. Rather, prewriting helps students realize they have a great deal of choice, even when a specified topic or piece of curriculum is involved. In good prewriting activities, students generate many possibilities and are then given a structured opportunity to choose from among them.

3. Most effective prewriting involves multiple steps arranged in a sequence that supports students' own thinking, not just one or two clever tricks a teacher pulls out of the bag. Often, the first step is to surface some shared concern or interest in the class through a brief piece of reading, a movie, a visitor to the school, or a good discussion that occurs in response to some topic or reading already being studied. Next, students can list questions and ideas that have developed in their minds as a result of the initial stimulus. Then they can generate material, using internal contemplation, group discussion, or outside data gathering of some kind. Finally, they can look for a focus in the material they've begun to amass before they begin actual drafting.

The order of these steps will differ, of course, depending on the circumstances. For example, data gathering may begin before question generating, especially if the topic is one the writers know little about. They may not be sure what questions to ask until they have gotten involved in the subject. We've offered a variety of sequences to illustrate some of the alternatives throughout this book, particularly in the chapters on assignment design, integrated activities, and collaborative research, as well as those provided later in this chapter.

4. Whatever approaches you use, prewriting takes time. Teachers in writing workshops are always surprised at how much time is required by the prewriting activities they find most powerful, and kids in the classroom are no different. For a short piece on a topic from students' personal history, fifteen minutes spent listing, choosing, and visualizing is the minimum. For the kinds of complex activities described above, where students are really exploring a subject in depth, several class periods may be used raising issues, brainstorming ideas, and gathering material.

5. Prewriting is just as important for transactional—persuasive, descriptive, and informative—writing as for personal, autobiographical pieces. Some of the current process experts on teaching composition give the impression that the only meaningful topics are personal, expressive ones. However, students can readily become engaged in academic and externally focused topics; teenagers are not totally self-absorbed and usually care passionately about some issues beyond their everyday lives. Not only is transactional writing important throughout schooling; it is a valuable avenue of personal growth, and a useful tool in life. Prewriting activities are an efficient way to make such writing meaningful and help students improve its quality.

One special task of prewriting for transactional topics is to help the writer deal with relatively new material. Unlike writing about family, friends, or important events in one's life, writing about an academic subject means grappling with information and ideas the student has not had time to contemplate or sort out over a long period. This is one of the main reasons that students' more formal analytic pieces are so often much weaker than their personal essays. A good prewriting activity for a transactional topic will thus include steps to help with the sorting, analyzing, and sense-making needed before students can write well about a new subject. It's an obvious but overlooked truism that the quality of students' writing is limited by the information they have or can get and the sense they can make of it.

Let us now review some of the basic kinds of prewriting activity in the repertoire of many good writing teachers. We are aware of three general categories of prewriting, each of which has been discussed in depth by other teachers, theorists, and researchers.

- Internal thinking processes, such as free writing, visualizing, and clustering.
- Group processes, such as brainstorming, small-group problem solving, and whole-group concept mapping.
- External data gathering, including observation, interviewing, surveys, and reading.

In the course of inquiry for a particular piece of writing, it's not difficult to make use of all three types. We'll provide brief descriptions of specific methods in each area and then some illustrations of how they can be combined in sequences that initiate students' thinking and culminate in writing some kind of draft.

INTERNAL PROCESSES

Free Writing

This approach, first described by Ken Macrorie and then elaborated by Peter Elbow, aims to help unblock writers stopped by the blank page or hindered by the urge to interrupt production with constant editing. It has been misunderstood by researchers who attempt to evaluate it as if it were simply the spontaneous drafting of a finished text. Elbow himself makes clear that free writing is just a good first step for writing.

As we noted in Chapter 6, the rules of free writing are simple. One sets a time limit, say five or ten minutes, and writes *without pausing* for that period. There is no stopping, no going back to scratch words out or correct spelling. The writer can put down whatever she wants, and if nothing comes to mind, can write, "I don't know what to say, I don't know what to say. . . ." or list colors, verbs, or anything else, until a new idea surfaces. She can stay with one topic, interrupt it to start a new one, or simply register the thoughts and sensations of the here and now. Two examples of free writing are shown in Figure 10–1 (*a* and *b*).

The aim of free writing is not to produce "good" writing, but simply to unlock the gates, to establish a flow. The writer may discard the entire sheet when finished, and just regard it as a warm-up or a dump of the distractions and preoccupations of the day. Students can learn a lot about how the mind works just by looking at the content of this mental unloading. But often a single good sentence or paragraph will be worth saving, a start on something the writer would like to say or a piece for the middle of an assigned topic.

Focused Free Writing

Focused free writing uses the same rules as described above, except that the writer begins with a specific topic. He may digress and interrupt his ideas but should attempt eventually to steer back toward the central focus. Focused free writing can be a good way to record initial reactions to a piece of reading or a class discussion.

Clustering

Clustering is an arranging of words in two-dimensional patterns, guided by a process of radiating associations. The writer starts with a circled word or phrase in the middle of a page, perhaps a topic choice of her own or a word connected with material being studied by the class. Then she writes words and phrases she associates with the first word, circling them, arranging them around the first word, and drawing lines showing the connections in her mind, like spokes in a wheel. Additional associations may arise with some or all of these new words and are added to the diagram. The writer can then use this clustering in a variety of ways: as an outline or list of subtopics she wishes to cover, as a scaffolding that leads her to the issue she really wants to focus on within the larger topic, or as a guide to a group of issues related to one another, in one region of the diagram. The method is described in detail by Gabrielle Rico in her book, *Writing the Natural Way*; an example is shown in Figure 10–2.

Figure 10–1 Two Examples of Free Writing

A

I'm glad it's over. I can't wait until tommorrow when I can finally rest. I'm so tired Sometimes it's hard to write what when you're thinking because you're thinking about writing I don't know about, oh shoot I need to get passes. I bet there's going to be hardly anyone at the meeting. I hope I get to hear Kim's tapes. I wonder who'll be at the get-together tommorrow. I hope Sehba's there. I'll have to call and see if she's coming. I wonder when I'll get my braces off I hope before Pictures are taken, my ID looks really dumb. That box was so heavy my arms hurt. I'm so sleepy. I wonder if the physics-quiz is going to be hard. I hope Mr. Thor is not mad because we didn't meet for Math Team yesterday I think he understands

Figure 10–1 (Continued)

B

> Ghosts, I found this confusing, What is the point, the idea? I know, I think, those people are so loud loud, aint they shut up, my life is screwed but I think I getting it together what am I going to do all these applications to fill and mail. How am I going to pass that physical fitness test. Will I run well today, will I get first place? Nah, not even close. What will my parents say. Stuck. Hell is life, why is life is heaven for other people. Other people do well but they got so many white hair but I dont, do they worry more than me or what!

Concept Mapping

Concept mapping is similar to clustering, except that its production is not necessarily associational. A student can begin with a list of subtopics, cause-effect relationships, or whatever aspects of his topic are relevant, and arrange these in a two-dimensional chart. As connections are drawn in, using lines from one item to another, these can be labeled to explain how the two items are related. This method is especially helpful for writers who are trying to learn and write about larger subject areas.

Poetry

Almost any mode of writing can be used to generate ideas for any other. For example, many business writing experts recommend that if one has a particularly complex or diplomatically sensitive memo to write, one should try drafting it first as a letter to one's spouse or close friend. We've experimented with *diamantes*, poems written in the shape of a diamond, as a means for doing the same thing: thinking about ideas for one mode of writing by composing in another. The structure is simple:

Figure 10–2   Clustering

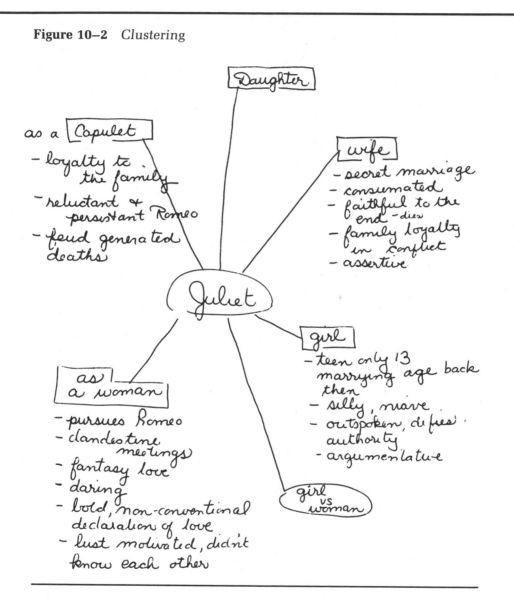

Daughter

as a Capulet
- loyalty to the family
- reluctant & persistant Romeo
- feud generated deaths

wife
- secret marriage
- consumated
- faithful to the end - dies
- family loyalty in conflict
- assertive

Juliet

as a woman
- pursues Romeo
- clandestine meetings
- fantasy love
- daring
- bold, non-conventional declaration of love
- lust motivated, didn't know each other

girl
- teen only 13 marrying age back then
- silly, naive
- outspoken, defies authority
- argumentative

girl vs woman

```
                       NOUN
              ADJECTIVE     ADJECTIVE
              VERB      VERB      VERB
PARTICIPLE    PARTICIPLE    PARTICIPLE    PARTICIPLE
              VERB      VERB      VERB
              ADJECTIVE     ADJECTIVE
                       NOUN
```

The first and last nouns can be opposites, or may be related in some other way, and the words between can build on the differences between them as well as the underlying connections. One colleague of ours applied diamantes to social studies, with results like this:

```
                        Washington
                  Heroic        Aristocratic
              Lead      Fight       Conquer
    Nurturing    Creating    Establishing    Stabilizing
              Defend      Struggle      Save
                Murdered      Commoner
                         Lincoln
```

Two samples from Robin Wolf's class at Deerfield High School show how well the activity works even in French, and how the substitution of a statement instead of four participles works for the middle line.

```
                          Vic
                  Sportif     Fatigué
        Courir    Faire du Vélo     Grappler
      J'adore la concurrence avec autre gens
          Le vélo    Les filles     l'argent
                 Occupé     Drôle
                   Concurrent
```

```
                         Tracy
              Energique     Contente
            Rire    Parler    Skier
            J'aime l'été à la plage
      Mes amis, mes bateaux, les garçons
            Amusante, Artistique
                      Élève
```

Journal Keeping

Any of the above activities, along with lists of possible topics and more directed leads, can be included in a regular journal. The journal has been popular in recent years as a place for students to write for their own purposes, without having to worry about outside audiences or evaluation. However, students can be asked to review their journals on occasion to hunt for entries that they'd like to develop into more extended, public pieces. Journals can lose their attraction after a certain amount of time, and this step helps make them seem more productive, giving students a fresh perspective on what they've accrued over a span of time. (In Chapter 7, we discussed journals as a place for self-initiated writing, and in Chapter 8 their use in writing-to-learn activities.)

Visualizing

Visualizing is a powerful technique through which students search their memories to recall sensory data from past experiences, to reconstruct scenes they have read about, or to create in their minds experiences from their own imagination. Because it works so well, evoking vivid details people have often forgotten, and because it requires some rather carefully worked out methods, we've set aside the next full chapter to explain it in detail.

GROUP PROCESSES

A number of the previous activities can be used as readily with a group as with individuals. Groups can create concept maps or clustering diagrams together, with the teacher or a student volunteer recording ideas on the chalkboard. There are additional techniques, however, that depend on the chemistry of a group, whether large or small, to make them work. Key to these activities is the importance of talk as people think, generate ideas, and make sense of information. They create audience and dialogue, so that writing is not done in mental isolation.

Topic Search Interview

Whether the writing is entirely of the student's own choice or related to a shared subject in the class, students can create lists of topic possibilities by interviewing one another in pairs. It's important that each speaker remain nonjudgmental and simply help extend the list, asking questions and exploring some of the essential elements of each topic. Often, one idea will remind the writer of a second and third, even if the initial one hadn't seemed significant in itself. Each listener can record the list as the other person talks, and then give it to the speaker to keep in his writing folder, to be consulted in the future when the well seems to have run dry. As Nancie Atwell describes in *In the Middle*, it's a good idea for the teacher to model a topic search of her own, to set the tone and demonstrate how ordinary day-to-day experiences and interests can become valuable topics.

Focused Interviews

Student interviews can draw out information for more specific subjects as well as for wider topic searches. As with the topic search interview, the presence of the interviewer provides an interested, questioning audience, someone who helps the speaker realize just how much she has to say. This is similar to the teacher–student conference, about which we'll have more to say later. For now, we'll just say that teachers should be aware that the methods they use in conferences provide a model for students to use with each other.

Brainstorming

The goal of brainstorming is to create as long a list of topics (or ideas, questions, concerns, data, whatever) as possible in a set time period. The formal rules for brainstorming are as follows. One person acts as recorder and writes all suggestions out on the chalkboard, using short phrases or single words. Participants call out their ideas, and all are written down, even if some repeat previous entries. No ideas can be evaluated or rejected. This not only keeps the list growing quickly but allows weaker ideas to lead to better ones through association, rather than cutting off the process. The class can work as a whole or split into several teams to see which can develop the longest list. After a long, rich list has been created, the group can select one or two of the most useful ideas or may sort the list into categories or otherwise use it to move toward specific writing activities.

Small-Group Problem Solving

Small-group problem solving works well for a number of reasons. It increases the amount of individual participation for a given time period, since fewer people need to contend for "air time" in a group of five compared to a whole class. It allows for student initiative and responsibility, since the groups can't all have the teacher sitting in with them. And it encourages friendly competition when the groups compare notes.

The groups can all be given the same problem or topic to consider, or each group can be assigned to tackle a different aspect of the subject. Brief oral reports can be taken from each group at the end of the discussion period so that all ideas become a help to the whole class, and the groups are made accountable for their work. Managing such group activities is an art, and we've provided some methods for training students to use groups effectively in Chapter 14. For a powerful justification of the method and some techniques to use, read William Glasser's *Control Theory in the Classroom.*

Debates and Discussions

Hot discussions on contemporary issues, disagreements on the flaws or virtues of a character, preference for one protagonist over another—good talk in the classroom—is always valuable as prewriting. Sometimes this can be planned (as in the "Franny" debate later in this chapter), and sometimes the teacher will want to take advantage of a passionate disagreement that unexpectedly develops. Any discussion can be stopped before all the participants' energy is used up, for students to free write their reactions. Bystanders to the disagreement may want, in their writing, to take sides or to comment on the exchange. Since it's almost impossible for everyone in a large class to join in, this step has the added value of recording responses that might otherwise have been lost.

EXTERNAL DATA GATHERING

Whether the topic is personal, social, or academic, outside information can be an important spur to students' thinking. Similar or contrasting opinions and experiences, data that reveal a principle, trend, or problem, concepts that help make sense of one's life—the world is full of stimulating stuff, and teenage boredom is merely a thin defense in the face of an adult world that is both attractive and a little threatening.

Surveys and Interviews

Once students identify a problem or question they're interested in, they can learn much from interviews. They can design written surveys to be administered to the whole class, to other students in the school, or to some segment of the larger community. They can prepare protocols for more in-depth interviews with one another or with people outside the classroom. Students may seek opinions from a broad sample of people to chart a controversy or portray a public attitude, or they may consult experts who can give them direct information about a problem. In either case, they'll need help designing their protocols and questionnaires, and they'll need to do some field testing on one another to learn what kinds of questions work well—otherwise, much time can be consumed gathering unusable results.

Observation

Sociologists and anthropologists learn to observe actual human behavior and analyze the patterns they see in it. Scientists observe chemical processes, animal behavior, complex ecosystems. Observing can provide rich sources of data for writing. However, beware of the old standard "how-to" essays, or the exercises in which everyone gets to peel and describe an orange; these are all too often introduced arbitrarily as writing drills, with no context or student engagement in any purpose for the writing. Such topics can become meaningful, however, if the teacher provides the steps that will make them so, and if the activities are relevant to students' lives and/or to topics they're already engaged with. For example, Jim Langlas at Wheaton North High School has his students compile collections of teenage how-to's—how to eat in the school cafeteria, how to get your mother to write an excuse when you're not really sick, how to wear out-of-date clothes and get away with it—based on students' observation and recollection. Obviously, it takes only a little preparation and the brainstorming of a good list of possibilities to make the activity work, and the writing calls for just as much detail and clear direction giving as any less engaging topic.

Reading

Researchers and teachers are discovering more of the connections between reading and writing. Of course, reading provides specific data and topics for immediate writing projects, but it can do much more than that. At a deeper level, immersion in certain kinds of reading helps all writers to assimilate the tone, flavor, structure, norms, and rhetorical strategies of particular genres of writing, a prewriting activity that's no less effective for being osmotic and unconscious. Further, reading helps students identify themselves as fellow writers. When kids come to see textbooks and novels not as fossils, but as writing done by other real people who struggle with their own writing processes and even get stuck occasionally, students can identify. Kids see their own stories, instructions, and explanations as the same kind of work as the published pieces they read—and they can learn about the craft of writing itself in a conscious way.

Writing needn't be just a response students provide after they've read an assignment. Prewriting can come *before* reading as well as after. Reading teachers know the value of predictive activities for improving students' comprehension of their reading. We've already mentioned dialogue journals that go back and forth between teacher and student or within student pairs; many teachers use these to help students become engaged in reading. Students can scan their entries later, to find an aspect of the book they wish to write about in a more extended essay or review.

PREWRITING SEQUENCED AND CONTEXTUALIZED

In isolation, the methods outlined above don't mean very much. And if they're introduced arbitrarily to start up an assignment that students aren't committed to in some way, then any teacher can prove to herself that "these ideas don't work any better than the old ones." So now we offer a few examples that are embedded in ongoing course work. Other activities scattered throughout the book provide as many additional variations as we could find room for.

A Debate on "Franny"

Bob Runtz of Hersey High School uses the following sequence not only to get students thinking about a piece of literature, but to set the tone for group work and classroom dialogue at the start of the year. Students begin by reading J. D. Salinger's "Franny" aloud in class, taking turns with short passages until the story is finished (it's around forty pages long). This in itself demonstrates that the class will be, among other things, a story-sharing group. Then each student writes a brief response beginning, "I sympathize with . . ." and chooses either Franny or her boyfriend to write about.

Next, students write a paragraph taking the side of whichever character they didn't choose the first time. When these pieces are finished, the students divide into two groups, according to the character they chose first, and the groups sit on either side of the room facing each other. Alternating sides, students now read their papers aloud. The teacher can join in, being sure to have written a paper for each side so he can join with whichever group is smaller when the division is made. Obviously, when the reading is over, students on each side will want an opportunity to rebut comments from the other side and to discuss the whole picture. There are many ways to structure this final step. One is to have a brief journal-writing session to help students focus their ideas and reactions.

The final arguments can be written at home as more extended essays and shared in class the next day.

Prewriting for a Prose Literary Topic

For a high-school British literature class, Barbara Dill, at Glenbard West High School, helps students respond to John Henry Newman's essay on education in the following way. First, they are asked to imagine that their school has been bombed and must be entirely rebuilt and reorganized. The class is divided into groups, which will act as school-board construction committees. They are to assume they've got all the resources they'll need and the power to carry out whatever they think best. The job of each group is to design a new school reflecting their ideals. The groups report to the class, and after discussion and comparison with Newman's ideas, students take some class time to free write on an aspect of the proceedings that now strikes them as important or an assertion they wish to make. Only now are they ready to begin organizing their thoughts to write about Newman.

Extended Topic Search

Teacher direction of a topic search needn't be limiting, but can open up possibilities for students who don't realize they have subjects they'd really like to write about. To help students choose topics for a longer paper, Robin Kacel, of Wheeling High School, finds she needs two full periods. During the first, she talks through a list of all the aspects of students' lives—home, parents, siblings, school, teachers, difficult or enjoyable subjects, jobs, friends, relationships, the most important person in their lives right now, church, clubs, future, dreams, ambitions, and more. As she slowly recites these categories, students jot down whatever words or phrases come to mind. Toward the end of the period, when this process is completed, they look over their notes and circle any words that turn up more than once, or any that now seem especially important. Overnight, they have the opportunity to consider this list further, think about possible topics suggested by the words, and consider whether there are others they'd prefer.

Robin also talks through her own topic search for the class, narrating her considerations, back and forth, about whether to choose one particular direction or another. She does this both so that students can see how such choosing takes place and so they can observe an adult writer at work. Struggling with her own writing efforts and modeling these for the class is, for Robin, an essential part of prewriting. She finds that it leads students to make free choices of their own more readily and thoughtfully.

The second day of Robin's topic search is devoted to brief conferences with each student, during which teacher and student together identify a topic. If this is to be a term paper, they find a transactional research subject related to one or more of the student's chosen items. The student may not be writing about a personal subject at all, but the academic content she studies will be meaningful because it relates to a personal concern. The preparatory work continues in a more focused manner from here. (See Chapter 19, on research writing, for further suggestions in this area.)

Obviously, there are many more possibilities and activities we could describe. In a good class, almost any experience or material encountered can offer the opportunity for reflection and dialogue using written language. However, once a teacher understands the structures and patterns of good prewriting activities, he can create his own at will, to fit the subjects, interests, and achievement levels in his own classroom. He needn't depend on books about teaching writing—this one or any other—to tell him what to do.

Chapter 11

Guided Imagery

It's early in the semester, but not the very beginning. The teacher is about to start a writing activity, and the class is mildly surprised when he asks them to put down their pencils. He explains that he will conduct an exercise to help them concentrate and create vivid images in their minds for their later writing. He asks them to sit back, relax, take a few breaths, and close their eyes if they wish. After further relaxation instructions, he asks them to imagine taking a trip down a wilderness river on a raft.

Speaking slowly, rhythmically, the teacher encourages students to gather confidence for this trip and then begins to describe the movement of the raft down the river, first through quiet water and then into more and more turbulent rapids. He asks them to feel the raft tossing and turning, to see the rocks and foam, and to hear the roar of the water. He even includes a stop at the shore before the roughest rapids, so that those who are uncomfortable can get out to walk past them. After the rapids, he continues, softly:

Your guide tells you it is time now to rest and seek new adventures, and he lands the raft at the mouth of a blind canyon. He tells you that you will be there for a time, and that you can explore the canyon. You move into it and find the tall cliffs on either side getting narrower and narrower above you until you are in the middle of a tunnel. It becomes darker and darker. What do you feel?

And without explanation, suddenly, light shines ahead, and you arrive at the mouth of a large cave, which is well lighted. The cave is guarded by a gatekeeper, who informs you that there is a treasure within, and you wonder what sort of treasure it is. You must prove yourself worthy of admission to the treasure cave by telling of something you have done, or accomplished, or achieved in your life. And you know that each of us has such a worthiness of some kind, and you now find what yours is. . . . You tell of your accomplishment to the gatekeeper as a ticket of admission, and she permits you to enter the cave. You are surprised and pleased that your treasure is something unexpected, yet very familiar to you, something you are happy to rediscover. What is your treasure?

*(Adapted from "Group Exploration: Guided Fantasy,"
in William Pfeiffer and John Jones,* A Handbook of
Structured Experiences for Human Relations Training,
Vol. 4, University Associates, 1973)

After a long pause, the teacher continues in a soft voice, telling the students that though they've enjoyed their treasure, it is time to leave it, and he brings them out to the river bank, where, night having fallen, they look up at the stars and contemplate all that has happened. Finally he instructs them to gradually return their attention to the classroom, and after a few moments, when all are comfortably refocused, he asks them to make notes about their experience of the trip, or about what made them worthy, or the treasure they found. They've just been through their first guided imagery.

From our work with teachers and students, we've found guided imagery to be one of the most powerful prewriting techniques available. Why? Because after using this unique device, people often produce writing filled with exquisite details, surprising connections, and insights that wouldn't be present otherwise. It's also a classic inquiry or environmental-mode instructional technique.

Guided imagery can be used for a wide variety of topics and genres: for personal writing about events or people in one's life, for engagement with and analysis of literature, for imagining experiences one has never actually had, or for reviewing previous experiences, whether autobiographical (the house one lived in as a child), practical (dealing with test anxiety), or academic (understanding a chemistry experiment).

What exactly is guided imagery? Many cognitive psychology researchers believe that information is coded both as symbols and as "images" in the brain (Sheikh 1983, Paivio 1971). Guided imagery is a focusing of consciousness on such images—not just thinking about events, but imagining them as if they are taking place in the present. The teacher (or other professional) directs this imagining in order to help people recall sensory data, feelings, and thoughts. The listeners are helped to relax first, and the leader provides verbal cues, but since the images are in the listeners' minds, much of the construction depends on them (more about this balance later). The word "imagery" is perhaps misleading, since constructed images are not just visual, but can include all five senses, as well as inner feelings and realizations.*

Guided imagery serves a number of vital purposes in teaching writing. Most essentially, as an incredibly powerful prewriting technique it helps people retrieve large amounts of material from memory. If students know something about the topic, guided imagery invariably generates a flood of information, demonstrating to them, often for the first time, just how much they have to say. Pages of notes may grow from one brief remembered scene. And if that much data is stored concerning just that one moment, it is awe-inspiring to consider how much memory of one's life is packed away in the normal adult (or adolescent) brain. This realization can help students develop confidence and trust in themselves as writers.

Even though much data is stored, however, most people tend to favor one or another of their senses and therefore miss information that could be perceived through others. Guided imagery encourages people to develop all the channels available—hearing, vision, smell, taste, touch, feelings (both physical and psychological), and ideas. Further, the process can be structured not only to retrieve this data, but also to encourage evaluation and thought about the data as well. Guided imagery teaches students the art of productive, quiet contemplation, a tool that may be foreign to much of the rest of their lives, but vital in academic work.

Guided imagery is especially valuable in that it combines teacher support and student initiative. The teacher sets the overall topic and provides essential prompts that inexperienced writers may need, but leaves most of the actual content decisions to the student. The students choose among many alternatives, draw on their own inner resources for the actual material to be brought to mind, and thus develop ownership of it. Two psychologists who have written much about methods related to guided imagery, John Grinder and Richard Bandler, explain why this individual ownership is inherent to the method. They stress that the directions a

---

*A considerable body of psychological research on mental imagery has been done—on its nature and its applications in psychological therapy, sports performance, memory enhancement, pain control, and other medical treatments. The concept was first elaborated in the 1930s, but began to receive wide attention only in the 1970s (Strosahl and Ascough 1981). Now, it serves as a major tool in a number of therapy methods (Shorr et al. 1980, Leuner et al. 1983). It has proven statistically to be the strongest component in stress inoculation therapy, a program for helping medical patients cope with pain. It has been shown to improve the mood of the clinically depressed. And study after study has explored and confirmed its role in improved memory and learning (Sheikh 1983, Purkel and Bornstein 1980, Shaw 1985, Waters 1982).

leader provides must be more or less *contentless*—that is, the words should invite the student to notice sensations or construct images but shouldn't specify what these are to be. If the leader makes the suggestions too specific, the process doesn't work, for sooner or later the leader's words fail to fit the student's thoughts, and the concentration is broken.

The hope, of course, is that students will learn to conduct their own memory searches and create their own spells to draw on mental resources. Teachers find that it becomes easier for students to respond each time they use the technique. In fact, as Grinder and Bandler point out, the guided imagery cues in the teacher's voice and other actions become imprinted in students' minds, so that they immediately shift levels of consciousness when the teacher begins. Those who use guided imagery regularly find kids love it and use it well.

Teachers ask questions about this technique, and so we need to offer answers to some of the "Yes, but's."

"Yes, but it sounds like hypnosis. Isn't that dangerous if I'm not professionally trained to handle it?"

Answer: Grinder and Bandler point out that changing levels of consciousness is routine, as we all know from the common experience of suddenly "waking up" in our cars after having driven for five or ten minutes through complex traffic while totally lost in unrelated musings. Even in school, much of what we do with students actually amounts to manipulating their levels of attention and consciousness. When we read a story or poem out loud, for example, we intend for students to screen out sensory data other than our voice and to experience images and feelings internally. Guided imagery is akin to some widely used relaxation techniques; but if it's hypnosis, it's very mild. Fortunately, it's impossible through such methods to force people to think about things they don't wish to confront. They naturally protect themselves, avoiding thoughts or memories psychologically too difficult to handle.

"Yes, but I'm not interested in this touchy-feely stuff."

Answer: We English teachers love to sit around and complain about how much TV our students watch and how it's stunted their ability to visualize anything, like a scene in a play or novel, unless an electronic picture is supplied by someone else. Well, guided imagery isn't an encounter-group tactic: it's a drill for developing a higher-order thinking skill—the ability to summon up complex and detailed mental images. Perhaps if we called it "Remedial Visualization," the technique would seem more appropriate for school.

"Yes, but it's just not my style—I'm not the 'psychological' type. Can I really make this work?"

Answer: This is a highly structured technique depending much more on the nature of the normal human mind than on particular personalities. Students (and people in general) already create their own hypnotic inductions when they daydream or when they try to imagine how any project will look when it is completed (building a birdhouse, rearranging furniture, decorating the gym for a dance), so they've already had plenty of practice. This is just a matter of adding one more skill to one's repertoire. Most teachers have a few basic patterns they follow in their classroom. One might as well add to the range and flexibility of these patterns in order to be able to choose what is appropriate to any particular teaching situation.

"Yes, but my students are too immature [or too noisy, too unskilled, too macho, too lacking in experiences worth talking about, too . . .]."

Answer: If you always think little of your students, then that's what they'll be. You may be surprised at what they can do in a new mode. You'll also be surprised at just how suggestible they are. If you think they'll giggle and make noises to break the concentration, use surprise to put them off guard. Example: one enterprising teacher, Shirley Meier, at Hoffman Estates High School, decided to eliminate students' embarrassment by asking them, before she began, to arrange their chairs in a circle facing outward. No doubt immature kids could still have made noises to disturb people (or to defend themselves), but in this new situation it simply didn't occur to them to do so.

The key to success with guided imagery is persistence: if you try it and stay with it, it will work. Harvey once taught this technique to a beginning teacher named Vit Briedas in an English Methods class. Vit's student-teaching assignment was in a tough Catholic high school with oversized classes of blue-collar jocks. When Harvey went to visit the classroom for the first time, Vit began introducing a guided-imagery activity to this unpromising assortment of students, telling them that they would later be doing a piece of descriptive writing. This was apparently going to be Vit's attempt to show his methods professor how much he'd learned in the class.

Things did not begin well. It was the last period of the day, just before a big basketball game, and when Vit started telling all those impatient bruisers to relax in their seats, close their eyes, and take a mental walk down a snow-filled street, there was an eruption of giggling and backtalk. Harvey sank deep in his seat at the back of the room, foreseeing impending disaster and regretting that he ever introduced poor Vit to this delicate technique.

But Vit just stayed with it, talking the students up and down that street, talking about how snow was gently falling on the ground before them, falling and gradually covering the grass, the occasional snowflake landing on your cheek with a slight, tickling sting. One boy near the front was still mocking the exercise and jabbing his pal in the side, so Vit walked slowly around his desk, still rhythmically spinning out gentle phrases, as many students closed their eyes, and Vit very slowly walked up beside the resistant student and quietly cuffed him on the back of the head. This was the most unusual fusion of authoritarian and progressive education we'd ever witnessed, and we certainly wouldn't recommend it to anyone. However, the kid did shut up, and in another minute, the classroom was totally silent. All of us—including the observer—were soon enjoying the experience of discovering a beautiful cardinal perched on a limb on that street we were exploring with Vit. And we found, each of us, that we could reach out our hand very slowly . . . and that brilliant red bird would step into our palm . . . and we could hold it up to our face . . . and look closely at his plumage . . . and enjoy the beauty of his color . . . against the newfallen snow all around.

If you believe it, students will believe it.

HOW IT WORKS

To explain how it's done, we'll work through one full guided imagery on an autobiographical topic. Then we'll discuss principles for designing your own scripts and provide examples of several types.

The teacher can begin by announcing a topic, an aim, or a time and place and then listing some of its many possibilities to help students identify a version significant in their own lives. The choice of topics is a sensitive one. The best, we believe, are topics that give some appearance of focus but that really open up a wide range of concerns and levels of seriousness, from the trivial to the deeply personal, from the comic to the cosmic. This combination of focus and choice provides support and comfort to the more insecure students, while gently urging all to engage in the difficult process of choosing. Autobiographical topics that we've found to be especially effective include "a person who has been important in your life," "a stepping-stone in your life," "a time you learned something," "an accident you had or witnessed," "a time you were hurt," "something you lost." We'll describe the "loss" assignment, because it is probably the deepest and most personally challenging of all these choices and as a result has led to much powerful writing in our classes.

The teacher begins by reciting a slow, methodical, and evocative series of choices, leading people to range through their memories, and to make lists of thoughts, scenes, words, images, and ideas as they come to mind:

One topic many people have found valuable to write about is a loss. This is a word with rich associations, so perhaps I can help you consider some of the possibilities. People experience many different kinds of losses in their lives.

What are some things you've lost? [Very slowly, pausing between each idea.] As a young child, did you ever lose a toy, perhaps a special dolly or blankie, a ball, a tooth, your mittens, a book, a pet, a big game? Did you ever drop something down the drain, into the snow, behind a radiator? As a more grown-up person, have you ever lost your coat, wallet, homework, glasses or contacts, a special piece of jewelry, your car in a large parking lot, your keys, watch—or maybe a job?

What ideas, feelings, or beliefs have you lost? Childhood myths and legends—Santa Claus, the Easter Bunny, the Tooth Fairy? Belief in the omnipotence and perfection of your parents? Have you lost trust, illusions? Have you ever lost your confidence, your cool, your composure? Lost your temper? Can you remember times you lost sleep? Lost yourself? Of all these things you may have lost, what are some that you'd like to regain? And which ones are you better off without?

What people have you lost in your life? As we grow up and change, sometimes we lose old friends. They move away and we lose track of them. All those faces in old yearbooks or class pictures—which of them have you lost? Have you ever lost a friend because of a dispute or a misunderstanding? Did you ever lose your little brother or sister in a crowd or in a store? Ever lose someone who died?

Students testify that this oral listing helps considerably to weigh the possibilities. An arbitrary search for a topic becomes a genuine light-bulb flash when one item triggers a significant memory. Listeners also realize that a wide range of possibilities is really welcomed. Those willing to take some risk feel invited toward the deeper possibilities. Those who find their hurts too painful or the risks too great, given the eventual audience for their writing, will choose something they can handle. The listing makes clear that the leader does not have one model essay in mind; the "What do you really want?" question, which many students ask (and teachers gnash their teeth over) is defused.

The teacher then checks to see if everyone has identified a loss and carefully observes to see who needs help. Individuals who are stuck must be assisted to find a loss they feel comfortable writing about; this help can come from the teacher, but often supportive students will take over, gently questioning the hesitant one and offering suggestions. If someone is torn between alternatives, assure her that she can try out one of the choices now and can always switch to the other one if it's not working out. Only when every writer has made a solid choice can the process move on.

The teacher then asks students to identify a significant moment related to their loss—the event itself, or a moment of realization if the occurrence was more gradual. Once everyone has found a focus, the class is ready for the actual guided imagery. The directions begin by helping people turn their focus inward. This is a relaxation step similar for all guided imageries. Again, it must be delivered very slowly and sensitively, with phrases offered at about the rate of normal breathing, so that students have time to perceive the sensations they are being invited to consider.

Now put down your pencils and relax, sit back into your chair, and get as comfortable as you can. You can take one or two deep breaths . . . taking a moment to let your body relax. I am going to give you some suggestions to help you do some internal research, to explore your own memory. While I talk, you may find it helpful to stare into space or to close your eyes, so you can fully appreciate the pictures that my words call up in your mind.

As you sit there, you can notice the pressure of your back against the chair . . . and your feet on the floor . . . and when your eyes are closed . . . you can hear the sound of the air rushing through the ventilator over your head . . . and the sounds of others in the room . . . and you may become aware of your own breathing . . . the air flowing into your lungs, and the feeling as you exhale. . . . And as you become increasingly relaxed . . . you can be pleased to discover . . . that you can take yourself back in time . . . and, using your memories . . . recreate scenes from your life.

Notice that this step refers people to sensations they are experiencing as you speak, but does not specify what the sensations will be. Thus, it invites people to focus, but to fill the focus with their own content. The teacher should alter the references to fit the particular physical situation, using the same contentless approach. If disturbances occur outside the room, don't try either to fight or ignore them, but simply incorporate them into the process: "And you can hear noises in the hall, but they seem distant, and they don't disturb your thoughts."

Try to establish a rhythm, so that your talk has the quality of a poem, with relatively long pauses between phrases. *Go slowly!* People need time to search their minds and reconstruct images at each step. You'll notice too that the phrases are often connected with "and"s. They are there on purpose, helping people to stay with you and to connect their thoughts.

And so now I would suggest that you return to the time and place of your loss. And as you arrive there you will notice that time is slowed down, making it easy for you to find yourself in the scene, and settle slowly into yourself. Now you can take a good, long, slow look around. What do you see? . . . Look down at yourself and notice how you are dressed. . . . Now turn and look to your right. What can you see there? . . . Now look over to your left and notice what's there. . . . And you can even turn all the way around and look behind you and notice what you see there. . . . You can notice the sounds in this place . . . and the feel of the air on your cheek.

Is someone else here with you? Who is it? And how do you feel about this person or these people? . . . And what are you saying? . . . And what are you doing? . . . And what are you thinking? . . . And feeling? . . . And now time begins to move on and you can experience your loss and the events that are taking place. . . . [Long pause.]

And as you finish experiencing this event in your life, you can think about what it means to you now, and you can appreciate the insights it gives you. . . . And now, you can gather up the sensations, ideas, sights, and sounds to bring back with you . . . and you can gradually return to this time and place . . . to this room, taking all the time you need.

And when you are fully ready, you can open your eyes. [Now change voice tone to normal.] And now you may want to pick up your pencil and make a few notes so that you will remember the many things you have just observed in your experience.

As students open their eyes and return their focus to the room—which may take a minute or two—they can begin listing some of the things they've just recaptured: ideas, feelings, images, colors, sounds, words. Kids should just list words or phrases without trying to organize or write whole sentences. After several minutes of listing, the teacher announces the actual writing assignment itself: to write an account of their loss in whatever way seems natural and appropriate to the subject. They should be told who the audience will be for their work, so they won't be surprised later and can take their own needs for privacy into account as they write. We generally ask students to read their work aloud in groups of three after they've completed a first draft, and writers may protest if they haven't been told this in advance. (We'll take up these further steps in later chapters.)

Here are some additional suggestions and guidelines:

1. Don't attempt a guided imagery until you have established trust and comfort among the group.

2. Plan for a time without interruptions, comings and goings, or other distractions. Chances are that all of these will probably occur anyway; if so, just incorporate them into your guiding words.

3. When you begin a guided-imagery exercise, be clear and direct. Use your personal power when you ask students to put down their pencils, relax, and join in a very different way of thinking.

4. Change your voice quality significantly when doing guided imagery. Usually, a lower, quieter tone works well.

5. The imagery should include all three channels of mental information processing—visual, auditory, and kinesthetic (physical as well as emotional feelings)—to stimulate memories in people who are stronger in one area than another.

6. Allow plenty of time for the return. Do not move to the next activity (listing, debriefing, whatever) until all have opened their eyes and given evidence of being ready to begin. Do not be surprised if some people are deeply moved by their experience.

7. Don't believe that people see or hear exactly what you tell them to. The associations created by your words will differ widely from one person to the next. You may be instructing them to look at the people in their moment, and instead they will hear sounds that happened after the event. It doesn't matter. All that matters is that the general tone and structure of guided-imagery activities help people look inward and recover abundant details.

One thing you can do to perfect your technique is to debrief students after you have conducted a guided imagery. Explain to them that this activity works differently for different people and may not work at all for some, so you'd like to find out just what *did* take place in their minds. If some thought of things very differently than the way you suggested, what did they experience? If someone got off the track at some point, when was it? This will help you learn what wording is effective and what directions are too explicit, too vague, or too quick to shift focus. As long as the debriefing is approached this way, nothing you do will be "wrong," and all of it will be fascinating, to the students as well as to yourself.

APPLYING GUIDED IMAGERY

If you want to create your own guided-imagery scripts, you can use the basic structure we've followed here:

1. Specifying, listing, and choosing a topic.
2. Selecting a particular moment or scene within the larger subject.
3. Relaxing.
4. Working through the actual guided imagery, including data from all three channels: visual, auditory, kinesthetic.
5. Contemplating the significance of the memories and gathering materials to bring back.
6. Returning to the present, making notes on data retrieved, and receiving the actual assignment.

Script for "A Time You Learned Something"

The following is a guided-imagery script for autobiographical writing that asks students to be more explicitly analytical, so the directions differ somewhat from those for the "loss" imagery. This is particularly valuable for getting to know students' needs, attitudes, and anxieties near the beginning of the school year. It would be quite simple to shift this imagery toward the experience of learning in any specific subject—"A time you learned something about books" or "A time you learned something in English" so as to explore with students their previous experience in your subject.

LISTING AND CHOOSING

Since learning is the main thing you're supposed to do in school, it can be useful to become aware of how learning has actually worked for you on some occasion. Then we can all share our data, to help us think about just how people learn. Perhaps I can help you recall a time you really learned something, whether it was in school or not.

People learn from experiences in all kinds of situations—in school, working at a job, in their family, throughout the many parts of their lives. And there are many kinds of things you learn. I'm going to suggest five different types of learning, and after I mention some examples of each kind, I'll pause for a moment so you can think and perhaps jot down a few notes about the different learning experiences in your own life.

First of all, you've learned many skills, such as cooking, basketball, playing the guitar, or repairing furniture. Think about what skills you have learned, and make a note about some that you value. . . .

People learn information—computer programming, football statistics, astronomy, religion. What subjects have you become especially involved with? Jot down a few that come to mind. . . .

People learn social skills, like selling, negotiating in a group, how to act like a student, how to have fun at a party, how to get along on the street, how to behave in a new job. Think of the social skills you know, and list a few. . . .

And then there are personal relations, like how to argue, how to ask for things from people close to you, how to get along (or fight) with your brother or sister. You can make a few notes about personal skills you've learned. . . .

Finally, there are beliefs about life that you have learned—beliefs about politics, about the nature of school, about human nature and how people behave. Now you can make a few notes about your beliefs. . . .

It may be recent or well in the past, but perhaps you have recalled some things you've learned and can choose one you'd like to think more about now. It would help if you can really remember what sorts of things took place as you learned it. [Long pause] . . . Does everyone have one in mind? [Confer with any uncertain students.]

ADDITIONAL PREPARATORY DATA GATHERING

Now let's think about how you learned—and you can take notes to record anything I ask about that seems important. Who was involved with you in this learning, helping you or creating the situation for you —perhaps a parent, a teacher, a friend, a grandparent, the kids on the block, your boss at your job? . . . Did that person say or do anything that made the learning easier—or harder? . . . Did that person give you any advice? Was it helpful or harmful? . . .

Where were you? Was it a pleasant setting, or perhaps a disturbing one? . . .

Were you aware of any obstacles—fears you felt, or information you lacked, or competition that discouraged you? If there were obstacles, do you feel that they were positive or negative influences on your learning? . . .

Were there any stages you went through? Did you perhaps avoid the learning at first? Did you do things wrong initially? Was there a period when thoughts were just "cooking" in your mind, before you understood? Was there a sudden realization, or was it more gradual? . . .

SELECTING

Now I want to ask you to select a moment from your learning experience that you'd like to recall in more detail—perhaps the moment when you realized something new, or maybe a moment when someone gave you just the help you really needed, or when you became discour-

---

aged, or found new resolve to keep trying. . . . Does everyone have a moment in mind? . . .

RELAXATION STEP

[Use directions similar to those in the "loss" imagery, above.]

GUIDED IMAGERY

And now you can take yourself back to the time when your learning occurred . . . and you can feel and see and hear things just as you did then. . . . And you can look around and notice where you are. Look to your left. What do you see there? . . . And now look to your right and notice what you see. . . . And look straight ahead of you and see what is there. . . . And you can notice any particular objects that come to your attention. . . . You may even notice things right nearby and things farther in the distance. . . . And you can hear the special, distinctive sounds of this place. . . . And you can look down at yourself, at your clothes and shoes and notice how you are dressed. . . .

[Prompts continue and finish, as with the "loss" imagery.]

With this task, more direction is provided before the actual guided imagery begins than for the "loss" imagery described earlier. Since the topic is one most people don't think much about, more preparation is needed so that students can analyze their experience as they visualize the scene. We've also included several directions that illustrate just how much detail is stored in people's minds. Some striking surprises can be generated from the prompt about objects in the distance, for example. On one occasion, a student from Jamaica was inspired to recall that as she sat daydreaming in school one day back home, she became entranced looking out the window at a brilliantly colored lizard on a branch, when the teacher suddenly broke her reverie with a request that she read an essay she had unfortunately failed to complete.

Huck Finn—A Script for Writing About Literature

We've already provided one guided-imagery script about literature, as part of the integrated activity in Chapter 3. That script uses details from a story by Hemingway but does not quote it directly. The following example is based on a shortened version of an actual scene in *Huckleberry Finn* and asks that students imagine their own ending for it. Thus, it might be most useful to use this activity *before* students have read the book, or at least before this particular chapter. Notice, too, that guided-imagery steps for literature may proceed in opposite order compared to personal writing. The students' act of choosing comes *after* the main visualization, whereas it usually comes first in an autobiographical task.

RELAXATION STEP

[The relaxation step is the same as for the "loss" activity above.]

IMAGERY

Now you can listen to, and imagine in your mind the scene I want to read to you from Huckleberry Finn, and you can see and hear and feel all that is taking place, just as if you are there.

[Read very slowly.] "Then we went loafing around the town. The stores and houses was almost all old shackly dried-up frame concerns that hadn't ever been painted; they was set up three or four foot above ground on stilts, so as to be out of reach of the water when the river was overflowed. The houses had little gardens around them, but they didn't seem to raise hardly anything in them but jimpson weeds, and sunflowers, and ash-piles, and old curled-up boots and shoes. . . .

"The nearer it got to noon that day, the thicker and thicker was the wagons and horses in the streets, and more coming all the time. By-and-by somebody sings out—

" 'Here comes old Boggs!—in from the country for his little old monthly drunk—here he comes, boys!' . . .

"He was drunk, and weaving about in his saddle; he was over fifty years old, and had a very red face. . . .

"Boggs rode up before the biggest store in town and bent his head down so he could see under the curtain of the awning, and yells—

" 'Come out here, Sherburn! Come out and meet the man you've swindled. You're the houn' I'm after, and I'm a gwyne to have you, too!'

. . . "By-and-by a proud-looking man about fifty-five—and he was a heap the best dressed man in that town, too—steps out of the store, and the crowd drops back on each side to let him come. He says to Boggs, might ca'm and slow—he says:

" 'I'm tired of this; but I'll endure it till one o'clock. Till one o'clock, mind—no longer.' . . .

"In about five or ten minutes, here comes Boggs again—but not on his horse. He was a-reeling across the street towards me, bareheaded, with a friend on both sides of him aholt of his arms and hurrying him along. . . . Somebody sings out—'Boggs!'

"I looked over there to see who said it, and it was that Colonel Sherburn. He was standing perfectly still, in the street, and had a pistol

---

raised in his right hand—not aiming it, but holding it out with the bar-
rel tilted up towards the sky. . . . and when they see the pistol the men
jumped to one side, and the pistol barrel come down slow and steady
to a level—both barrels cocked. Boggs throws up both of his hands,
and says, 'O Lord, don't shoot!' Bang! goes the first shot, and he stag-
gers back clawing at the air—bang! goes the second one, and he tum-
bles backwards onto the ground, heavy and solid, with his arms spread
out. . . .

"Colonel Sherburn he tossed his pistol onto the ground, and turned
around on his heels and walked off. . . .

"Well, by-and-by somebody said Sherburn ought to be lynched. In
about a minute everybody was saying it; so away they went, and yell-
ing, and snatching down every clothes-line they come to, to do the
hanging with."

And now you can imagine for yourself what comes next, what you
think the mob does. . . . You can notice all sorts of details in your own
story . . . where the people go . . . what the scene looks like . . . what
various people say . . . and what actions you observe. . . . And you can
let the events flow in your mind until you come to an ending and you
realize the final outcome of your story. . . . [Allow a minute or two for
contemplation.]

And after you have realized what your ending is, you can bring your
thoughts to an end, and return to this room . . . and take up your pen-
cils to make whatever notes you need so you can remember what you
imagined and how your story went. [Allow three to five minutes for
note making.]

The assignment now is to write your own conclusion to this story.
When we're finished, we'll compare endings with one another, and
with Twain, to help us learn what the story means to each of us.

This guided imagery is, of course, really just good literature read
aloud—though it includes preparation, in the form of relaxation, and
concludes by asking students to imagine their own ending. However, we
include it to emphasize how powerful reading aloud can be, no matter
how old the listeners, and to show that, after all, guided imagery is closely
related to literature and poetry.

Guided Imagery for Nonfiction

It shouldn't be difficult to see how guided imagery can be used to make
situations and issues vivid for *any* material kids study. The following
sample concerns a well-known anthropological study students find fas-

cinating, thought-provoking, and not too difficult to read: *The Forest People*, by Colin Turnbull. Turnbull spent a year with a pygmy tribe in what is now the Republic of the Congo. Turnbull describes in narrative form a culture focused on music and on a very nonsuperstitious religion. The pygmies are especially interesting because they live virtually without any form of government or even tribal leadership, guided only by the customs and pressures within their small communities. The encroachment of the modern world, however, threatens this peace-loving people's health, their social organization, and thus their existence. One possible guided imagery, to help promote discussion or writing after the students have read most of the book, runs as follows.

RELAXATION STEP

[Use the relaxation step described earlier.]

GUIDED IMAGERY

And you are surprised to find that you are transported, just for a short time, to the Ituri forest, and you can feel the warm, humid air, and the damp clinginess of your clothes, and you can see huge trees, with their gigantic trunks rising many stories high, with green foliage just at the very tops. . . .

And you hear sharp, hollow tapping sounds, and children's voices, and men and women talking . . . and then bits of song. . . .

And now you come upon the Ba Mbuti camp, with the sun filtering down through the trees, and spiraling light as it hits the columns of smoke from several fires, drifting lazily upward. . . . And the light dances down the coils of blue smoke and seems to leap from place to place on the leafy floor of the forest, as the trees sway in the breeze high above. And you listen and hear many sounds—birds, monkeys, bees, the rustling of a nearby stream. . . .

And you find yourself among these very small people, and magically you can understand them. . . . And since you've read about them, you know what is going on. . . . And you look around and notice the small huts covered with huge leaves, and objects lying about—small chairs, nets, baskets, pots. . . . And you hear people singing and telling stories as they sit at their fires.

And you see people cooking over the fires, and working on objects they are making. . . . And you are offered food. And at first you are worried, because you don't know what it is . . . but you get your courage up, and taste it . . . and you're surprised at how good it is, a sweet sauce, with tasty, tender chunks of meat. . . .

And somehow you are able to converse with your favorite person in

this village you have read about. . . . And you think about how differ-
ent your life is from the life of these people. . . . And you think about
what may happen to them in the future. . . . And you realize what you
want to say. . . . And you can experience whatever happens next, as
the two of you talk. . . .

And when you are finished, and when you have appreciated the in-
sights you have gained from your discussion and from your visit to
this tribe, you can return to this room . . . [finish as with previous
imageries].

Guided imagery is a powerful method because it draws so naturally on students' creative abilities while helping them integrate concrete experiences with more abstract thinking processes. It involves students of all levels, allowing the teacher to provide plenty of support for students who need it without depriving them of their own initiative. Though it doesn't solve all the problems of teaching writing, it ensures that whatever students are working on will be significant to them and thus worth the effort. Because it combines all these things, it's one of the most elegant teaching methods we know.

Chapter 12

Drafting:
Supporting
Writers
at Work

There's a great deal we don't know about how people actually get writing done. Researchers have tried to break the barrier and monitor the unconscious thoughts that writers turn into words on the page, but it's not a simple task. Some investigators have asked students to compose aloud, verbalizing all their thoughts and musings as they proceed. Some have charted visible actions, such as pauses, as students write. Others have used "stimulated recall"—that is, they videotape the writer and the paper he's working on, and afterward both writer and researcher view the tape to recall the internal process. However, all of these methods provide only hints and inferences. It's very unlikely that composing aloud works exactly like composing silently. With stimulated recall, a writer's report of what he was thinking will obviously omit any processes outside his consciousness. Perhaps this inaccessibility explains why it seems harder to help students with their actual drafting compared to the things we teachers can do during the planning and revising stages.

One piece of research that does help us understand the drafting process vividly is Mike Rose's *Writer's Block: The Cognitive Dimension*. Rose used stimulated recall to probe the thinking of students who had serious writing blocks compared to others who experienced little blocking. He found that those who were blocked used unproductive thinking patterns of several kinds:

• Invocation of nonfunctional, rigid rules rather than more functional or flexible rules.
   • Misleading assumptions about how the writing process works.
   • Conflicts between several contradictory rules or assumptions.
   • Lack of strategies for getting writing done.
   • Premature editing.

Detailed case studies showed that students with writing blocks often re-called rules from previous teachers or textbooks and applied these rules rigidly, incorrectly, or in ways that prevented them from proceeding. Once they did begin to write, they'd turn to editing as soon as they finished a sentence or two, thus interrupting and ultimately forgetting their train of thought. In contrast, competent student writers approached assignments with a willingness to adjust their own mental rules about writing in order to follow the demands of the task as they emerged.

The implications for teachers are many. We need to think not just about how our advice and corrections are ignored, but also about how they may be followed all too carefully, creating conflicting demands and dead-end pathways in kids' heads. We need to find ways to help students become flexible so they can deal with each new and different writing task, and we must do this without usurping the initiative, writing the paper for them, or making it into a mirror that reflects only our own directions and re-quirements. We need to shift the concern with correctness to its proper place—the final proofreading of a finished piece—and separate it from the work of thinking and drafting. We need to help students become aware of their own writing processes and ways to vary them, to undo the common student belief that ways of thinking are a fixed part of one's personality.

WAYS TO SUPPORT DRAFTING

Obviously, everything thus far in this book aims to make drafting a pro-ductive process. Creating a supportive climate and classroom community, designing meaningful assignments, and providing good prewriting activ-ities all help prepare students to write and clear away obstacles to suc-cessful work. If students are engaged with explaining something they care about to an audience they truly wish to reach, in a classroom where they know their ideas will be respected, they're more likely to write without hesitation. They will tend not so much to worry about set procedures for writing, but will search for those that work for a particular piece.

However, we also need specific ways to help students when they reach the drafting stage in their writing. This stage can be exciting and produc-tive, so if students do get stuck—as most writers do sooner or later—or if they simply don't know how to proceed effectively, we ought to be able to help them discover and follow their own line of thought. Here are some approaches.

In-Class Time for Writing

In many social settings, students find little time or space in their lives for contemplation. Some students may not really know how to focus their thoughts, and if you've conducted an effective prewriting activity or helped students identify their own topics, it can be essential to get right to work at a time when the teacher is there to help. We've described in-class workshop settings in Chapter 6; we'd like to stress here just how productive they can be for fluent drafting.

One important advantage to the drafting workshop is that the teacher can focus on individual needs. While students are at work on their own writing, their problems are likely to vary tremendously, and few whole-class activities will be relevant to more than a couple of students at a time. Brief conferences allow the teacher to monitor, listen, encourage, suggest thinking processes or writing techniques as needed.

During in-class writing time, students themselves can choose tasks appropriate to their topics and work styles. Along with actual drafting, some may need to stop to read, gather more data, or brainstorm additional ideas. Those who find they can only write in the comfort and quiet (or noise) of their own room or other favorite place can use class time to talk. Many writers discover what they want to say through discussion, and plenty of prewriting and small-group activities depend on this. A corner of the room can be set aside for two-person peer conferences, structured perhaps with a few rules about talking quietly so the rest of the class can concentrate, and recording outcomes on a brief self-evaluation sheet.

The greatest concern some teachers have about in-class, loosely structured writing activity is that it consumes much time and appears to be difficult to control or use productively. There are many small management methods good teachers have evolved to help make a workshop work. Nancie Atwell describes how she ensures productive use of time by having each student state in one brief phrase, at the beginning of the period, what she plans to work on. Many teachers find that it's effective to circulate among the students and kneel or pull up a chair to hold quick writing conferences. This gives the teacher easy control over time, makes monitoring of activity possible with very brief glances, and allows him to choose the students he will speak to without having to call out names. Looking at overall time allotment, students learn grammar skills more permanently when they've discussed them in one-to-one conferences, so they don't need much time on whole-class grammar lessons—which should free up time for the drafting/conferencing sessions.

Teacher–Student Conferences During Drafting

One of the most effective ways we can help students is through individual conferences. As Nancie Atwell points out, the longer we wait to give help, the more our intervention can seem punitive, an act of "correcting" what has been done wrong. The question is, how can we support students' drafting processes without interrupting or dominating them? And then there's the other side of the coin: how can we stand back, not be intrusive, and yet still be helpful?

One way to solve this riddle is to think of conferences not so much as opportunities to give students advice, but as occasions to help them verbalize aims, feelings, problems, and worries during writing. By asking questions that reveal the writer's processes and purposes, one may be able to help far more effectively than by hearing or reading the writing. Advice is then more likely to be attuned to the writer's needs. By suggesting thought processes the writer can use, rather than prescriptions for words on the page, the teacher can give help and yet still leave it to the student to solve the problem.

Donald Graves has described the short "process conferences" he holds with younger writers, and these work well for teenage authors too. Graves suggests some specific ways teachers can help writers think and make decisions, rather than simply telling them what to do:

• Sit on the same side of the table with the student, signaling collaboration rather than opposition. Let the student hold the paper and decide to angle it or hand it to you if he wishes.

• Ask questions and help students talk, rather than just read over a paragraph and give a comment. Opening questions can help the student start off the conference and explain what she is trying to say in her writing: "OK, Jill, tell me what your paper is about and what part you're working on right now." Questions can signal the teacher's interest in the ideas, draw students out, and encourage them to consider more information: "I didn't realize a computer could do that. Do you need some special program or equipment?"

• Process questions help students see where they are in their work and how they might proceed: "OK, so you say you don't like this part. Tell me how you got it written. What were you thinking about?" Focus questions can encourage students to identify their main idea or the structure they are creating: "So what's the main thing you're really trying to say here?" Students' answers to these questions can help them make their own discoveries about what is needed to improve their work.

• Search for questions students can answer, rather than questions that put them on the spot. Conferences should encourage students, not just prove the teacher is smarter. If the student thinks the paper is already perfect even though problems are apparent, ask what it is that gives him the most satisfaction with it, or how he thinks a reader will react to particular parts. This can give you valuable information about what he's trying to achieve and what approach might help him understand the difference between his own perception and that of an outside reader.

• Wait after asking a question. Give students time to think, and don't jump in immediately. Silence is valuable.

• If the student wants simply to read a chunk of the piece aloud, listen. Not only can you offer a response at the end, but you can notice those lovely moments when the student hears an error or thinks of a change, picks up a pencil and jots down a correction in mid-reading (and thus doesn't need outside help at all). This is revision in action.

• Teach skills late in the conference, and focus on just one, so that the student will remember the item clearly.

• Listen and learn from students. Conferences not only help students write, but help the teacher understand how they think, discover what is blocking them, or realize that a valuable idea is hidden under the surface confusion.

• Tape-record conferences periodically, to monitor the process and your own teaching methods. Give the program some time before judging whether or not it works.

Conferences, like any other strategy, can heighten teacher control and discourage students, or they can develop student responsibility and promote growth. Thus, they epitomize the central issue explored in this book. Graves says it well:

How hard it is for an activist to conduct conferences! Everything is reversed. I have to give up the active, nondelegating, pushing, informing role for another kind of activity, the activity of waiting. . . . But the rewards, the new energy as the learner teaches me, keep me going. The margin of writer control increases while my presence decreases. . . .
The top teachers, I've found, whether in the center of the city, or a rural school, have an insatiable appetite for learning. When teachers learn, the [students] learn.

Build Awareness of Writing Processes

To help students identify writing strategies that work for them, structure activities that develop kids' awareness of their own writing process. Encourage self-observation, using a writer's journal in which students make notes about how they got particular pieces written. Pose specific questions so the journal entries can be productive: "What led you to think of this idea?" "How did you get started?" "Which parts were difficult to write, and why?" Then take time to discuss these matters in class and use the opportunity to show students that people's writing processes differ widely.

These are also useful questions to ask in conferences, of course. And students can learn to ask them of one another when they confer about their writing. Most serious writers are exquisitely conscious of the idiosyncrasies, procrastinations, and useful pretenses in their own writing process, and students may begin to see themselves as writers when they develop the habit of thinking about this. Such a debriefing process has always been important in sports, and many teachers are finding it to be an essential step in their teaching. It helps ensure that even when students have difficulty, they can learn from their problems.

Demonstrate Methods for Sustaining Momentum or Getting Unstuck During Writing

The person who has written most about the intimate details of the writing process is Peter Elbow. In *Writing Without Teachers*, he suggests "desperation writing" for times when one feels unproductive. The trick is to go ahead and write down the bad, uninteresting thoughts one has, using focused free writing, and then comb through them, writing out any ideas one finds, each as a *single sentence* on a separate 3-by-5-inch card or bit of paper. One can now arrange these cards in piles, compare pairs, or otherwise look for relationships. As Elbow puts it, usually at about this point sanity returns and ideas begin to flow. A few of the other techniques he suggests include approaching a piece as a dialogue, temporarily changing the audience for the writing, or writing out the history of how one's ideas about a topic evolved.

Allow Some Mental Space

To reduce premature editing, allow some mental space, so there are not too many requirements or instructions for students to fulfill at once. For example, audiences can be valuable for motivating writing, but if students worry about the audience too soon, they may not be able to explore ideas they're uncertain about, for fear that they'll be received badly. Too many instructions and lists of criteria for evaluation of the final product can have the same effect. Provide students enough structure to go on, but save some of the evaluative guidelines for revision time. Everything can't be perfected at once.

Similarly, encourage students to circle words to be looked up for spelling and to leave blanks for vocabulary they can't think of promptly, so they can keep the rhythm of the writing process going. Of course, this is an idiosyncratic matter. Some writers find that if they are distracted, particularly by an associated idea that doesn't quite fit in the piece, the best thing to do is to take several minutes to draft the digression. This way, the digression can be saved and the main flow of the writing continued.

SUMMARY

The drafting stage of writing is a complex and seemingly solitary moment. Writers often shuttle from detailed production and elaboration—just getting words down on the page and saying what one wants to say—to reconsideration of larger aims and questions—"Now that I've said that, does it say what I wanted?" or "Now that I've said that, do I still agree with my original idea?" Peter Elbow describes the difficult moment when a writer has made an argument but has begun to realize that she actually believes the opposite. It seems as if all that drafting time has been wasted. Instead of seeing such events as unproductive, we need to help students to realize that this is the most interesting moment of all in drafting. It's called *learning*.

Chapter 13

Revising

Students seem to hate revising. They whine, "Why do it *again*?" They moan, "You mean I'll have to copy it over?" They cajole, "I'm sick of this—can't I start another piece instead?" Sometimes they even come right out and say, "Who wants to sit around looking at all their own mistakes? Besides, all this revising never gets me a better grade anyway."

In school, revision time usually means you did it wrong at first, and your punishment is to correct lots of errors marked in red. When teachers force revision in the customary way, the results are predictably disappointing: kids grudgingly re-skim their text, fixing up a couple of minor surface errors, often leaving the gravest proofreading problems untouched, and, much worse, completely neglecting the real issues of rewriting: order, logic, detail, support, word choice, metaphor, point of view, and all the rest.

Many students have learned to hate revision simply because of what it has always meant and felt like in school. Yet we know that revising is a vital step, a skill and mind-set for all good writers. How can we make it more meaningful for students, help them to use it, help them take possession of it as one of the tools of their own writing craft?

Perhaps the answer is that beyond showing students *how* to revise, we must also must show them *why*, creating a setting in which revising is a natural and valuable activity. We must provide a more positive definition of *what* revising is, and arrange the *when*—time for pieces to rest before they are revised, a way of deciding which pieces are worth spending more time on, and then more time for the actual work to be done.

The following principles summarize some strategies teachers can use to provide the why, what, and when of revision in the classroom. Students will be encouraged to revise when:

1. They write often about topics of *genuine personal meaning*, topics that they have chosen for themselves.

2. *Writing is regularly read aloud*, allowing the classroom community of writers to partake in the fundamental human urge to share stories, and allowing individual authors to hear, develop, and revise the voice of their own work.

3. They often have the chance to write for *real audiences* inside and outside the school.

4. The environment is full of the *tools and supplies* of the writing trade—paper, pens, pencils, scissors, rubber cement, typewriters (or word processors), dictionaries, thesauruses. Simple equipment innovations can remind writers to revise: use of a "Rough Draft" rubber stamp tells students (and nervous parents, if they are concerned) that some pieces will get further attention at a later stage, and the habit of double-spacing such early drafts (whether typed or handwritten) facilitates revision later.

5. *Models* of writing in process are displayed in the room, including kids', professional authors', and the teacher's.

6. *The teacher writes* while students write—not necessarily always, but often enough to show her own struggles and to let students look over the shoulder of an adult writer at work.

7. The *teacher confers with individual students* often. Conferences as short as two or three minutes may be very useful to writers; the teacher must create the workshop atmosphere that makes such individual attention feasible.

8. For early drafts, the *teacher's responses focus on content*, meaning, support, clarity, and detail—not to judge what ideas are "correct," but to help students develop and explain what they wish to say. Grading can fix and kill a piece of writing and should usually be held until the end of a project. Mechanics are appropriately taught either later in the process or when students request help.

9. Students write *knowing that revision will take place*; revising must be seen as a normal, integral, nonpunitive part of a larger process, in a setting where their ideas are respected; but they'll also choose what to revise, for not every piece deserves revising.

10. Students' writing is *routinely saved in folders*, so that they can return to work on individual pieces over days, weeks, even months. Saving the writing in a folder enacts respect for the work and implicitly asserts both that cooling-off periods are necessary and that repeated rewriting is a vital step for most writers.

11. *Students work with peers* as mutual audiences, editors, helpers, collaborators. Since literacy is socially constructed, communication with

others is needed both in the here and now and reflexively to facilitate kids' integration of literacy skills.

Now let's look at the three major elements for promoting revision in more detail.

CREATING REASONS WHY

Revising depends on having a purpose. Is the student revising to create a perfect product? Or to communicate more clearly to a particular audience (and if so, to whom, and with what purpose)? Or is the student revising to understand or develop his own ideas more clearly for himself, as a learner? It makes a difference. Unless there is a well-defined purpose for students' writing (whether the teacher creates it or helps students to create it themselves), revising will be arbitrary, for any number of alternative versions could be appropriate. Without a purpose for writing, revising will seem to be a matter only of "giving the teacher what she wants." Encouraging revision thus begins with the very conception of a writing assignment, including such essentials as finding real audiences for students' writing *beyond* the teacher. The most important factor in whether students will seriously revise any given piece of writing is whether they care enough to continue working on it.

If students are to care about revising a particular piece, they must want to make it better, to go back and look at it again, contemplate it, be involved with it. They have to *own* it and think of it not just as the teacher's topic and the teacher's responsibility, but theirs. It must connect with something inside them. At the same time, they need to develop a sense of how their writing is perceived from the outside, what it means to be a reader who is trying to understand something that is not yet in his own consciousness.

Obviously, encouraging this inner and outer involvement, creating students' ownership and connection, can't begin with just the revising itself or even with a writing assignment, for it depends on relationships in the entire classroom. We've already talked a lot about classroom climate in this book, and creating a positive climate will promote both these bases, ownership and audience, for revising. Later in this chapter we will suggest some specific climate-building activities that can promote the involvement and awareness students will need in order to revise effectively.

TEACHING WHAT IT IS

In a way, all writing is revising. Lil Brannon, Melinda Knight, and Vara Neverow-Turk (1982) argue that writing and revising aren't separate—

writers regularly look back, as they write, to see where they've gone so far, determine whether it's where they wanted to go, and decide what to do next. Theorists and researchers call this a "recursive" process.

But revising is also a distinct stage. Revising offers students a chance to look critically at a completed draft of their work. One of the advantages of revising as a formal stage is that knowing we can revise later frees us to pour out rough ideas in the first draft *now*. We needn't always stop and judge ourselves during earlier drafting. Instead, we can concentrate on generating material, achieving a syntactic flow, and creating something— even if it's an imperfect something—to work with. As some researchers have found (Perl 1978), unskilled writers tend to stop in the middle of every sentence, worrying too much whether their initial work is correct, so their writing is even more disconnected than it might otherwise be. The greatest value of free writing is that it *separates* the generating of material from the work of critically judging and improving it later. Knowing that there will be a chance to revise alters the writer's approach to the first draft, lowers anxiety, and allows a trial of possibilities that might eventually turn out better than one's immediate thoughts (Elbow 1973). If ideas seem weak at first, it's not a bad turn of events—it's something to work from.

Revising is rethinking. Students usually think of revising as fixing spelling and grammar. However, good writers are even more interested in revising for meaning, seeking to be clearer and more effective for their audience. Students rarely attempt revisions of the latter type spontaneously (Bridwell 1980); yet since these are most likely to affect what the student has to say, it seems as if they could command the most interest.

Focusing students' attention on content also helps dissociate revising from error. Working on ideas means one is trying to understand more, to look deeper, to see things from a different perspective, not just to find what is "wrong." As Peter Elbow says, "Producing writing, then, is not so much like filling a basin or pool once, but rather getting water to keep flowing *through* till finally it runs clear" (Elbow 1973). Such work can be very satisfying for students, once they've begun it. Fixing grammar, spelling, and mechanics can then be considered proofreading, the very last step a writer takes before publishing a piece.

At least some of the time, revising can be a purely positive activity. Think of a painter like Monet painting haystacks repeatedly, in every kind of light. Each painting is a re-vision—not a correction of something that was wrong in the previous painting, but an opportunity to see the subject literally in a new light. One teacher applied this concept effectively by asking her kids, once a week, to write portraits of a classmate, all writers focusing on the same student. A different student was chosen each week. The portrait subject would ultimately receive all of the descriptions of him or her, bound together, as a keepsake. By the time the class reached the last portrait, they were much more skilled at the job than when they began.

However, revising is not easy. Most of us don't want to give up the words we worked so hard to create or face the fact that our work is not perfect. Sometimes a draft contains contradictory ideas, or it doesn't yet quite say what the author wants to say. Or maybe the writer isn't yet sure what he wants to say. Teachers can help students face this confusing process by talking about it with them and guiding them sympathetically through it.

WHEN REVISING SHOULD OCCUR

Donald Graves points out what is obvious to all artists and serious writers: *Not every piece should be revised.* He says students should, on average, revise one piece out of five they start, and that students, not teachers, should pick the pieces to be fully polished. When students choose, they can focus on the pieces that are worth revising, that hold the most interest for them, and that are most likely to yield new insights when revised. This certainly helps promote a sense of ownership and helps students learn to make decisions about their own work. It means that final results are likely to be better as well, because students can try many starts quickly, and then work hardest on a few that seem most promising. Trying to revise everything is a little like literary necrophilia: some pieces die young, and they should be left in peace.

Revising takes time. If teachers don't allow time for it, students will believe it must not be very important. We're talking about two kinds of time. First, writers need time to gain perspective—time for their work to rest and then to be contemplated in some kind of context. Looking back over a number of compositions, a student can see how she has progressed, how her interests and feelings and methods have changed since she last took stock. This self-awareness is an important part of learning and of taking responsibility for one's own growth.

And then students need the time to actually work on revising—specially set aside, in-class time. This may include regularly scheduled writing workshop sessions as well as activities in which students obtain responses from helpful readers (something most professional writers find essential). This means using methods like peer critiquing, which eats up plenty of time.

In the following sections, we'll provide as many concrete techniques as we can, to help actualize some of the aspects of revising we've described here.

SETTING THE CLIMATE FOR REVISION

Following are four "oldie but goldie" activities for building a positive climate for writing at the beginning of the year, focusing especially on revision of content. These activities are meant to help students think of revision in several different ways:

• In the largest sense—that is, revising as learning, and changing one's ideas.
• As a process of discovering choices and alternatives and then deciding which ones best express the writer's thoughts.
• As a process of getting more in touch with an audience and with the experience of *being* an audience, thereby discovering what the needs of the audience are.

Comparing First and Last Impressions

On the first day of class (or the first day of any new unit, project, or book to be read), our colleague Jim Vopat has students write down whatever they think they already know about the subject and their feelings about beginning the endeavor. If they don't know anything, they guess or speculate. Students share what they have written in small groups, and a recorder in each group writes down points of consensus, points of controversy, and questions people have. The recorders report these to the class, and the teacher collates points on the board. This becomes an agenda for inquiry during the unit, and the class returns to it periodically, as various answers to questions are discovered and misconceptions cleared up. Meanwhile, the teacher seals the students' initial writing in an envelope, to be opened several weeks hence—in the middle or at the end of the unit. Students can then write about their own changes of perspective when they open these letters to themselves.

What is revised here is each student's concept of the topic, more than the particular piece of writing in the envelope. However, after students have gone through this process for the first time, the teacher can point to the experience and say, "Now this is what I hope will happen, at least some of the time, when you are writing—not just creating a product to get a grade, but discovering new concepts and changing your own ideas about the subject."

Building Personal History

The following activity, originated by Phyllis Stimac, extends over a longer period of time and uses the student's personal history, rather than course subject matter, as the material. During the first week of the semester, ask students to list all the important incidents in their lives that they can think of, using single words or short phrases. Over the next four weeks, ask students, once a week, to write a short piece with everyone using the same genre—a fable, a childhood memory, a narrative of an event—drawing on a different item from their list each time. From the second week on, allow time after each piece is written for students to look over their previous writings (which are kept in a folder) to add to, change, or just contemplate what they've done. Obviously, the students gradually build a segment of autobiography and learn to handle one variety of journal entry as well. Be sure to share your own entries with them. After four or five weeks, students choose one entry to polish and turn in. Finally, they can write a journal entry about why they chose the item they did to revise, and another entry evaluating how their writing has progressed or changed.

Comparing Story Endings

A similar exploration of choices can be carried out using literature, rather than autobiography. Read a very short story aloud, stopping at a crucial point before the ending, or give out a photocopy with the ending omitted. Students each write their own ending. You can help them develop it by using guided imagery to focus everyone on the details, feelings, and issues of the story, as described in Chapters 3 and 11. Volunteers read their endings aloud, and you read yours as well as the original.

So far, nothing really new. But what's important is what you do next. Ask students to write a journal entry about why they think they chose their particular ending. If people chose widely differing endings, they can also be asked to discuss what the story seems to mean to various groups or members of the class. The journal entries are now the real topic of discussion, helping students to see how different interpretations of the story led to the different endings. Finally, how many now want to change their own ending? People should discuss not only *what* they'd change it to, but again, *why*. The aim is not to guess the "right" ending, but to see what the choices are, what significance they have for each person, how they express or alter the meaning of the story, and how changes reflect students' growing understanding of what the story is about.

The Writer as Audience

Once an initial level of comfort has been reached after the beginning of a semester, you can help students learn to see their own writing as their audience would—a major part of the revising process. Mark Huegelmann, of Orland Junior High School, starts this activity with students writing a short essay telling something about themselves or recounting an experience they've had, with names left off the papers. He explains that the papers will be shared aloud and that authors will eventually be asked to identify themselves, so students can avoid topics that might embarrass them.

When they are finished with a draft, Mark collects and shuffles the papers and gives them out for students to read aloud to the class (if you need to guard against inappropriate language or content, take the papers home and read them over first). Students then try to guess who wrote which one. Of course, individual writers hear their piece read aloud by another person, so they get a sense of what it's like to be the audience for their own work as well as for the others'. After each piece has been read and the author guessed, the teacher can ask students to explain how they arrived at their answers. The responses may focus on particular incidents or actions typical of the person, but may also focus on style. Students can become aware that the *way* they write often says as much as *what* they write. When the sharing and discussion are over, students can revise their drafts, using the realizations they've gained from the session.

USING REAL AUDIENCES

Many writers use a first draft essentially to get their ideas down and then revise to make those ideas clearer to someone else. The changes will depend upon who the audience is. Obviously, more explanation and background will have to be provided for someone unacquainted with a topic than for someone who's an expert.

Providing a real audience is one of the most organic ways for a teacher to create a reason for students to revise. Until the student writes for a real audience besides the teacher, revising is in a sense just an exercise, guided mainly by the teacher's authority to demand particular standards. A committed poet may invest much time getting the words right just for his own satisfaction, but for most of us, it's the need to communicate that forces us to reconsider what we've said from a particular reader's point of view and try to make it clear for that person.

Why is it that the teacher does not seem to students to be a "real audience" for revising in the same way? This is a frustrating question for most of us, and we'd like to offer the following hypothesis (which we wish some doctoral candidate would research to confirm or deny). Most school essays meant only for teachers' eyes aren't written to inform the teacher about the topic. Rather, at worst they're a means to test the student's knowledge of content the teacher already knows intimately, and at best they're a vehicle for the student to learn and to expand her own ideas about it. In the first case, revising seems beside the point because, as students are prone to plead, "You *know* what I meant"—and the real truth, often, is that you do. In the second case, when the writing records ideas essentially for oneself, there's no need to revise because the words don't function as explanations, really, but simply as reminders, as cues to what is in one's head.

The effect of a real audience is as crucial for adults as for teenage students. In the Illinois Writing Project, we've enjoyed over the years the sure-fire shock that comes when we ask a group of teachers to write a letter to a trusted friend about a student who has frustrated them and then to revise the letter so it can be sent to the child's *parents*.

It's easy for teachers to lose sight of the significance of audience and purpose in students' writing. After all, the student's *real* purpose is to learn to write, isn't it? However, you can't write writing; you write about something, to someone. A number of studies have shown that students do write differently to different audiences, changing sentence length and complexity to adjust to audience needs. One fascinating study (Hays 1981) found that students who wrote with an awareness of an audience and purpose worried less about surface appearances and concentrated on the ideas in their writing. You can find concrete suggestions for audiences and how to help students think about them in Chapter 15.

SOME NECESSARY PROCESSES

Teachers are sometimes disappointed when students who are given the opportunity to revise don't see that changes are needed and simply settle for fixing a few minor surface errors. Obviously, if students don't know how to carry out the task, just assigning it to them won't yield very useful results. What are some of the skills of revising? The writer must be able to:

- Reread and get a sense of how the writing "sounds" to a reader.
- Compare the result to the original purpose and, if the two differ, decide whether to revise the result or recast the original aim.

- Identify the strong, valuable aspects of the writing, the parts to leave alone or to build on.
- Ask questions of the text as a reader would, in order to identify parts that need expansion or clearer explanation.
- Conceive of alternatives and choices, different ways to think about the topic, areas that merit expansion, and different ways to express a particular idea.

These processes can be taught by modeling them and by providing guided practice. Students can try evaluating their own work and then pairing up to critique each other's writing, indicating what the reader considers the strong parts and what questions she has, and talking through possible alternatives. Brief focus lessons can help students learn to ask various types of questions, such as the following:

- *Expansion:* "I was really curious about your uncle's store, and I wanted to know more about what he sold."
- *Deletion:* "I didn't understand why you included this part. It didn't excite me, and I really wanted to move on. Is there something you were trying to say that I'm not getting? Or is there a particular reason why you want this part in here? Or do you think it should be taken out?"
- *Clarification:* "I was confused when you said he came there as a young man. I thought you already said that his family moved there when he was small. Which was it?"
- *Cause and effect:* "I just really wondered why he would go off and join the army like that. Why did he do it?"

As students hear such questions asked of their writing over a period of time, they will begin to internalize them and to learn to view their own writing more as an audience might. However, it takes time to acquire this awareness. Don't expect it to develop after one or two sessions.

MODELING REVISION OF CONTENT

You can show students some of the ways that revising works by displaying successive drafts of your own writing or student samples. Circulate copies of the initial draft first and let students discuss what information they'd like to have added. They can then compare their own criticisms and suggestions to the changes that were actually made by the author.

Keep in mind, however, that it's always different being an outsider, not knowing what information may have been left out, and what alternate directions are possible. Comparing a reader's suggestions to the writer's own knowledge of the material can in fact provide a good object lesson, showing how tricky it is to give meaningful advice on writing. The process can thus help prepare students for peer critiquing. Furthermore, when the sample comes from a previous year's work or other outside source (Brannon, Knight, and Neverow-Turk's book *Writers Writing* has some excellent examples), students are often far more cutthroat than when the writing is their own or their classmates'. Nevertheless, their own criticism helps them recognize an audience's needs, even if it isn't easy for them to take the same hard-boiled view of their own work.

Use group composing to show how many choices are available when a writer is revising content. As the whole class makes suggestions, someone records the group's composition on the board. Even though the exposition ultimately follows in one direction, there will always be plenty of discarded alternatives along the way, and a second recorder can keep a list of these for later reference. Then, after a draft is done, individual students or small groups can work on various branching points to see how the story or argument works out when it goes off in a new direction. A new computer program called "For Comment" formalizes this process, allowing up to sixteen editors to offer revision suggestions about a single document draft. The program codes each suggestion separately, and creates a "paper trail," which allows the original author to try out and choose among all the suggestions from his would-be collaborators without permanently altering the original version until he's ready.

You can model the revising process yourself. Shelly Reece, a friend who teaches in Oregon, actually composes right on an overhead projector, letting students give him a topic and observe his writing process. Shelly tries to vocalize his internal thinking, decision making, and feelings as he works, so students can "hear" all the noise that zooms through a skilled writer's mind during composing. One can do the same thing revising a draft.

COPYEDITING AND PROOFREADING

So far, we've focused on revising ideas and expression. But usage, spelling, and mechanics are important, too. We know that readers often judge writers at least in part by the surface appearance of writing, even when this is mostly irrelevant to the content. We worry about our students succeeding with other teachers later and out in the "real" world—even though most of those later teachers will require little writing, and employers probably won't spell too well themselves. But there's no escaping the fact that a well-edited paper signals the writer's caring and that it's easier for readers to attend to ideas when the surface doesn't distract them. How can we promote good editing and proofreading? More than any trick or clever teaching method, it's essential to remember the basics, even if we've stated them several times already:

• *Kids care about the details when they care about what they are saying.* Many teachers notice that students' grammar and mechanics improve when the argument grows passionate—or at least their willingness to go back and clean things up increases with investment in the piece. Students' drafting work should focus on what they want to say. Editing and proofreading are the last steps in the process, but investment in the previous steps will make these last ones more meaningful.

• *Kids need to know that the teacher also cares about what they are saying.* Start off the year, the unit, the conference, focusing on content. Go on to feedback about clarity and correctness only after you've made it clear that the ideas are important to you. If you start by discussing mechanics, students will think that's what you care most about, and they'll be correct.

• *Kids must feel the classroom is a safe place to reveal their weaknesses to a teacher or peer.* One teacher we know plumbed the depth of this truth when she suddenly realized that the students who always improved the most in mechanics—even on tests—were boys who had girlfriends with good editing skills. To put it another way, without a trusting community, students may be reticent to seek help.

• *Kids take editing seriously when the occasion for the writing makes editing meaningful.* When pieces are to be published for circulation to other students in the school, parents, or the school board, editing will matter. Sad but true, we teachers are not as meaningful an audience for teenagers—we're too familiar and too invested in the outcome. When we do assign writing that's directed to us, it is usually meant primarily to promote students' own exploration of subject matter, so it may be that on such occasions they should simply do more writing, rather than spend time editing.

When the setting is right, it won't be so difficult to teach actual usage and mechanics skills through conferences and short focus lessons, *as particular items are needed.* If students are writing dialogues or dramatic scripts, for example, they will have good reason to show who is speaking, so it will be appropriate to teach the use of quotation marks and accompanying punctuation. If students are strongly invested in writing letters to the school board about athletic policy, they'll see the purpose of proofreading to check commas and periods so that the board will pay attention to their arguments and not be distracted by nonconventional patterns.

USING CHECKLISTS

One concrete way to guide inexperienced writers through revision (or peer critiquing sessions) is to provide them with a checklist of elements to consider. There's no one best checklist to guide students in revising: what you use depends on the time of year and the writing activity kids are engaged in. When you create your own checklists, start with simple ones and expand as students become proficient. Help them do a good job of noticing one or two important things, and build on that. Begin with content, and add items on clarity and correctness later, after students have learned to focus on what they have to say. Include items that ask about strengths in the writing as well as questions and problems. As students learn to ask various kinds of questions of their texts, add these to the checklist (see Figures 14–1 and 14–2 in the next chapter for examples of lists for earlier and later in the year).

Adjust checklists according to the mode and purpose of the writing. If the paper is meant to be informative, the reader should consider whether she has learned something. If it's persuasive, ask if she was persuaded. If it's a news story for the class newspaper, include the journalist's five "wh" questions—who, what, where, when, and why.

Adding to or recasting the checklist is something the class should participate in. This is their chance to think about what characterizes good writing of various types. And their active role means that, in still another way, they are taking responsibility for the quality of their work. They will be measuring it by their own standard. Then, before they use the new checklist on their own work, let them try it out, as a group, on an anonymous student writing sample and then on a professional piece. This provides good critiquing practice, lets students field-test their standards, and illustrates that the same terms they use to analyze their own writing can be used to think about "real" literature as well. The implicit, crucial message is that they are writers just as much as the established authors whose works they read.

USING FOLDERS

Folders are one key to gaining control over time. When students store all their work in one place in the classroom, it's easy for them to review all their pieces and decide which of many first drafts, sketches, and beginnings merit revising. Thus, some pieces can get the rest time they need before revising, others may never be touched again, and one or two that the student is especially involved with may become the focus of epic struggles.

Students can store revising checklists, their own personal lists of possible topics for future writing, usage reminders, and vocabulary and spelling words in their folders, to be updated as they conquer one set of problems and advance to new ones. And both students and the teacher can look through the folder to get a long-range view of progress. Once the year gets going, students will probably need two folders: one for finished, polished pieces, and another for work in progress.

MANAGING INDIVIDUAL CONFERENCES

Conferences are not impossible. Obviously, before you can run one-to-one conferences, you must have a valuable activity happening for the other twenty-nine kids who aren't in conference with you. If you've established a regular daily or weekly writing workshop in your classroom, this automatically gives you a natural time for conferencing, while students are productively engaged in their writing. You can also work in conferences during various small-group activities (not necessarily writing activities), simply by pulling kids out of their groups one at a time.

Some teachers fear that a workshop setting will mean lack of control, with students not on task, but we see this as an essentially routine classroom-management issue. Teachers constantly have to create and enforce norms about all sorts of classroom procedures. They know that they must be serious and consistent and let students know they value the norms they are trying to establish. So it is with conference time; if you let students know that you want this time used constructively by everyone, you can make the right behavior take root, just as you do with dozens of other parts of the school day. Clearly, the folder system described above can make this process easier: anyone who claims he has nothing to do should go back to the folder, identify a piece that is worth developing or revising, and get to work on it.

We've already described teacher–student conferences for drafting in Chapter 12. How are they different when the focus is on revising a completed draft? Perhaps most essentially, when the student has a whole draft in hand, the main question is now less likely to be "Where is this piece headed?" and instead will be "What has this piece become as a whole, and how are the parts interrelated?" It may be harder for students to contemplate major changes in direction, particularly if the time left is short or if the time lapsed since completing the first draft is too brief to gain a new perspective. Yet, because ideas change and because writers often discover their real direction only when they've gotten some words onto the page, the original beginning of a piece frequently does not fit with the developing middle and end.

How can the teacher continue to take a coaching, rather than a copyediting, role and once again help students without pointing out and solving all their problems for them? Again, as in conferences for drafting, use the conference to ask questions and learn from students so that the students become more aware of their own aims, and you are able to make your help relevant. Only this time, the questions may be a little different.

The initial question may well be "What are you planning to revise?" Even when the whole class is working on a project or unit, the more you can allow students options about what to revise, the more meaningful the work will be. Then your questions can help inform both you and the individual students about what they're trying to achieve: "What's your purpose in writing this?" "Who is your audience?" "What parts do you feel good about?" "What parts do you think need work? What makes you think that?"

The teacher can adopt a coaching role, on the sidelines, rather than an editor's role. "Have you read this to someone else?" "How did you feel about their reaction?" If the reader/listener didn't respond well at some point: "Why do you think she reacted that way? Is there something you can say differently to help her, or do you think she's so unsympathetic to your ideas that you'll never reach her?"

There may not be time to hear or read entire pieces if you are to get around to everyone. Therefore, use the conference mainly to discuss the process, rather than read the words. Then, when it's time to focus on polishing and mechanics, don't be trapped into editing whole pieces. Conferences can be used to run a spot check on one paragraph for each student. Or if a student has a particular problem—say, run-on sentences—that you and he have noted on the list in his writing folder, you can spot-check just for these, on one page. Be sure the student has done his own editing job first, so that you are helping him see what he missed, not doing his job for him.

Remember that in conducting revising conferences, you are not just trying to get good products—you are not the editor of a professional magazine. Rather, conferences provide an opportunity for you to model the kinds of question asking and problem solving that students can learn to do for themselves and provide for each other in peer conferences. Your aim is to help them become independent of you.

Chapter 14

Peer Writing Groups

Peer-group work is probably one of the most complex methods for teaching writing. But it's also one of the most rewarding, because students simultaneously write for a real audience, become a real audience, talk over alternatives, learn from one another (by comparing similar efforts as well as by receiving suggestions), get to know their classmates well, and form a working community. Unfortunately for teachers, small-group activity is one of the trickiest of classroom strategies to implement, since it asks students to work together in a very unusual way: responsibly, independently, collaboratively, noncompetitively. Recognizing the difficulties involved, we no longer call this peer editing or critiquing. We've learned that editing is the aspect least likely to succeed early in a group's formation. Further, we believe, the key value of peer writing groups is that they provide a source of ideas in the prewriting stage and responses to drafts.

GENERAL PRINCIPLES

The main thing we've learned about peer writing groups is that they work beautifully and powerfully *if you take enough time and energy to prepare them.* If you just plunge in, cheerily announcing to your class, "Hey, let's try editing each others' papers today," disappointment will quickly follow. We all have our horror stories of peer editing groups gone astray. So here are some principles we've learned about the gradual and delicate process of developing effective student writing groups, mostly taken from the experience of teachers in the writing projects and in-service courses we've led.

186

Make-up of Groups

Some teachers like to let students form their own groups according to natural friendships and affinities. This often works well in very homogeneous classes, with some gentle nudging and finagling by the teacher. Other teachers find that with heterogeneous groups students learn from one another and from hearing a variety of perspectives. They carefully mix sexes, general ability levels, and strengths in the different aspects of writing (creativity, editing skill, critical insight). In any case, groups should stay together long enough to develop and make use of a working relationship. When problems arise in a group, the teacher shouldn't immediately offer to change group memberships, but rather encourage the students to try to settle the problems themselves first.

Group Size

Three is a good number for peer groups. It allows each writer to get two opinions but helps control time by limiting the number of papers to be read in each round of work. Four may be a more realistic number if many students are regularly absent or pulled out, since it means that at least three in each group will usually be present.

Room Arrangement

There's no way to avoid the disturbance of moving chairs and the noise when everyone's reading aloud in close quarters. However, if group work is regularly scheduled, students can get in the habit of arranging their chairs in tight, knee-to-knee circles the moment they walk into the classroom so they can go right to work.

Scheduling

Don't try to initiate critiquing on the first day of the semester. Give the class time to get to know one another and to get comfortable with your course. Groups will need to go through a sequence of training activities like those described below. Once you begin, however, groups need the opportunity to work regularly. You won't get much payoff from a once- or twice-per-semester approach. For a given assignment, students can meet once to share ideas and get started, once to work on developing and revising content, and once to proofread.

The Student Reader's Role

Giving help is not a simple process, and both teacher and students need to understand just what is involved. When peer response is most effective, students aren't just hunting surface errors in one another's papers. They are at once fellow inquirers and mutual audience. In fact, roles change as they move through the writing process. When they sit down to brainstorm at the beginning of a writing activity, students are co-workers, encouraging each other onward. They need to be good listeners. Especially for longer projects, just talking through their ideas with someone helps students find a focus. When reading first drafts, groups serve as interested audiences: they focus on ideas, discuss the subject itself, ask questions, tell writers what parts worked, as well as where they were confused and what they'd like to hear more about. Later, when they are proofreading, the students finally become editors, looking for grammar and spelling errors and helping each other polish the pieces.

Helping Students Give Concrete Responses

Perhaps the most frequent problem teachers encounter is that students tend to give one-line comments at one of two unhelpful extremes: either "It's perfect the way it is" or "It stinks." These kinds of remarks reflect the tricky social dynamics that have so often torpedoed teachers' casual attempts to implement peer editing. Here are some ways to help kids make their responses more concrete, reasonable, and constructive:

•   Provide critiquing guidesheets (see the examples in Figures 14–1 and 14–2) designed to fit the assignment being read and the prevailing stage of peer-group development. These sheets help kids stay on task and treat each paper equally.
•   Establish a basic formula. Example: students must identify one part that's good and explain why, must ask at least one question, and must indicate one place where they'd like to hear more. Expand and revise the formula as students become more adept.
•   Readers can state briefly what they think the writing says. Just to say, "It's good," doesn't reveal what has been communicated. If the readers summarize the ideas, the writers can see whether they communicated successfully.
•   Have each writer specify and request the sort of criticism wanted. This makes it easier for peers to bring up negative reactions, because they've been explicitly solicited.

Figure 14–1 *A Critiquing Guidesheet for Personal Writing*

Writer _____   Reader _____

Peer Critique Sheet: Personal Narrative

Be as specific as you can in answering these questions. Your comments will help the writer improve his or her paper.

1. What event did the writer focus upon?

2. Why do you think the writer chose this topic?

3. How did the writer feel about the incident when it happened? How do you know?

4. How does the writer feel about the incident now? How do you know?

5. What part of the paper did you like best? Which part impressed you the most? Why?

6. What, if anything, confuses you about the narrative as written?

7. What would you like to know more about?

8. What would you change about the content or arrangement of this paper?

_____

Figure 14–2   *A Critiquing Guidesheet for Transactional Writing*

Opinion Paper: Writing-Group Evaluation

Writer _____

Readers _____

_____

FOCUS: Is the opinion of the writer clear?
What does the writer believe?

(Writer: If this reader's response does not reflect your intent, ask your group where you went wrong.)

Does the writer remain on topic throughout the paper?
Yes ___ No ___   If no, where does s/he go astray?

ELABORATION: Does the writer anticipate the needs of the audience?
Yes ___ No ___   If no, what more do you need to know? If yes, give an example of something the writer said that you needed to know to grasp his/her idea.

Does the writer clearly show how or why s/he has reached his/her opinion? Yes ___ No ___   If no, what still confuses you?

ORGANIZATION: Has the writer arranged material effectively?
If not, what alternatives would you suggest?

If s/he has, what was especially impressive?

Has the writer linked ideas where necessary? State where links might be inserted.

GENERAL COMMENTS: Explain what impressed or concerned you about the paper that the other questions don't let you state.

Giving and Receiving Criticism Constructively

Once students learn to be more concrete in their responses, they may begin to experience another problem: the writer doesn't want to accept criticism readers have given. This is a sensitive issue, because although it's important for students to feel ownership, simply liking what one has written doesn't make it communicate successfully. To address this problem, try the following:

- The use of guidesheets can signal the fact that everyone is being treated the same, that everyone is being asked to seriously consider the advice they are being offered and no one is being singled out or picked on.
- Readers should give "I" messages: not "Here's how you must change it" but "Here's how it strikes me." As Peter Elbow says, "The reader is always right and always wrong." Readers know their own reactions but can't be certain what the writer intended.
- Readers should ask writers who their audience is and what purpose they have. Readers can then try to respect the writer's aims and help achieve those, rather than rewrite the paper their own way.
- Tell students it's really up to them what to do with advice. Not all advice is good. Different audiences will respond differently: that's life. Often readers' complaints reflect some problem in the text, but the changes suggested may not seem like the right ones to the author. On the other hand, if a writer wants to reach a particular audience, she'll need to listen to them. As Peter Elbow also says, "The *writer* is always right and always wrong." The writer may know what she is trying to say but can't be sure particular readers will get it.

TRAINING STUDENTS

Peer writing groups usually don't work well the first time you try them. As a result, this is probably the single most abandoned element of the process paradigm; many teachers and even a few researchers will tell you that they tried peer editing, and it doesn't work. The basic reason it is so hard to implement is that in our schools, students aren't often taught or encouraged to work cooperatively or to give respectful, insightful, constructive criticism. This is peculiar, since almost all the work of real adult life is done by groups of people—offices, departments, staffs, teams, partnerships, crews—who must work collaboratively and exchange feedback if high-quality work is to be accomplished.

Anyhow, you cannot expect kids to work in peer groups automatically. You'll have to do some training, but students will draw on this valuable experience throughout their lives, so the time is well spent. The training activities we are about to describe are very detailed and elaborately sequenced. Most classes will not need to have each experience; you can select those activities that seem necessary for your group. In general, the less cohesive the class, the more training it will require. Conversely, we've seen some well-developed classes prepare themselves for peer-group work quite quickly by focusing mostly on step three, below. No matter how tough the class, if you invest two or three class periods on this training, peer groups will work.

Step One: Practicing Collaboration

According to David and Roger Johnson (1984), the leading theorists of collaborative learning in education, students working in groups must be able to:

1. Give direction to the group's work by:
   a. Stating and restating the purpose of the assignment.
   b. Setting or calling attention to time limits.
   c. Offering procedures on how most effectively to complete the assignment.
2. Express support and acceptance both verbally and nonverbally through eye contact, enthusiasm, praise, and seeking others' ideas and conclusions.
3. Ask for help or clarification of what is being said or done in the group.
4. Offer to explain or clarify.
5. Paraphrase and clarify another member's contributions.
6. Energize the group when motivation is low by suggesting new ideas, by being enthusiastic, through humor, etc.
7. Describe one's feelings when appropriate.

Teach these skills by assigning groups to work together to generate a joint written product (interviewing each other to write profiles, doing some research, reviewing a short article), giving specific roles to each student in each group ("encourager," "summarizer," "questioner," etc.). Rotate roles on successive days, so everyone practices several roles. A large number of small-group activities designed to build general collaboration skills can be found in books on this subject; see, for example, Louis Thayer (ed.), *Fifty Strategies for Experiential Learning*, Books 1 and 2 (1976 and 1981).

Examine the process together after each session. Each student can give one positive comment to each other member of the group, mentioning something helpful that person did. A survey form can help (with such questions as "How many in your group contributed one or more ideas today?"). Observe the groups yourself, and sometimes appoint one student in each group as observer for the day (this person should report to the group, not to you). Discuss the principles and how the enterprise is going. Obviously, writing is a valuable tool in this self-observation, as well as a meaningful task for the groups.

Step Two: Collaborating on Prewriting

Now begins the development of students' intellectual and affective skill at actually helping each other with writing. First in pairs, then in small groups, students listen to each other's writing ideas and orally offer suggestions in a format structured by the teacher (perhaps on a written guidesheet). Listeners must help individual authors verbalize their idea, brainstorm it, think up new ideas or examples or details, anticipate difficulties, and identify sources for information. This focus on constructive work should be practiced before students ever begin evaluating one another's work.

Step Three: Responding to Training Papers

There are heavy risks involved when peer writing groups begin to critique their first paper, so that paper should come from *outside the group*. Ideally, this first "training paper" should be from an unknown, unnamed student so that members of the group will be able to respond to it uninfluenced by friendships, loyalties, reluctance to hurt, or other limits.

To begin, hand out copies of the same paper to all the newly formed peer writing groups. (If you aren't ready to actually put the kids into their groups yet, you can begin instead by having all class members read the paper and discuss as a large group the ways they might respond to it when they do get into an editing session.) One member of each group reads the paper aloud and others offer oral response to the content, using directions given in a guidesheet. Then have students immediately regather as a whole class to discuss the paper and compare responses. Some of the issues described above (under "Helping Students Give Concrete Responses" and "Giving and Receiving Criticism Constructively") will no doubt come up. This discussion gives the teacher a vital opportunity to model appropriate and sensitive comments for specific papers and helps to standardize what goes on in the groups. Work through enough training papers to ensure that students are offering specific, insightful, and diplomatic responses.

You can provide further modeling by having several students role-play a response session, using another outside paper. Students can also respond to a training paper *in writing*, exchange these written responses in their groups, and discuss their reactions. Perhaps especially important is the model you provide when you respond to students' papers in conferences. If you give extensive, controlling advice that makes the paper into one you would write, groups will generate the same kind of criticisms. But if you take care to keep responsibility in the writer's hands, student responders will learn to do that too.

Step Four: Peer Response

Now students can move on to respond to papers by their peers. If the groups are developing slowly or the teacher feels cautious, the groups can work through stages in their response, focusing in early sessions on content only. Response would be restricted to overall meaning or message; students would simply practice what Graves calls ''receiving'' the writing—providing a holistic, human hearing for what the author has tried to say. Later, when trust is stronger, peer editors can pay increasing attention to clarity, organization, or structure. They can help the writer answer such questions as: ''Is it clear?'' ''Does it make sense?'' ''Have I provided enough details or support?'' ''Are things in a meaningful order?'' ''How does the tone strike the reader?'' In adding these dimensions, the teacher may again elect to use training papers from outside the class with a guidesheet. Practice can first be oral and then involve written comments.

Once students have established patterns of reviewing the content of each other's work respectfully and insightfully, they can begin to look at papers as copyeditors, offering whatever help they can with proofreading. If needed, give practice with an outside training paper and guidesheet—first responding to content, next to clarity, and finally to correctness, focusing on several recurrent or troublesome patterns of error (the training paper should be chosen with these elements in mind). Then students can move on to comment similarly on papers by group members. As students learn more usage skills, they may at some point be able to copyedit each other's papers directly. However, they should beware that marking on the surface of someone else's work should never be done without a clear, unforced invitation from the author.

Step Five: True Autonomous, Flexible Collaboration

People in writing groups (not just "editing groups" or "response groups") at this point can now read and respond to each other's work at all stages of the process and at all levels of feedback, guided by the texts at hand and the wishes of the authors. Guidesheets are a thing of the past, and the teacher monitoring of the groups' daily operation is no longer necessary. The classroom's peer writing groups are part of a community of authors that supports and gives energy to the work of writing.

TROUBLESHOOTING

Peer groups at times need support or intervention. Ways to provide this:

• As the Johnsons (1984) point out, reminding students that you are observing their processes often helps them become more aware of their own group process. Use a guidesheet to make your own observations concrete and accurate.

• Provide regular self-evaluation and group-evaluation forms, so that students can explicitly examine their own participation patterns.

• Allow time periodically for groups to discuss among themselves how they are working as a group, using group-evaluation forms as a basis for discussion.

• When a group has problems, encourage the students to try to solve them before you intervene. Guide students to be constructive when dealing with a shy or dominating member: "We want to help everyone in the group use this skill. How can we help each other?"

• When you do intervene, do so strategically. Comment on good practices to reinforce them. Reteach group skills when you see it is necessary. If one student dominates, appoint that student to observe who contributes, to enable him to become more conscious of the issue.

• Remember that whatever happens in groups depends critically on the climate in the room and the expectations about writing created by you. If writing means mainly guessing what the teacher wants to hear about a piece of literature, groups will focus on guessing what the teacher wants. If writing means mainly perfect grammar, groups will worry only about correcting grammar. But if it means explaining ideas the writer cares about to an audience that really wants to learn what that writer has to say, groups will struggle to help each other achieve that. If revising means fixing things because the teacher says everyone must do so, groups will hunt for easy changes to make. But if revising means students choose the pieces they care most about and refine them to communicate their thoughts fully and clearly, the work of groups is likely to be genuine.

Chapter 15

Publishing

A roomful of students listens as one boy reads his recollection of being called to the office at summer camp to learn that a favorite grandparent had died. Though the topic and the reading aloud are both of his own choice, he has taken a risk, and for a moment the emotion makes it hard for him to continue. There's a longish silence in the room as he composes himself. A couple of students brush away tears. Some teachers fear such emotional moments, but this one sits quietly with the rest of the listeners. It's clear that the subject is important to the boy and to the rest of the students as well. As he finishes reading his vivid and touching reminiscence, there are quiet comments of sympathy and appreciation. Several more students volunteer to read next, perhaps to help him feel that he's not alone. The group has felt the power of words that matter, and they say so when class is over. . . .

Several junior-high kids show a visitor a shelf of bound student-made books and collections of essays by the class and by students from previous years. Efforts by older siblings are pointed out. Mixed in is an album of photos from a class picnic put together by a parent who was inspired to contribute when she saw the kids' books. It's all part of the history of the class and the school. . . .

A sophomore high-school class is in the midst of their work on a magazine project, with four groups of seven or eight students clustered in each corner of the room. Each magazine is focused on a special interest or range of related topics (with titles such as *Fast Food Worker*, *Makeup Magazine*, *Soccer*, and *Teen Rocker*), and the groups are at the stage of arguing out editorial policies and choosing topics to research. Using the various kinds of knowledge in the class—artistic talent, word-processing skill, and so forth—the magazines will come out looking near professional, and will be filed in the school media center. . . .

196

James Britton, early on in the recent burst of theorizing and research about writing, argued that nothing is more counterproductive than the "dummy runs" that constitute much of kids' writing experience. Writers need real purposes for writing and real audiences to receive their work. For us as teachers, this means finding audiences other than ourselves— beyond the four walls of our classrooms—and getting students' writing out to them.

It also means helping the students themselves become a supportive and energizing audience for one another's words. The sharing of stories, information, and accounts of problems is one of the most natural and powerful ways to build a community, whether it's a social group, a management team, or an academic class. And a community, in turn, creates a strong need to go on sharing, an audience that members want to please, to influence, to learn from. We see this regularly in our own professional relationships. Bring three or more teachers together to work on some task, such as the improvement of composition teaching in their school, and notice how quickly they get to telling stories related to the problem and how difficult it is to stop them from doing it.

In Chapter 2, we listed four reasons why a variety of real audiences is important for student writers. We'd like to recall that list and add a fifth item as well:

1. An audience provides that special jolt of *motivation* that comes from knowing the work is real, and not just another school hurdle.

2. It provides students with *practice* adjusting their written discourse to the needs of a reader, one of the most fundamental yet unteachable skills writers use. So far as we know, the most effective way to learn this skill is to do it, observe the results, and adapt one's next effort accordingly.

3. Students get *real feedback* from audiences, which helps them to learn what works with different kinds of readers and different sorts of writing tasks.

4. Writing for real audiences creates *natural pressure to edit* the work—not because an English teacher will lower your grade for sloppy proofreading, but because you don't want the effectiveness of your message to be compromised.

5. When the class serves as audience for one another, students begin to connect their experience as readers and listeners with their own efforts as writers. This in turn leads them to notice, in their reading, how professional writers solve particular problems; and when the whole class shares writing on a similar topic, they realize options and alternatives they might use in their own pieces. Reading and writing become deeply interactive.

By "publishing," then, we mean communicating in writing to any and all audiences close to or distant from the students and having that writing actually reach its intended target as often as possible. Publishing can mean formal acceptance by magazines or newspapers in the community or the school and entry in contests, but it also means much more: student-made anthologies, placed in the library; letters sent to authors, government officials, friends, or grandparents; plays videotaped or put on for the school; pieces read aloud in class. The use of writing to help with the ongoing inquiry in the class also counts as an important kind of publishing. Students can compare interpretations of literature they've read, conduct panel discussions that start with prepared position statements, read aloud to the class quick explanations of particular concepts being studied—all are ways of publishing that help with the learning process of the classroom community. It's important to see publishing as more than just a narrow kind of performance, as in state writing contests or laminated, bound tomes.

Once students have chosen a publication effort they really wish to carry out—a cause, a project they want to see through to completion, an idea they want to convince someone of—revising, polishing, perfecting grammar and mechanics become natural concerns, rather than just catering to teachers' pet peeves. Students want to make a good impression, and teenagers are all too conscious of the social appearance of what they do. It's appropriate at this point to care about appearance and details of one's writing.

The most obvious way to help students learn about writing for other audiences is to find some, have students write to them, and let the students see what responses they get. Here are some audiences and outlets for junior-high and high-school writers:

• Classmates as audience—but take time to help students learn how to listen, be supportive, ask good questions, and acquire the skills of being a good audience.

• Students in the class next door, down the hall, in another course or class, or in another building; or the students of a friend who teaches in another town or state.

• Little kids in a nearby elementary school—send them fairy tales, animal stories.

• Students coming into next year's class—give them advice about how to succeed.

• Students who will have to do the same project or unit in the future—provide them with study guides for English as well as other subjects (math, biology, history, etc.).

• Classroom bulletin boards and displays—individual students can have the spotlight for a week, to post their best pieces, autobiographies, early writings, printed materials on favorite subjects or hobbies, or whatever. Special-interest groups can prepare displays on their obsessions, with their own explanations, charts, how-to essays, and the like.

• The shelves of the school or community library—to circulate bound student books, class anthologies, and student literary or topical magazines.

• Special displays of student work—books, essays, poetry, combinations of art and writing, set up at local libraries and other institutions.

• Theater audiences made up of the class, other classes, or the whole school—present plays and scripts live or videotaped. At one high school we know, the drama department presents a writer's showcase of dramatized student pieces chosen from throughout the school, for a long weekend run every year.

• Students throughout the school or other community groups—conduct surveys and questionnaires to learn opinions and attitudes. (Designing good questionnaires is tricky, so be sure to have students pilot-test questions on each other and, if possible, on a sample subject or two.)

• People the class is interested in—local TV personalities, organization leaders, successful businesspeople—send letters asking about their lives, their work, their policies.

• Government officials—send them letters about particular issues, events, community needs. Consider all possible levels and branches—national leaders, special agencies like the Center for Disease Control, legislators who are knowledgeable about particular issues, state administrators, local mayors, aldermen. Students can brainstorm concerns they want to ask about or lobby for.

• Good teachers they had in the past ("You may not remember me, but . . .").

• Friends, relatives, and parents, both near and far—the writing can be a holiday message, simply a letter, or a piece that grows out of a memoir about a person or event of importance to the writer.

• A friend, advisor, or pastor who helped the writer out at one time ("Did I ever tell you how important it was when you . . .").

• The author of a book the writer has read, especially if the author is alive and willing to respond.

• Textbook publishers—send critiques suggesting improvements for the next edition of the composition text, the chemistry book, or other school materials.

• Local corporations ("What's your policy on industrial waste?" or "What sorts of jobs do you have open, and what should we be studying to prepare for them?").

• The editor of the local newspaper, or a local newspaper columnist.

(Proofread outgoing letters carefully, to avoid being ambushed in print. Many journalists love to stick it to the school system by lambasting the grammar errors of student correspondents.)

• Local newspapers—may run feature articles on class activities, local organizations, and/or people. If a newspaper won't publish them, type and bind them and get local doctors, dentists, and beauticians to add them to their waiting-room reading table.

• The school board—send them reports and inquiries ("Here's what we've been studying in junior English." "When are we going to get our new gym?").

• The principal and other building administrators—may be given suggestions, questions, and reports. Let them know that your class expects replies, either in writing or in person.

Make it real. Just mentioning an audience doesn't necessarily make it meaningful. There are "as if" audiences and actual audiences. But even the actual ones may be only "as if" for many students. Teenagers haven't always had the social experiences to sensitize them to the reactions of some audiences. Theorists argue that a writer's sense of audience is a kind of fiction anyway. We don't *really* know how someone is going to react to what we are about to say. But by hearing responses in social situations over a period of time, most of us get better at anticipating responses, and students can be helped to develop this skill.

Help students get to know particular audiences. A cautionary tale: Linda Cannon, an energetic and thoughtful teacher at Fremd High School, had students write stories for younger children and sent them to an elementary classroom taught by a friend to get a live response. The students were crestfallen when the evaluations came back: the children found the stories dumb. Linda realized that next time she'd need to acquaint her students with the world of third-grade readers before they composed their stories. An in-person visit works wonders to solve this problem, followed by a later visit when writing can be shared aloud.

Here are some ways to build audience sensitivity:

• Bring in a visitor for the class to interview—a personnel manager from a local corporation if students are practicing résumés or job applications, a local politician if the students are writing letters about local problems, a drug counselor if they all want to write about drugs, or a parent whose job is related to some ongoing class project.

• Use role playing—one student can argue his own position about a school policy, and another can play the school principal or a board member responding.

- Debates—when students prepare arguments for one side of an issue and then hear the opposing side, they can learn how to anticipate doubts or questions their readers may have.

A caveat: Be sure students don't become overwhelmed by their consciousness of an audience. As Peter Elbow points out (1973, 1981), writers can be *intimidated* as easily as they can be motivated by audiences. It doesn't help to imagine a critical eye constantly looking over one's shoulder. Include the concept of audience in your initial explanation of the assignment. However, when drafting, students may need to turn inward to figure out what they have to say. The revising stage is often a better time to look more consciously outward.

Part IV

Evaluating
Writing

Chapter 16

The English Teacher's Red Pen: History of an Obsession

A few years ago one of our teacher-consultants in the Illinois Writing Project devised and led a workshop that climaxed when every teacher in the room got to break a red pencil in half and ceremonially throw it in a passing wastebasket. It was a testament to Marilyn Weincek's theatrical skill (not to mention her taste for in-service brinksmanship) that the teachers took this didactic drama in a constructive, symbolically liberating way. Neither of us has ever been tempted to conduct that ceremony ourselves, but the fittingness of its imagery has lingered in our minds.

In Chapter 17, we will review many alternative methods of responding to, evaluating, and grading student writing. But because this part of writing instruction is so fraught with intense feelings, expectations, and value conflicts, we want to pause first and offer some background and history to provide a context for understanding this issue. In our experience as workshop leaders, the implementation of the process model of writing most often founders on the rocks of evaluation; teachers who enthusiastically experiment with a wide variety of assorted prewriting and revision activities balk when invited to try out a similarly broad selection of evaluation strategies. We English teachers seem to believe that there is really only one right way to evaluate student writing, and this profoundly self-limiting idea is the subject of the next few pages.

As writing teachers we don't usually notice how obsessed we are with evaluation. But others notice. To us, it seems only normal and responsible to spend twenty or thirty or forty hours a week of out-of-class time correcting kids' papers. We think that a student paper with two or three hundred red circles and marginal comments is nothing special; it is simply another workmanlike bit of English teaching. To us, intensive correction is the standard, responsible, professional way of responding to a piece of imperfect student work.

But we don't often notice that our approach to marking papers is dramatically different from what most of our colleagues do in the name of evaluation. Think about this. What other teachers have as their unabashed goal to correct every error that every student ever makes on every piece of work they ever attempt? What other kinds of teachers sit home through long weekends working their way through stacks of student papers that rise high above the arms of their La-Z-Boys and absorb every free minute of time? What other teachers routinely miss family outings to the zoo, the movies, the ball game, and Grandma's house because of all the papers they have to mark? What other kinds of teachers ask school administrators for—and sometimes get—reduced class loads because of all the papers they must grade? And what other teachers expect everyone else to feel so sorry for them because of their overwhelming paper load?

Or, to turn it around: Of all the teachers of all the subjects taught in junior and senior high school, which group spends the greatest proportion of their professional time on evaluation activities? Right, the English teachers. In no other school subject do teachers spend so much of their teaching time on activities related to evaluation, grading, marking, correcting, and giving judgmental feedback of all sorts. Oh sure, some math and science teachers fall in love with their own complex point systems and always seem to be sitting around the faculty lounge pounding on a calculator and deducting another sixteenth of a point from someone's score on their table-covering spreadsheet of student grades. But, grading computations aside, most other teachers' evaluation of student work—reviewing, marking, and grading the actual products—on average occupies a comparatively small proportion of their professional life. These colleagues do not often tell stories of whole weekends spent grading tests on the Constitution, lab reports, or figure drawings. In fact, evaluation in other subjects customarily consists of brief items or samples, some of which can even be scored by the Scantron machine or a personal computer. None of the national professional societies in these subjects has issued any official call for more paid paper-marking time, as the NCTE has.

Given that we writing teachers approach the evaluation of student work in such a different way from most of our colleagues, one crucial question promptly presents itself: does it work? Does this unusual and elaborate and time-consuming and costly approach to the evaluation of student writing work? Does it help students learn to write well? As the data from the National Assessment demonstrate, as the research collected by Hillocks and others shows, and as the reports of introspective teachers confirm, it doesn't work very well at all. We haven't created a nation of skillful, confident, fluent writers—in fact, most critics say we have accomplished the opposite. We have raised a countryful of well-schooled adult people who write poorly, who hate to write, who avoid writing when they can, and who, when they meet English teachers at parties, nervously joke about having their grammar corrected. Indeed, the impact of our evaluation activities on people's lives can be discovered right between the cheese dip and the rumaki, if you dare to reveal your occupation to strangers: most adults remember their English teachers as people who made them feel bad about writing and about themselves.

Why do so many of our former students end up both incompetent and hurt? Perhaps they feel they've played a twelve- or sixteen-year no-win game with their English teachers. Notice that in evaluating the mechanics of writing—spelling, punctuation, capitalization, usage, and so forth—we typically enforce *a higher standard of student performance than in any other subject in school.* On a math quiz, a student who gets 80 percent of the problems correct will probably get a B; if a student shows 90 percent comprehension on a history test, she'll probably get an A. But if a student misspells every tenth word in an English paper, many English teachers will give that student a C or even an F. The stories are legion of teachers who pridefully announce their idiosyncratic and arbitrary rule: "I'll read your paper only until I get to the third error, then I'll stop and send it back," or "If you have more than two errors in your paper, it's an automatic F." This behavior—and even its milder, everyday forms—underscores that we hold a much higher standard when we evaluate the mechanics of students' writing than any other kind of student work in school.

Indeed, it is only in the mechanics or surface features of writing that perfection is unabashedly upheld as an appropriate goal for the evaluation of teenage students. We once heard a high-school English teacher announce passionately in a workshop, "I'd rather have my students write one paper a year that's 100 percent perfect than have them write hundreds of papers that have errors in them." In every other branch of school teaching except ours it is well recognized that students must be evaluated on the basis of developmentally appropriate expectations and that sound evaluation is based upon a reasonable, proportionate sense of what mastery or competence means at any given level. But English teachers try to rate students on the standards of adult, polished, professional, public prose, a standard that is impossibly daunting—and inaccurate, if we consider the fact that real professional writers actually get a lot more collaborator assistance in polishing their work than kids do in school.

Further, our obsession with perfection in mechanics actually undermines our teaching of, and students' attention to, the more fundamental aspects of composing—content and clarity. What our intensive correction of mechanics implicitly teaches kids is that correct writing is good writing:

you can write almost any bunch of ideas in school, and if they are neat, well punctuated, and correctly spelled you're likely to be rewarded. Ask most students what good writers do and most often they'll answers, "Good writers don't make a lot of mistakes."

We've said or implied a dozen times in this book that the key to engaging students with writing is to keep meaning at the center of the process, to always ensure that kids experience writing as a way of communicating, of getting something done for themselves. But when our evaluation efforts center obsessively, punitively, perfectionistically upon the mechanics of writing, we push meaning out of the center and enshrine correctness as the reason for writing. There's no surer way to make students treat writing like other pointless, arbitrary school hurdles. Indeed, that is essentially what we have done in the teaching of writing in this country; we have taken what is potentially the most personal, energizing, and richly meaningful subject in the whole curriculum and sucked the meaning out of it. We've degraded our subject and in so doing have created a nation of wounded, unconfident semi-writers.

At about this point in the argument, a faint voice built into each of us begins to whisper, "But if you don't correct all those errors, the errors will take root and students will *never* learn to write correctly!" Notice what this worry implies: we assume that writing is a totally different kind of school subject, something unique that requires a completely different sort of evaluation procedure, one with far more comprehensive and frequent correction than any other skill or content we teach in school. But is it true? Does it take more feedback and correction to learn how to write than to learn anything else? Does writing require more response than reading, history, art, driver's education, or science? Is writing somehow more complex, or more demanding, or different in quality from all these other sorts of learning? Conversely, will evaluation strategies that usually fail in other subjects somehow work with writing? Clearly, there are no rational reasons for believing that the answers to any of these questions support what we traditionally do.

Still, it is undeniably true that writing is a tremendously complex activity, and the question remains: how *do* people learn to write if not by intensive correction of their errors? In fact, people can and do learn to write in the same basic way they learn any other complex and valuable skill: by making real attempts to use the skill in appropriate contexts. The fact is, in real life we rely very little on external evaluation and much more on practice—unmonitored, unsupervised, uncriticized practice—as the key way of learning almost everything important: talking, walking, relating to others, riding a bicycle, playing an instrument, and so forth. In every one of these complex activities, the main mechanism by which learners advance is by practicing—trying out—the activity to the best of their current ability in real-life situations and then making use of whatever fragmentary, naturalistic feedback ensues to shape their next attempt.

For example, parents do very little evaluation or correction of their young children's early speech. They don't give two-year-olds feedback about their placement of adjectives relative to nouns or about the quality of their subordinate clauses. Instead, parents almost invariably respond to whatever *content* they can derive from the child's attempted utterances, however "incorrect" the form may be. Parents don't worry about negative particle inversions ("I no like broccoli!") taking root or becoming permanent; they understand intuitively that a highly efficient natural learning process is at work that will eventually eliminate various categories of errors, overgeneralizations, and immaturities. Junior will not go off to college saying "I no like chemistry," but it won't be because his parents started correcting his earliest errors in the crib.

In real life, we don't believe that one must be constantly monitored and corrected in every attempt to learn. On the contrary, when we consciously structure optimal learning situations outside of school, we tend to provide a rather low ratio of evaluative feedback to unmonitored practice. Think of the way we teach piano. The customary arrangement is that the pupil practices perhaps five or ten hours per week and then sees the teacher for a single hour. And during that session the teacher does not just evaluate, criticize, and give feedback; she also listens, plays the instrument a bit to model, talks about feelings and attitudes, plans the practice schedule for the following week, and attends to a variety of other matters. Even when the teacher is evaluating, she does not stop the student to point out and criticize every single misplayed note or passage. Instead, the effective music teacher is selective—she skillfully focuses the pupil on a few problems at a time, ones that are within the student's reach to attend to and correct.

Perhaps the most important school-related analogy we ought to consider here is reading. Not only is reading an inseparable component of literacy, but it is also a subject that—all media exaggerations and hysteria aside—American schools have succeeded well in teaching to the majority of kids, and one that most adults feel reasonably confident about. Our ideas about evaluation in the field of reading are very different from our prevailing ideas about evaluating writing.

In evaluating reading, teachers try to assess a student's ability to construct meaning from a text, and they use a variety of techniques to check this: oral reading, conferences, group discussions, study questions, pencil-and-paper comprehension tests, standardized reading inventories, and other methods. All of these measures are usually made in terms of classroom, grade level, or age-related norms of developmentally appropriate competence. Children are expected to produce oral reading samples only occasionally, and these samples are not intensively corrected. Indeed, the best reading teachers tend to be very selective in calling kids' attention to errors or to miscues. The skillful teacher carefully focuses the child on a few developmentally appropriate issues at a time.

Most practice of reading is actually unsupervised, unmonitored, and unevaluated. If a first grader comes back to class on Monday and reports having read an issue of *Scientific American* over the weekend, the reading teacher does not say, "Oh, my dear, you shouldn't have tried to read that without me there to check your reading. Think of all the miscues you must have had. Think of all the comprehension errors. All of your mis-readings and misunderstandings will probably take root now and be with you the rest of your life!" Instead, because most reading teachers have faith in unmonitored practice and selective evaluation, what they do say is, "Great! What did you find out?" Their attitude is "Go ahead, kid, try to read anything you can get your hands on at whatever level you can handle. If you comprehend just 2 percent of that *Scientific American*, wonderful. And by the way, I'm proud of you that you would try something so grown-up and so challenging!" In writing, on the other hand, we think that every word that every kid ever writes must pass beneath a teacher's red pen. And kids who risk writing anything imperfect, exploratory, play-ful, or over their heads are told, in effect, "This is terrible. You flunk. Don't try this again until you can do it perfectly."

These analogies to learning in reading can be extended indefinitely; we hope the point is established. Unmonitored practice with limited feedback works very nicely in learning to read (and for most other pursuits in life), and we have no reason to think it won't work in writing too. Now we don't mean by all these comparisons to sanctify the field of reading and the corps of reading teachers. There are still plenty of retrograde reading teachers and programs. But the fact is that there are broadly accepted standards for the evaluation of reading that are more sophisticated, flexible, and developmentally sound than the complementary assortment of ideas we have in the developing field of writing.

There are still a couple of half-answered questions in the background. The first one is: why doesn't our traditional approach to evaluating writing work, given that we devote so much time and energy to it? The other question is: if it doesn't work, why do we keep doing it?

Why doesn't intensive correction work? Why, as the research collected by Hillocks strongly demonstrates, does students' writing *not* improve as a result of intensive correction any more than it grows with other, lighter forms of teacher response? One of the things we English teachers rarely do is simply stop and reflect on the outcomes of our traditional, labor-intensive form of evaluation, to ask ourselves, "When I return papers to students, do those students subsequently master the errors that I've marked in red? Do the issues and weaknesses raised in my marginal comments get attended to and improved?" When the question is put this way, most of us begin to grumble about the low return of results for all the time we put in. The students just don't seem to improve; they don't pay attention to all those carefully circled errors. So much of our exquisitely detailed feedback goes unheeded. And all of us have shared this painful English-teacher experience: we hand back a kid's carefully marked-up paper, he takes one look at the sea of red ink, crumples it up, and tosses the paper—along with perhaps 10 or 15 minutes of our scrupulous, uncompensated, out-of-class time—into the wastebasket.

Obviously, students who discard their papers can never learn from whatever feedback they contain—and this common classroom event gives us a hint about why intensive marking of papers is ineffective much of the time. A student's throwing a corrected paper away is just an extreme and dramatic manifestation of the factors that make intensive correction a problematic form of evaluation: it is overwhelming, unfocused, demoralizing, and non-meaning-centered.

Intensively marked papers often give too much feedback. Students can't see through the mass of marks to notice the related sets or patterns of errors they need to work on. In our attempt to be scrupulous, we overload the learner. Imagine yourself trying to learn any new content or skill this way; if your instructor insists on telling you every aspect of everything you did wrong on every attempt you ever make, you will probably feel overwhelmed and unable to sort out the key elements you need to focus on in your next attempt. If you've ever seen (or been) a person trying to get up on water skis for the first time, you know what we're talking about. A wet, scared, exhausted person floats unstably in the water while four or five well-intentioned people in the boat bombard her with feedback about her prior attempts: "You let go too soon!" "Keep your knees bent!" "Pull yourself up!" "Put the tips of the skis together!" "Just let the boat pull you up!" "Lean back!" "Relax!" "Hold the rope in the middle!" If you're on the receiving end of all this advice, it's simply too much. When it overloads you, you cannot use any of it, and it ends up being worse than no feedback at all.

Notice that intensive correction is also overwhelming for the teacher. All those complaints English teachers make about the paper load are real. If you grade all student papers in the traditional, comprehensive manner, it takes huge amounts of time. With a student load of 125, a teacher who makes a single writing assignment and then spends ten minutes on each paper has committed more than 20 hours of out-of-class time. Ironically, such marking takes so much time that it tends to limit the amount of writing one assigns—after all, a teacher cannot assign more writing than he can responsibly evaluate in the waking hours of his life. But if "responsibly" means intensively correcting every word that every student ever writes, the teacher-evaluator becomes a bottleneck in the process; you begin to constrain the amount of writing practice students get. And since research says that students grow more from practice than from correction, this becomes an insidious professional trap. To be blunt: the traditional red-penciller role makes the teacher into another reason why kids don't write enough; it tricks us into spending most of our time on our least effective instructional activity; it saps precious time from much more powerful strategies; and, to boot, it leaves us feeling frustrated, impotent, and unappreciated.

An element that's needed in feedback for writers and water-skiers alike is *focus*: as the research shows, the best way to respond to weaknesses in a piece of student writing is to direct the author's attention to one or two related sets of problems at a time. Thus the student's attention can be steered unambiguously toward issues that stand out clearly and can be attended to. Such a limited and selective approach may not be a popular form of evaluation. Parents and taxpayers may insist on old style of comprehensive marking, just like everybody in the boat enjoys shouting their pet pieces of advice to the would-be skier—but it's still bad evaluation. Should professional educators knowingly use a bad form of evaluation just because some of their noisier clients prefer it?

Another problem with intensive correction is morale. Most students—most people—have a hard time separating marks on their writing from attacks upon their person. We easily recognize and accept this fact with young children. Primary teachers tend to be very sensitive to this issue, and the best ones almost never make the kinds of intensive marks on the surface of students' work that we in the higher grades commonly do. In fact, many primary teachers will tell you that the surface of a kid's piece of writing should be inviolate, that it's an expression of a self, a work of art or artifact that should never be defaced by anyone else's markings or revisions.

This is a view that we teachers of older kids need to give respectful consideration. We assume, of course, that our students have developed to the stage where they can "take it" when their paper comes back to them all marked up. But can they? If we think about the darkened faces, the crumpled-up papers, and perhaps most importantly, the steadfast, universal, passive-aggressive resistance of teenagers to revising their writing, we know that issues of morale are deeply involved when we put our pens on students' papers.

Even more powerfully, we should think back over our own history as writers, perhaps as college students; recall a time when we got back a heavily marked-up paper from a professor; and try to recapture, as fully and honestly as we can, the feeling that we had at that moment. Did we gratefully and delightedly turn to the task of incorporating all those helpful hints into our next paper? Or did we instead experience a general, very personal feeling of hurt and embarrassment? Did we ever look at the paper again? If so, for what reason? If we couldn't constructively use this sort of response as college students, how can we expect our teenage pupils to show such emotional maturity? Furthermore, it's good to keep in mind that we weren't normal kids. Teachers, by and large, are people who liked school, succeeded there, and for whom the customary school ways of doing things usually worked. Even those of us who do recall learning a lot from intensive correction must ask ourselves: even though it did work for us, does it really work for most typical teenage writers?

Closely related is the issue of meaning. One of the things that discourages kids about intensive correction is that it seems to value form above content. And even though we sometimes *tell* students things to the contrary in our lectures and pleadings, what we *do* communicates something else. If we spend more ink on mechanical errors than on content comments, we are communicating that we value the mechanics more. And since our standards for the mechanics of writing, compared to other subjects in school, tend to be very, very high, it is easy for kids to see writing as a game that is not about content but about following a large number of arbitrary rules.

Then what about that other lingering question? If it doesn't work, then why is the intensive marking of student papers so deeply embedded in our school culture? How can something so wrong or counterproductive be so durable? One small and immediate set of reasons concerns our need to have something to evaluate by, something quantifiable. Obviously, spelling and punctuation errors provide relatively unambiguous pieces of data that can be reliably tallied and translated into some sort of score. Content, organization, focus, logic, support, tone, style—all the other attributes of writing seem harder to quantify and more subjective. These subjective elements, of course, are always factored in implicitly when teachers attach letter grades to pieces of writing, but we all seem insecure about how valid, how scientific, how trustworthy our holistic judgments could really be. (In the next chapter, by the way, when we talk about designing analytic scales, we'll argue that teachers' so-called subjective judgments of student writing are typically based upon very rational and valid ingredients that can quite easily be surfaced, specified, discussed, explicated, and defended.)

But the larger reasons for the intensive marking of writing in American schools are historical. We tend to forget that the subject we now call writing—which essentially consists of teaching students to compose their own original texts in a variety of discourse modes—is a relatively new school subject. Indeed, throughout most of the educational history of this country, the middle member of our beloved Three R's stood not for "writin'" as we now teach it, but for *handwritin'*. In the colonial schools, it was simply not a matter of concern for elementary or secondary pupils to be composing their own stories, poems, or reports.

In fact, composition originated in American schools in the nineteenth century as a kind of fusion of four much older strands of curriculum: penmanship, spelling, grammar, and rhetoric. With the rise of industrialization and the rationalization of its attendant bureaucracies, it became much more important for many people to be able to generate clear, effective, original documents and correspondence. Gradually, this demand came to be reflected in school curricula. But as schools moved to invent and develop this new subject of composition, some of the values and habits attached to its precursor subjects stayed with it.

For example, the learning and evaluation of penmanship have, from Sumerian times, stressed surface features. Of course this makes sense, since making handwriting conventional, neat, and attractive is the purpose of the subject. There's nothing nitpicky about evaluating handwriting, within reason, on the basis of its appearance. Much of the writing (penmanship) instruction in American schools of the nineteenth and early twentieth centuries involved the careful, neat copying of other people's words—often the texts of literary greats or historical figures.

Similarly, in the traditional study of formal grammar it was reasonable to evaluate students on whether they could remember sets of rules or abstract terms. After all, this grammar was being consciously taught as an end in itself, as a self-contained system the mastery of which provided discipline for the mind; only in a more general way was it seen as an aid to better writing. Spelling instruction has had a similar history in American schools. Spelling has been taught both as an adjunct to reading and as a special, separate body of knowledge that polite and educated people need to master—not so much as a tool for writing. The traditional American approach to spelling, composed of weekly word lists, tests, and spelling bees, never stressed students doing many original pieces of their own writing.

The trouble is, of course, that now we're asking kids to do something quite different. Composing one's own original texts isn't primarily a task of using neat handwriting, reproducing words from a spelling list, or remembering (or consciously applying) grammatical terminology. When writing in the modern sense is the aim, these subskills are of minor significance compared with the larger task of making clear, coherent, original messages in written language. Unfortunately, as the teaching of writing evolved, many of the methods and criteria formerly used to evaluate these minor elements were inappropriately applied to evaluating students' whole, original compositions. Thus, even to this day we attach a disproportionate significance to the surface appearance, grammar, and spelling in students' compositions.

The fourth root of composition, rhetoric, presents a somewhat different case. Rhetoric was actually taught very rarely at the elementary and secondary level, far less than either penmanship or grammar, although it was clearly the traditional school subject with the closest affinity to what we now call writing. After all, the study of rhetoric was concerned with the composition of speeches, the structure of arguments, the nature of evidence, ways of affecting an audience, the creation of figures of speech, and related matters. But classical rhetoric was also limited in its applicability to the emerging subject of writing in a number of ways: it was based more upon speaking than writing; more upon ceremonial than original discourse; more upon conventional, fixed forms of discourse than those invented by the author or dictated by the material at hand. Indeed, we can trace our teacherly faith in fixed frames for writing (like the five-paragraph theme) directly to classical rhetoric.

These historical considerations begin to explain how we got off on the wrong track with the evaluation of writing. But why has it taken us so long to recognize the error? We still haven't accounted for the incredible durability of this approach. Obviously, intensive correction has remained in our practice not just as a mistake or an oversight, but because it continues to serve some other purposes well. We still correct papers intensively today, not because it is a good way to teach writing, but because it is a way to teach certain elements of the so-called hidden curriculum, that implicit agenda of social values that schools embed in various procedures, rules, and structures. Writing offers a perfect opportunity to teach neatness, punctuality, orderliness, obedience, and perhaps most centrally, the willingness to take criticism from adult authorities appropriately (i.e., without protesting). There is nothing unusual about a school subject being turned to these corollary purposes; social studies inculcates patriotism, Latin teaches memorization, health classes provide a host of socio-moral teachings. The problem is that *our* subject—writing—has too often been harnessed to other goals that are not just irrelevant, but sometimes directly contradictory to the nature of what we are trying to teach.

If you look at writing as a school subject that's only about a century old, its not surprising that we're still having some problems fine-tuning this upstart chunk of the curriculum. Comparing our field's brief history with the millennia of teaching reading, math, languages, science, art, history, and other subjects, it is no wonder that we're still trying to figure out what kind of evaluation works best. In a sense, the paradigm shift we talked about earlier may be reviewed as the next stage in the growth of our emerging field: the arrival of a new and more appropriate set of values, approaches, and methods for actually teaching the modern school subject of composition. The so-called process model, viewed in this context, far from being a radical or partisan innovation, is simply the next developmental stage. We certainly needn't be intimidated by the weight of one paltry century of tradition.

One of the juicy ironies of this whole professional predicament, of course, is that we English teachers can't easily change our way of evaluating student writing now because everyone else expects us to do it the old way. Parents, taxpayers, school administrators, board members, and everyone else who is metaphorically looking over our shoulders believe that the only proper way for English teachers to evaluate any piece of student writing is to mark every error they can find with red ink. And where did these people get this bedrock faith in intensive correction, this expectation that now traps us and restricts our opportunity to try new ways of evaluating? From us, of course, and from our professional ancestors. The profession of English has raised up successive generations of citizens who believe that the evaluation of writing equals the intensive correction of its mechanical errors.

When these adults we have trained become parents, they may even challenge those of us who neglect to mark every error in their own children's papers. Sometimes they even pick up the phone and call up their kids' English teachers: "I see from your comments that you read little Dixie's paper, but there are three spelling errors here that you didn't circle. How come?" All of this faith in Mom, apple pie, and intensive correction, amusingly enough, manages to coexist comfortably with the fact that these adults hate to write, avoid writing when they can, and in fact aren't very good writers. What they are now demanding from us, in essence, is: "What you did sure didn't work for me, so I insist that you do it to my children."

Unfortunately, even the adults who are skillful writers sometimes lack insight into the things that really helped them develop. They often give their English teachers—or the more memorable things they did—more credit than is due for their growth. "Oh, I remember old Miss Fidditch—when you got a paper back from her it was covered with red. But you really learned something." From all we know about language learning, child development, and evaluation, the chances are that people who recount such memories didn't learn how to write from Miss Fidditch's bleeding over their papers, but in spite of it—probably from a combination of other less dramatic, more enduring, more embedded factors in their lives. But what's important, of course, is what people *think* they know about learning to write. And what these people, along with most other adults, think tends to paint us contemporary writing instructors into a corner.

This means that if we teachers are going to insist on our rightful professional latitude to try new forms of evaluation, we must educate not only our students but their parents as well. So be it. We are educators by trade, so the job of educating another group is no big deal. In fact, our Writing Project has had great success in communicating the new paradigm to parents and building community support for its related pedagogy. In Chapter 17 of the book, we detail some of the strategies that teachers and districts have used to accomplish this.

To convince ourselves and others that intensive correction is not the only way, and to undergird our own confidence in trying new approaches, we may need to recall what evaluation is for. It is to help kids learn. One of the most helpful concepts in educational evaluation is the distinction between formative and summative evaluation: formative evaluation provides feedback or help to students that allows them to grow and learn further; summative evaluation doesn't aim to generate future learning, but merely quantifies what has been learned up to a given point. Summative evaluation isn't actually educational: it's just required periodically to give a quantified report to learners or outside parties about what has been learned.

The vital, day-in-and-day-out interactive educational kind of evaluation is formative, including all of the many kinds of responses that teachers can give to kids that help them to grow and learn and move toward the next stage of development. Good formative evaluation stretches and challenges kids to operate in their "zone of proximal development." It neither underestimates their capacities nor asks them to perform feats far beyond their developmental level, but rather gets them to work in the range between the known and the unknown, right at the border of their ability. Students should always be encouraged to stretch, to increase their range, to try new forms, take chances, incorporate new elements. Good evaluation sustains morale, energy, and enthusiasm while challenging kids to explore new possibilities.

Writing is a subject in which the role of formative evaluation is dramatically evident. Everything a skillful writing teacher does aims at getting students to keep working, to continue the process, to reach and stretch, to try new ideas, new genres, new voices, new personae. When writing teachers work with kids' early drafts, their formative evaluation is meant to help kids resee their work, to revise it toward a clearer and more polished product. It's hard to think of a field where formative evaluation is more clearly and tangibly central than in teaching writing.

If we could prove that intensive correction works, that it is good formative evaluation, that students' writing grows reliably and measurably as a result of such feedback, we could start weighing its costs in morale against these gains. But the research, the history, the feeling in our hearts—all of these sources tell us that the formative gains just aren't there. What intensive marking provides, unfortunately, is only discouragement—or the message that writing is a perfectionist's game that growing, exploring writers can't really win.

As red-pencillers we purely serve the hidden curriculum, teaching kids to accept criticism passively, reminding them of their inferior status, stressing issues of orderliness and appearance over content. If we let ourselves be harnessed to these mundane aims of socialization, we sacrifice the credibility of our subject in students' eyes; we undermine their opportunity to know that writing is making and sharing meaning, a magnificent tool that can enrich their lives. We make ourselves look like uncaring bureaucrats. It's a heavy cost for us, and them, to pay.

This book does not suggest that teachers snap their red pencils in half and completely abandon their traditional way of marking student papers. There are times, a few times, when such an approach can be helpful to some students. In the final stages of copyediting a piece for publication, for example, this could be a wonderfully helpful and caring kind of response. But intensive correction is not the best or only kind of response for a given draft of a given paper by a given kid. Teachers need choices; we need a range of alternatives that will help us give growth-inducing feedback to different pieces by different student writers at all different stages of development. We cannot be trapped with a single way of responding but instead must each develop for ourselves a wide repertoire of evaluation strategies, drawing from this expanded set of choices according to our professional judgment of what a writer needs to grow.

Making this repertoire of choices real is what Chapter 17 is about.

Chapter 17

Responding,
Evaluating,
and Grading

If we are to find alternatives to red-penciling grammar errors and stamping uncommunicative letter grades on student papers, we will need some concepts to help us identify these alternatives and decide when they're appropriate. In this chapter, we'll sketch out such a conceptual framework and then offer some practical applications.

We can begin by thinking about teacher response in the broadest of terms. In human language generally, including the particular communication involved when teachers respond to student work, there are always at least two levels of meaning between speakers and listeners. First, there is the overt message presented: "You did a good job." "I don't understand this part." In addition, a second-level message tells us how to interpret the overt one. A wink tells the listener, "I'm only kidding." A pat on the back may imply, "I know there are problems with your piece, but I hope you won't let my comments discourage you. I want to see you do well." The seemingly simple statement "This part doesn't seem to fit" may really mean "I like to prove I'm tough and picky" or "Now you're in trouble" or "I want to help you make this your very best," depending on the context created by previous events in the classroom. All people unconsciously cope with these two levels of communication all day long, as they speak, write, read, and live their lives.

Thus, the effect that any particular teacher response may have on students depends on far more than the spoken words, written comments, or grading system the teacher may use. We've explored the larger context that influences the meaning of our words in Chapter 4; now we can use it to analyze the various teacher responses to pieces of student writing.

219

THE TEACHER'S ROLES

One way to describe responses within a context is to consider the many different roles teachers assume as they communicate with students about writing. What are some of the teacher roles we believe are most likely to permit truly effective response to writing—that is, response that helps students to care about their writing, to work hard and improve it, to develop their abilities?

Teacher as Listener and Learner

If students are to take their words seriously, then the teacher must too. Every teacher must find that part in himself that can be genuinely interested in students' own real thoughts rather than looking only for endorsement of his, the teacher's, ideas. Comments and responses must communicate an interest in students. This isn't always easy because the teacher is not of their generation and may not share all their cultural background. But unless a teacher has real contempt for his students (and we sometimes do see this), he can know that every person has moving and deeply significant stories to tell and that all of us share the essentials of the human condition.

Teacher as Adult/Protector

A classroom should be a safe space, where it's acceptable to take risks and try out new voices, so students can expand their abilities. This is not an assertion that we should go easy or that students should not be expected to work hard. It is simply a reflection of learning theory, a recognition that if taking risks is punished, students will tend to play it safe and try only what they already know how to do, rather than stretch their abilities. Creating a safe space may require some norms for behavior by students as well as by the teacher. Elaine Giermak, of Deerfield High School, puts it this way: "My students sometimes complain about my rules—for example, they aren't allowed to call anyone 'stupid' in my room—but they know that they'll be respected here." This role also points up the importance of teachers' sharing their own writing with their classes and receiving feedback on it. It models the taking of risks, as well as demonstrating the writing process itself. If such risk taking is not reinforced through comments given early in the writing process, later evaluation may discourage the expression of direct and honest thought.

Teacher as Encourager and Guide

A classroom can be safe and still be challenging. It's important to expect that students will grow, improve, look deeper, and expand their ideas as they write and revise. This means asking students repeatedly to explain their reasons for what they say, using these reasons as points of discussion in the classroom and sharing carefully chosen student writing models (perhaps from other classes) that illustrate what is possible without discouraging people. The teacher must be a good observer, looking to see where students are in their work, what challenges they are ready for, and which ones might be so difficult that they discourage rather than stretch people.

Teacher as Coach

All of us get frustrated with the basic student maneuver that resurfaces when students receive feedback before revising papers: "Just tell me what you want, teacher, and I'll do it." Students learn how to write for that special audience called teachers, but this doesn't always help them understand the workings of language. If a teacher can find ways to serve as a coach on the sidelines, rather than judge, jury, and executioner, she can get out from under. This is when having another audience in addition to the teacher is especially useful.

But it's not always easy being a coach. Teachers retain the ultimate power of grades, plus the sheer strength of adulthood and expertise. In this context, it's not hard for a teacher to usurp ownership when she thinks she is only giving "helpful advice." Lil Brannon (1985) tape-recorded teachers in conferences with students and then interviewed both teachers and students afterward, to see how each perceived what took place. It was clear that "suggestions" from a teacher sometimes completely overpowered the student's initiative when the teacher thought she was just helping the student out of a blind alley.

To avoid this trap in conferences or written comments, the teacher can report her own confusions and questions, rather than suggest what the student should do to respond to them. Suggest *processes* rather than specific ideas or words, as one of Lil's more effective tutors did in speaking to a student: "But if you have questions—like, you say, 'That doesn't make sense'—write that down and start trying to figure out why it doesn't make sense." Sometimes allow a student (if she's strong on confidence) to struggle and perhaps do less than perfectly, so that she can discover that there *are* problems with a particular strategy. She may even find an interesting solution the teacher hadn't conceived of.

Coaching instead of judging means that it's important not to grade drafts before the process is finished. After trying it both ways, Elaine Giermak reports that when drafts received a grade, revision became a dreaded remedial process of making up lost ground. Students were much more enthusiastic about revising when grades were given only after all work was completed.

There are, of course, roles that are more problematic for encouraging students to write. We had better take note of these, too.

Teacher as Expert

Teachers are also seen as experts, and this is a two-edged sword. Our expertise is needed. We have much to give our students. We may care passionately about particular authors or topics, and as we communicate this caring to students, we model what it means to be engaged, knowledgeable adults. At the same time, it's intimidating for a student to write to an expert who knows a lot about the subject. The student may think more about what statements will seem least inadequate to this expert teacher, rather than work out real ideas of his own. This is yet another reason why other audiences are valuable in school. When the student is writing to another person, the teacher-expert becomes a valuable resource rather than an adversary.

Another way to mediate this role is to realize that true experts usually feel themselves very much to be learners, not absolute authorities who have all the answers. The more teachers can model their own learning processes, the more students can see evaluative comments as helpful suggestions from a fellow learner, rather than judgments that make students worry about revealing their inadequacies the next time they write.

Teacher as Copyeditor

In the previous chapter, we considered why the time-honored role of English teachers as copyeditor remains so important in American schools and why it is self-defeating. As we pointed out, it deprives students of the chance to internalize this important role for themselves. Once all the errors are found and marked by you, there's little left for the student to do or learn as far as grammar and mechanics are concerned. Besides, copyediting eats up valuable time you need for other things. Spending hours with a red pen creates a bottleneck, making it impossible to assign enough writing to give students sufficient practice.

Because this is such a deeply ingrained yet unproductive role for us, and because students *do* need to learn to polish writing for wider audiences, we must consider very thoroughly what sorts of evaluation can effectively replace the copyediting role. Later in this chapter, we'll offer a number of ways to mark papers so that students really learn how to edit and proofread their own work.

Teacher as Judge

We couldn't entirely avoid the notion of teacher as judge even if we wanted to. Kids want to know how they're doing. Their parents want to know. The community requires us to give out grades. However, there are several different kinds of judging. Formative evaluation can help students perceive characteristics of their writing so they can improve as they revise their work. Grades, on the other hand, tend to put an end to further effort on a given piece. In school, grades mark the end of a piece of work. Once a grade is given, any further revision seems like punishment or, at best, an effort to make up lost ground. Grades may be necessary, but we don't need to put them on *everything*, and we can certainly hold them off until the last rounds of revising and proofreading a piece are finished.

One of the most important implications in this range of roles is that teachers may need to gather information and react to it in many different ways at various stages of the writing process. Timing is critical. Evaluation doesn't mean just one thing, but different things at different times. While many of the roles will be involved throughout the process, some will be more dominant at particular times. The chart in Figure 17–1 suggests how we might think of the relationships.

Figure 17–1   *Evaluating Writing as a Process*

Stage:	PREWRITING	DRAFTING	REVISION	PUBLICATION
Writer's focus:	Ideas	Fluency	Clarity	Correctness
Kind of assessment:	Observing	Responding	Evaluating	Grading
Teacher roles:	Listener; encourager	Encourager; coach	Coach; expert	Expert; editor
Goal of feedback:	Probing for interests; motivating	Encouraging; suggesting; processes	Questioning; challenging; evaluating	Judging; grading

To summarize the options in a more linear way: whatever else we do, we must *observe*; listening, learning about the topic from the writer and discovering what her needs are (e.g., does she need encouragement at this moment or a new challenge?). We can then *respond* to an emerging draft as adult encouragers or fellow learners, focusing on content, on what the writer has to say. Later, we can *evaluate*—that is, label and describe parts of the writing and how these affect us, indicating where we have questions, what meanings are not clear. And finally, we can *grade* the finished, polished writing by putting a summative letter or number on it. Using these four categories and the more detailed role descriptions that go with them, we can now offer some specific ways to provide feedback that will fit students' needs as they move through the stages of their own writing process.

OBSERVATION

One of our main purposes for reviewing students' work is to determine their progress and needs so we can decide what to do next in our teaching. It's natural to jump immediately to response or evaluation, which involves communication from teacher to student; but it's also important to realize that before we ever offer a word of feedback or put a mark on a page we must always observe individual students and groups as writers, assessing what we see and gathering information to guide ourselves.

One way we use this data is to form a mental picture of the student's abilities and achievements, and of course this picture becomes a part of our judgment, the summative grade we will give him. But it also determines how we will communicate with the student in our effort to help him learn. Teachers often ask, "What kind of evaluation will influence students to improve their writing?" But the answer, they quickly realize, is: "It depends on where that student is." Is the student ready to go through an editing or proofreading process, or is he sufficiently confused about his ideas that checking commas will only distract him? Can a student handle comments on all the possible usage needs in a paper, or would he learn more by solidifying his command of one or two?

To say that we ought to observe carefully to learn students' needs may not be as obvious as it sounds. Observing means that teachers must use their most highly attuned listening and visual skills, gathering data from all sorts of classroom interactions. Not only do we usually gather our impressions without thinking too consciously about how we obtain them, but it's surprising how often students are given advice based only on the written draft they've produced, without any reference to their conceived aims.

Observation often does not involve marking papers in any way. It may not be appropriate to grade personal journals, for example, since they are messages only for the writers themselves; but a teacher can read those parts of journals not labeled "private" to learn about students, about what they're interested in, how they feel about themselves and their writing.

This is one reason individual conferences are so valuable, even though they are time-consuming. It's not just that students discover how to improve their writing, though we certainly hope that will happen. But in addition, the teacher receives a great deal of collateral information about individual students—about what topics are meaningful to them, about their attitudes toward writing, about where they get stuck, about what they're trying to achieve in their writing, so that any advice given is relevant to their purposes. The teacher need not actually read much of the writing for this kind of assessment to take place. Just listening to students talk about their work provides much information.

To understand the importance of observation is to understand how our power to teach does not really depend on, but extends far beyond, our power to give grades. One of us learned about this from an especially masterful piano teacher, Annabelle Leviton. When Steve had difficulty with a particular Mozartean trill, Annabelle didn't scold him or try to explain what he was doing wrong. She first asked him to play it again and watched his hand very closely. Then she designed an on-the-spot exercise that would lead him to use his hand in a different way and said, "Try this a few times," which he did. The difficulty disappeared. Annabelle's evaluation of Steve's playing didn't involve any expressed judgment at all. It simply led from careful observation to the next teaching activity she realized she needed to devise.

Given that observation is the first step in responding effectively to student writing, we can go on to consider the various ways we communicate to students once we have attended closely to their effort.

RESPONSE

Writers write to be read, to have their ideas, values, and selves recognized in some way. They don't communicate just to be told they did a good job of communicating. Peter Elbow (1981) illustrated this best:

You can feel the difference vividly if you write a regular essay assigned by your teacher and then go on to write something directly to him: . . . asking him . . . to contribute money to your political campaign. . . . It's a relief to put words down on paper for the sake of results—not just for the sake of getting a judgment. "Getting an A is

*results," you may say, but see how you feel if you write your teacher
for a contribution and get an A instead of a check.*

The most important reaction a teacher can provide for students' writing
is a response as an interested reader. Perhaps the writing reminds the
teacher of an experience of her own, of something else she read, or of a
question that has always bothered her. If the writing is about subject matter
the class has studied, perhaps it leads the reader to focus in a particular
way on that subject matter, or raises further issues in her mind. "The
model," as Mayher, Pradl, and Lester put it in *Learning to Write/Writing
to Learn*, "is simply human conversation. Someone says something which
in turn makes us ask for more information, suggest alternative directions,
seek further clarification, or connect our own images and ideas."

Donald Graves calls this kind of teacher's role in conversation "receiving" the writing. Elbow (1981) calls it "reader-based feedback," as distin-
guished from "criterion-based feedback." While the terms sound fancy,
the point is not. As Elbow explains it:

*Reader-based feedback gives you the main thing you need to improve
your writing: the experience of what it felt like for readers as they were
reading your words. . . . Because reader-based feedback emphasizes the
practical question of what the words are doing rather than the theoretical question of how good they are, it is less evaluative and judgmental.
It usually leads to more listening and learning, less arguing.*

Whether or not this kind of response leads to actual improvement in
any given piece, it sends the most important of messages to students,
encouraging them to care about writing and to invest themselves in it:
"Your ideas count. They are worth putting down. They have an effect on
someone out in the world. They have an effect on *me*." Furthermore,
everything you do in this area provides a model for students, so you are
encouraging them to respond to each other in similar ways. Thus, your
response helps to create a community of interchange, dialogue, and interest in writing.

If you start with this kind of response at the beginning of the year (or
semester), you will make clear to students that meaning is what is most
important to you in their writing. Once that's established, you can move
toward other kinds of reaction without being misunderstood. However, if
you start by mixing response with evaluative comments on content, marks
on usage, and grades, students will assume it's business as usual: grammar
matters most, never mind what they have to say. It's not enough to do it

well and in balance; you have to deprogram kids from their previous expectations.

EVALUATION

Evaluation involves comparing a student's text to some kind of criterion or expectation. We're distinguishing evaluation from grading, using the dichotomy of formative and summative. Evaluation is an attempt to help writers understand what their writing does and says, so they can work on it further. Grading, on the other hand, simply rates students on some kind of scale and puts a final label on a finished paper.

If evaluation needs criteria—some description of what makes a particular kind of writing good—what criteria should you use, and how should these be communicated to students? One of the major contentions of recent composition theory and research is that writing (and, indeed, all language use) varies considerably depending on the user's purpose and the customs and requirements of the particular subject area. Up-to-date textbooks (such as those published by Scribner-Laidlaw and Allyn and Bacon) provide checklists with criteria designed to fit each of the particular assignments covered.

You may have your own lists of items that seem especially important for the topic you intend to use. It's particularly valuable, however, to ask *students* to develop these criteria. This makes them more conscious of the important elements and demonstrates that these are not just the whims of English teachers, but aspects of language that we've all internalized from reading, conversation, debates, discussions—from our constant human involvement with language. Evaluation is no longer just the province of teachers, but an activity in which students share a meaningful role.

In choosing criteria for evaluation or guiding students as they choose criteria, the most essential step is to look at the *purpose* of the writing. What you focus on, what you seek to help students improve, must be related to the kind of task you've asked students to carry out (or that they've chosen for themselves). Otherwise, the evaluation may negate your teaching effort and confuse or discourage students. Just to recall the basic list of purposes we outlined in Chapter 5:

1. *Writing to show learning.* This is primarily a form of testing, to see if students have done their homework.

2. *Writing to learn writing.* Here, mastery of the conventions of written language is the focus—structures, organization, forms.

3. *Writing to communicate.* This entails writing to inform or persuade someone else; it needs to be clear.

4. *Writing to express the self.* This type of writing may be private or expressed to others; much writing for other purposes often begins here.

5. *Writing to create.* Writing can be used to create an aesthetic object or to enjoy the basic human pleasure of storytelling.

Obviously, writing that is meant to help students think through a topic they are struggling to understand should not be evaluated in the same way as a polished piece meant to explain the topic to the public at an upcoming school event. Writing to be submitted to a contest, letters to the editor of the local newspaper, booklets being bound and added to the school library—for such published pieces, editing and proofreading are important and deserve comment. On the other hand, for an initial free-writing reaction to a chapter in *The Scarlet Letter*, meant to help initiate class discussion, evaluation of proofreading would be an unnecessary, time-consuming distraction.

Or, as another example, writing that expresses a student's self cannot really be evaluated as if it were just a practice exercise for learning how to organize material. One teacher we know was reminded of this when she assigned a particular formal task and received from a Vietnamese student a moving account of his first full—and very terrifying—day in America. She knew immediately that it simply wasn't appropriate to cover the paper with red marks.

The list of purposes for writing suggests, then, that there is a hierarchy of concerns a teacher should attend to, similar to the one we described in the chapter on revising. The most important concern is *content*; many types of writing can benefit from focus on it. Help students learn how to perceive particular qualities and features and revise them before moving on to *clarity*. Then, when students have made sufficient progress, add *correctness* to the list of criteria you are using to react to papers.

Content

Let's focus first on *evaluation of content* in early drafts of the students' writing. How can teachers comment on content without taking initiative and responsibility away from students? The most essential step is to avoid being prescriptive. Evaluative comment can readily register a need or tension without stating specifically what the writer ought to do about it. A reader might say, "I went along with you fine at the beginning, but then I got lost somewhere on page three," or, "I was really interested in this part, and it seemed like you knew a lot more about it. I'd sure like to hear some more." Asking questions and reporting on confusion are useful forms of evaluation because they leave decisions to the writers, but encourage them to take some kind of action.

Because the ideas for a piece of writing are in the student's mind, not the teacher's, it's difficult to give useful prescriptions without altering the purpose and direction of the piece. We recently observed a junior-high peer critiquing group, along with the teacher, trying to help one of their number who was unsure (as a result of teacher comment) how to end her account of a week spent in the hospital with a broken back when she was small. Everyone had ideas and questions, but nothing seemed to satisfy her. Then someone asked what happened when she came home. It turned out she was confined to a bed for six months, unspeakably bored. No one visited her, and even the tutor only came once a week. "I was never so happy to get back to school!" she announced. We all looked at each other, and she knew, too—she had just found her ending. What helped the student was not the giving of good advice, but the attentive drawing out of the student's own knowledge until she herself found what was needed.

Clarity

Content belongs to the students: teachers' reactions to it should aim to help students discover and explain what *they* have to say. *Clarity* is a more public matter, and evaluating it is appropriate as the student works on a second draft. Now the question becomes, "Is it clear to someone else?" Pieces that are to be shared with a wider audience can meaningfully be evaluated for clarity. Again, questions are probably better than prescriptions. Conventions that help with clarity—patterns of organization, focusing statements, transitions, and so forth—can be taught, using models and activities that generate them naturally (see the integrated activities in Chapters 3 and 18). Then students can be asked to look for these conventions in their own and others' papers, using self- and peer evaluation before the teacher's comments are provided.

If students are confident enough, you can model the evaluation and revising of a student paper on an overhead or a hard copy. But be sensitive to morale, and do *not* do this to insecure kids or very weak papers. To start building trust and modeling appropriate comments, edit one of the *teacher's* papers together as a class first.

Reading aloud is especially valuable at this stage. Students can read their own pieces or have them read by others. You'll find that students will often begin making corrections as the reading proceeds, without need of comment from anyone. Convoluted sentences, gaps in logic or explanation, need for connections, all tend to stand out in oral reading. Writing is thus reconnected with students' own linguistic competence for discussion, debate, and storytelling, and they can hear what works. A cooling-off period between first draft and oral reading helps give writers a fresh perspective for this self-evaluation.

Correctness

Correctness is the focus for final editing and polishing of student pieces that are to be published in some way. Students should have the chance to choose their best pieces to be worked on and evaluated at this level. As we've suggested, probably only a fraction of their work might be evaluated for correctness. Teach usage and mechanics not by drills, but by focusing on one item at a time in students' actual writing. Pick the single most pervasive or serious pattern of errors and mark some instances of that error only, drawing students' attention unambiguously to that problem. In further proofreading or on the next paper, they should be expected to focus on eliminating this particular kind of error.

As a way station between teacher marking and self-evaluation, comment selectively and leave some mistakes for students to find. Copyedit just one paragraph that contains the most significant errors as an example. Or place a symbol in the margin by the line that contains the error, leaving the student to do the work of finding it. Brief, individual conferences in which you point out one or two errors verbally can serve the same purpose.

Let students keep a proofreading inventory. Make a standard form that contains all the mechanical errors of concern in your course. Have students fill out one copy for each assignment you return to them. This means they get a tally (or, more efficiently, an estimate) of their errors. These can be kept in their folder or transferred to a chart.

What about proofreader's marks? Students can find these confusing and impersonal, one more desecration of their work, and one more obstacle to communication between teacher and writer. But if you present them constructively and involve students in actively learning and using the marks themselves, they can be a valuable tool. Many students get excited when they first start using carets and "stets." Make a chart or poster and explicitly review the marks. Explain, "This is how real authors and editors communicate about mechanics." Teach these marks for the kids, not just you, to use, emphasizing that these are special tools of the craft of preparing writing for a public audience. Stress some of the most useful icons, like the caret, the delete mark, "stet," and so forth. Show them examples of professionally copyedited manuscripts, if possible. If students have a language-arts text or handbook, page references to the text can indicate what the student needs to study before final editing of the paper.

Even though we are repeating ourselves, we want to stress some procedural principles for all aspects of evaluation:

1. *Focus on one element at a time.* Although students should be writing whole essays (or letters, scripts, or whatever) all along to engage with real purposes for writing, they can't easily analyze every aspect of their writing for refinement and revision all at once. Choose an important aspect of the form they are using (say, introductions), go over some model of it, and provide a guiding question or two about it to help individuals evaluate their own work or to help groups conduct peer critiquing. Then focus your own comments on their introductions when the papers come to you. As you go on to new elements, students will be responsible for all those previously covered.

2. *Photocopied or dittoed checklists are extremely handy.* Students can write out their own self-evaluations on a checklist and hand it in to you along with the paper. Peer writing groups can use the lists. Use them yourself. Start with just a few items: one positive response to content and one question the reader may have. As new items are covered, appropriate questions can be added to the sheets.

3. *Don't plan to evaluate everything.* This only increases students' dependence on the teacher. Contrary to popular belief, errors are not like weeds that spread by their own growing power. Remember how much faith we have in unmonitored practice in almost every other school subject, not to mention out-of-school learning. Students will get fuller writing practice if you assign more first-draft writing than you could possibly evaluate. Keep it in student folders in the classroom. Ask students to choose their best piece to revise and to submit it to you for comments first. Or have students bring one paper to you for a brief individual conference focused on one feature, while they submit others to their peer writing groups. If a feature needs attention in repeated spots in a paper, the same principle of selectivity should apply. Mark just one instance of the error and ask the student to find and work on the others.

GRADING

Teachers often feel trapped by grades. Because grading is final and judgmental, we worry, justifiably, that grades will discourage students; but we also fear that without grades, the work won't really matter. Separating grades from response and evaluation is a first step in reducing this conflict. Grading then becomes only the last (and occasional) event in a dialogue between teacher and student. Again, timing is everything.

Adding student control and responsibility is an important step in making summative evaluation of writing more valid. When students choose a portion of their work to polish and submit for a grade, rather than have everything graded, the judgment becomes more meaningful. Room is created, too, for risk taking, experimenting, and personal inquiry, in pieces that don't have to be ultimately submitted. We agree with Donald Graves that 20 percent of total output is a good-sized sample for the teacher to grade. A portfolio of such selected and polished work provides an excellent basis for giving a course grade.

Obviously, the next question teachers are likely to ask is: "How do I get kids to care about the other 80 percent of their work? How do I reduce their grade dependency?" In part, this returns us to the context and to all of the rest of the writing process. Grading time is too late in the game to address this question. Good assignments, prewriting activities that generate involvement, student ownership and authority over topics, attentive peer audiences, meaningful classroom interchange about subjects that matter to students—all contribute to make written expression meaningful rather than just a cold exchange of scholastic currency.

However, if you're desperate, grade "by the pound" for everything, or for all the unrevised drafts in the folders. For grade-dependent students who can't be weaned from their need to be paid in the coin of grades for all work attempted, assign a new letter grade for each and every substantively written draft or revision. You may wind up with eight or ten grades in the book for one repeatedly revised assignment, or grades for a number of pieces begun but never revisited.

Use self-grading for at least a portion of the credit on some papers or on students' overall portfolio of work. Kids can submit a form on which they indicate a grade along with explanations of strengths, weaknesses, and aspects they think they should work on next time. The class as a whole may be asked to vote on some pieces, using ballot slips for anonymity (perhaps the authors should remain unidentified as well).

Some teachers try to reduce the conflict in grading by using split grades: one for form, one for content. This helps somewhat, but it also raises new questions. Students will calculate the average, or try to psych out which grade is "really" more important. And the underlying focus on the grade, rather than the ideas or the learning of the craft, remains. Another way to approach this problem can be found in the evaluation categories outlined by Charles Cooper in *Evaluating Writing* (edited by Cooper and Lee Odell). Essentially, Cooper describes three kinds of scoring:

• *General holistic:* a score that in one way or another evaluates the paper as a whole, based on a broad impression.

- *Primary trait:* a grade focused on just one aspect of a piece of writing—for example, how it presents an argument.
- *Analytic scale:* a list of aspects of the writing, each of which receives a separate score.

Each of these kinds of grading serves a different purpose. *General holistic* provides a quick label but gives little or no information to the student about why or how the piece created the impression it did. *Primary trait* scoring is helpful when the teacher (or the student) has been stressing a particular aspect of writing, and information is provided about how the student handled that aspect. *Analytic scale* scoring allows the teacher to indicate the student's success at working with a number of elements within a single piece of writing.

We believe that for many teachers who are wedded to intensive correction (or forced by their situation to continue it), the analytic scale may be the most promising and appropriate step in a new direction. Because it is a holistic form of evaluation without any marking on papers, teachers can analytically score many papers very fast, eliminating bottlenecks and permitting them to assign more writing. At the same time, though, an analytic scale can provide students with some relatively sophisticated and detailed feedback on their writing—weighted subscores on several elements of writing effectiveness. One of the best-known analytic scales, designed by Paul Diederich, is reproduced in adapted form in Figure 17–2.

The Diederich scale has gained wide acceptance for its applicability to many types of expository writing, and once teachers internalize its eight criteria, they can scan and score papers so fast that it seems downright magical. Two or three minutes a paper would be a typical rate. Indeed, one of the biggest problems faced by teachers new to analytic scoring is reassuring themselves that it's really legitimate, as valid and useful as the old slaving-and-bleeding approach.

While you may want to use the Diederich scale just as it is for some writing tasks, it's important and remarkably easy to design your own scoring scales as well. This is a great teaching activity because it helps you and the kids realize what the goals are, for a particular writing assignment. Figure 17–3 is a generic analytic scale you can use to practice with. Down the left-hand column you can list traits that, when combined, would constitute a successful piece of writing for the assignment at hand. Under "Weight," you can insert a multiplier that allows some factors to be more important than others. It's a good idea to have everything add up to 100 (percent) for simplicity in record keeping. This may take some time to set up, but in operation such scoring scales save a great deal of time, while still giving students detailed feedback on their writing.

Progress on the issue of grade dependence will be slow. We're surrounded by a rank-conscious, competitive society. By ninth or tenth grade, bright kids are concerned about getting into college. Many parents exert pressure. To promote learning in such a context, teachers need to set a policy of providing plenty of writing practice and support without intensively correcting everything themselves, and they must stick to it. Meanwhile, they can also do everything within their power—reading their own writing, asking questions about what matters, urging groups to ask questions—to help students find real reasons for writing: discovering, thinking, trying to make sense of their lives and of the exciting, disturbing adult world toward which they are moving.

Figure 17–2 *The Diederich Scale*

1—Poor   2—Weak   3—Average   4—Good   5—Excellent

Reader _____

Quality and development of ideas	1	2	3	4	5
Organization, relevance, movement	1	2	3	4	5

_____ × 5 = _____
Subtotal

Style, flavor, individuality	1	2	3	4	5
Wording and phrasing	1	2	3	4	5

_____ × 3 = _____
Subtotal

Grammar, sentence structure	1	2	3	4	5
Punctuation	1	2	3	4	5
Spelling	1	2	3	4	5
Manuscript form, legibility	1	2	3	4	5

_____ × 1 = _____
Subtotal

Total grade: _____ %

Figure 17–3 *A Generic Analytic Scale*

Writer _____   Title _____

Grade Level _____   Subject _____   Type of Assignment _____

Reader's Name _____   Date _____

FACTOR (Traits)	SCORE	WEIGHT (Multiplier)	TOTAL POINTS
	5 4 3 2 1		
	5 4 3 2 1		
	5 4 3 2 1		
	5 4 3 2 1		
	5 4 3 2 1		
	5 4 3 2 1		
	5 4 3 2 1		
	5 4 3 2 1		
	5 4 3 2 1		
	5 4 3 2 1		
		TOTAL	

Scoring Key

5—Excellent 4—Good 3—Average 2—Weak 1—Poor

Point Totals Converted to Grades:

_____ to _____ = A   _____ to _____ = B   _____ to _____ = C
_____ to _____ = D   _____ to _____ = F

HANDLING THE PAPER LOAD—AND SHARING IT

We've talked about English teachers' fatal attraction to martyrdom. If we care deeply about our subject and our kids, we are frequently in danger of burning out. Thus, we may fear that more attention to writing, more care in responding, evaluating, and grading will add still more burdens to our work. Throughout this chapter, we've tried to say that you don't have to do it all. You *shouldn't* do it all. Not everything ought to be graded, and not all the responding and commenting should be done by the teacher.

Perhaps another way to express it is this. You can view your efforts in two different ways. One way is to focus on the papers, the outcome. Your interventions are meant to help students turn out better and better papers. You work very hard to make it happen, and sometimes it does. But this way, all the responsibility is on you, the teacher. The other way to see your work is to focus on the students. You want them to think in new ways about their writing. Perhaps today's work will show improvement. But what's even more important is that students want to write after they leave your class and will approach that writing with both involvement and care about craft.

If you choose this second approach, then you won't be satisfied just to correct papers. You will want the students to be able to extend, improve, and correct their own work. You'll want them to learn to ask questions of their own and others' writing, to be a good audience for one another, and to internalize that audience so they can see their work from a reader's point of view. This approach doesn't just lighten your load and catch mistakes; it shows student writers how audiences react to words. It not only involves students in the process, but helps them to practice, and helps you to see, their process of internalizing that audience. And it places responsibility for writing where it truly belongs: with the student.

Part V

Writing to Learn

Chapter 18

Integrated Activities for Learning Subject Matter

We've introduced the concept of extended, integrated reading-thinking-writing-speaking-listening activities and provided an example of one in Chapter 3. Descriptions of others are scattered throughout the book. Because integrated activities make writing a tool for learning, help teachers fit writing into a crowded curriculum, and help classes become cooperative learning communities, we'd like to explore their use further now.

Integrated activities share a number of essential characteristics. All are inductive experiences that provide a progressively deepening engagement with the material at hand. All involve a rhythmic alternation among various classroom groupings, cognitive processes, and purposes and modes of language use. While the content may be provided by the teacher, students are helped to find personally significant connections and implications in the material. Students' writing may range from expressive to transactional to poetic within a single activity.

Thinking processes include all thirteen categories in Raths' list given in Chapter 8 of this book (or anyone else's thinking skills model, for that matter); these range from summarizing and comparing to interpreting, criticizing, looking for assumptions, to decision making and designing broader investigations. Students alternate between working alone, in pairs, in small groups, and in whole-class sessions. The teacher may at moments assume a presenter role, but is more often a facilitator, resource, group manager, and collaborator. Real, tangible outcomes are stressed—reports, letters, position statements, performances—all of which can help other members of the class think about the topic as well as communicate to people in the larger community about it.

A VARIETY OF ACTIVITIES

Since we've already placed a literary activity first, in Chapter 3, we'd like this section to be especially useful for teachers of other subjects. This doesn't leave the English teachers out, however, for it's important that all of us encourage students to write often on a wide variety of topics. In any case, once you see the pattern in these activities, you'll be able to design your own for particular subjects and pieces of reading you intend to teach, whatever your discipline. And you'll no doubt begin to experiment with the structure of the activities—the length of time needed, the order of the tasks. If you don't have time to use every step, you'll be prepared to decide which are expendable and which aren't.

Celestial Mechanics—A Science Topic

The following activity involves three to four periods of class time, if executed completely. Much shorter versions are possible if the writing is not carried to a final draft—and there's still plenty students can get from a shorter version.

1. Begin by asking students to list, on a card or sheet of paper, everything they know about the movement of the planet Earth in space. After three or four minutes, ask volunteers to call out some of the items to be listed on the board (e.g., that the Earth rotates on its axis every twenty-four hours, that it revolves around the sun every 365 days, etc.).

2. Next, hand out the two quotations below and read them aloud to the class. Clarify any immediate questions caused by the antique vocabulary or syntax.

The doctrine that the sun is the center of the world and immoveable is false and absurd, formally heretical and contrary to Scripture, whereas the doctrine that the earth is not the center of the world but moves, and has further a daily motion is philosophically false and absurd and theologically at least erroneous.

—Report of the Examination of Certain Doctrines of Nicholas Copernicus, *qualifiers of the Holy Office of the Inquisition, Rome, 1615*

Methinks, that in the discussion of natural problems we ought not to begin with the authority of Scripture; but at sensible experiments and necessary demonstrations. For nature being inexorable and immutable, and never passing the bounds of the laws assigned to her, as one that nothing careth, whether her abstruse reasons and methods of operating be or not exposed to the capacity of men; I conceive that concerning natural effects, which either sensible experience sets before our eyes, or necessary demonstrations do prove unto us, ought not, upon any account, to be called into question, much less condemned upon the testimony of texts of Scripture, which may under their words, couch senses seemingly contrary thereto.

The intention of the Holy Ghost is to teach us not how the heavens go, but how to go to Heaven.

—Mathematical Collections, *Galileo Galilei, 1615*

Now ask students to write one sentence that summarizes the two quotes. A few volunteers then read their summaries aloud, to help the class discuss and clarify the basic facts and events involved.

3. Next, ask why we take what Galileo and Copernicus said for granted. How do we in fact know that the Earth moves? Suppose representatives from the Flat Earth Society were present. What could we say to argue with them? Students may point to the existence of day and night, the movement of the stars, or the changing seasons. But all these were well accounted for by the ancient Ptolemaic model, with its spheres rotating systematically over a flat, stationary earth.

Galileo said that explaining scientific phenomena depends either on sensory data or demonstrations. So what verifiable sensory information or conceivable demonstration would show that the Earth actually moves? The assignment now is for students, working in teams of four or five, to develop a one-paragraph statement that would prove to a modern skeptic that the Earth is moving (either rotating or revolving). Allow about twenty minutes' work time for this.

4. Reconvene as a whole class to read the statements aloud. Invite the class to join with you in role-playing the skeptic. You will probably find that few if any groups could think of immediate empirical proof. In fact, some may have resorted to writing a poem, a threat, a statement to the effect that "I know the world moves because my teacher/mommy told me so," or a quote from a song (such as Carol King's "I Felt the Earth Move Under My Feet"). A very few may remember seeing a large pendulum in a science museum (called the Foucault Pendulum) and being told that somehow its movement showed the Earth was rotating.

In fact, all of the proofs are indirect ones. Any visible direct observations, such as flying west in a jetliner at sunset and seeing the sun go down more slowly, can just as easily be explained by movement of the heavens as of the Earth (thought the jetliner argument does suggest that the Earth is round—for if it were flat, the sunset would not be affected much by the plane's movement, unless you were near the edge of the Earth).

Here are several pieces of evidence, for those who are not science buffs. The Foucault Pendulum is one. As the day progresses, the pendulum changes the direction of its swing, rotating completely in the course of twenty-four hours. The inference is that while the Earth rotates, the pendulum continues to swing in the same direction, no matter what takes place around it, thus appearing to change direction. The whirlpool pattern you can observe as water goes down in a bathtub is another piece of evidence. This motion is accounted for by adding up all the forces acting on the water: gravity pulls vertically downward, but because the earth is round, material located on the sloping sides of the planet is pulled in a direction *not* perpendicular to the axis and so experiences an extra twisting force, called the Coriolis effect.

In addition to the actual question of proof, it is valuable to discuss the experience itself. Even if most groups didn't figure out valid proofs, many will have recalled more data and asked more questions than they realized they knew and will have discovered that the questions of scientific proof can be elusive. The activity illustrates how we take our own beliefs for granted, how indirect scientific concepts can be, and what a magnificent accomplishment it really was to determine the mechanics of the solar system. Students can more easily grasp the mind-set of "primitive" peoples, past or present, who may not share our beliefs but who have grounds for their own that seem at least as understandable to them as ours are to us.

5. Now hand out an appropriate reading about Galileo. We've learned much from *The Discoverers* by Daniel Boorstin, which reviews some of Galileo's discoveries and aspects of his life. It focuses on a crucial astronomical discovery that Galileo reported in one of his early works, *The Sidereal Messenger*: that there are moons rotating around Jupiter. This was a very indirect, yet important, piece of evidence, which established that some bodies in the universe did revolve around other bodies beside the Earth. The reading also makes clear the political and personal nature of the debate Galileo was engaged in—an aspect of science students may not have thought about before.

SEEING THE INVISIBLE/DANIEL J. BOORSTIN

The Greeks developed the notion that the earth was a sphere on which man lived while the heavens above were a rotating spherical dome that held the stars and moved them about. The spherical nature of the earth, as we have seen, was demonstrated by such commonsense experience as the disappearance of departing ships below the horizon. The spheri-

cal nature of the heavens was also confirmed by everybody's naked-eye experience, day and night. Outside that dome of stars, according to the Greeks, there was nothing, not space, nor even emptiness. Inside the sphere of the stars, the sun went around the earth in its daily and yearly courses. . . .

To understand the paradoxical beginnings of modern science, we must recall that this beautiful symmetrical scheme, much ridiculed in the modern classroom, actually served very well for both astronomer and layman. It described the heavens precisely as they looked and fitted the observations and calculations made with the naked eye. The scheme's simplicity, symmetry, and common sense made it seem to confirm countless axioms of philosophy, theology, and religion. And it actually performed some functions of a scientific explanation. For it fitted the available facts, was a reasonably satisfactory device for prediction, and harmonized with the accepted view of the rest of nature. In addition, it aided the astronomer's memory with a convenient coherent model, replacing the list of miscellaneous facts then known about the heavens. More than that, while this much maligned geocentric, or "Ptolemaic," scheme provided the layman with a clear picture to carry around in his head, it helped the astronomer reach out to the unknown. Even for the adventurous sailor and the navigator it served well enough, as Columbus proved. . . .

Of course the traditional geocentric system of Aristotle and Ptolemy and so many others over centuries had its own weaknesses. For example, the system did not explain the irregularities observed in the motions of the planets. But the layman hardly noticed these irregularities, and anyway they seemed adequately described by the supposed movement of each plane within its own special ethereal sphere. Astronomers were adept at explaining away what seemed only minor problems by a variety of complicated epicycles, deferents, equants, and eccentrics, which gave them a heavy vested interest in the whole scheme. . . .

In July 1609 Galileo himself, who happened to be in Venice, had heard rumors that there was such an instrument as a telescope, and at the same time heard that a foreigner had arrived in Padua with one of them. To satisfy his curiosity, he immediately returned to Padua, only to find that the mysterious foreigner had already left for Venice. Having learned how the foreigner's telescope had been made, Galileo at once went about making one for himself. . . .

With a grand gesture, instead of trying to sell the device, Galileo made a gift of it to the Venetian Senate in a ceremony on August 25, 1609. In return the Senate offered Galileo a renewal for life of his professorship, which was to expire the next year, and an increase of his annual salary from 520 florins to 1,000 florins. This bargain produced resentment among his envious fellow academics, who would plague him the rest of his life. They objected that since others had invented the telescope, the most Galileo was entitled to was a good price for his instrument. . . .

What Galileo viewed through his telescope when he first turned it on the heavens so amazed him that he promptly published a description of what he saw. In March 1610 The Starry Messenger (Sidereus Nuncius), a mere pamphlet of twenty-four pages, astonished and troubled the learned world. . . .

Now the telescope "set distinctly before the eyes other stars in myriads which have never been seen before, and which surpass the old, previously known, stars in number more than ten times." Now the diameter of the moon appeared "about thirty times larger, its surface about nine hundred times, and its solid mass nearly 27,000 times larger than when it is viewed only with the naked eye: and consequently any one may know with the certainty that is due to the use of our senses, that the Moon certainly does not possess a smooth and polished surface, but one rough and uneven, and just like the face of the Earth itself, is everywhere full of vast protuberances, deep chasms, and sinuosities."

Next, the telescope settled disputes about the Galaxy or Milky Way: "All the disputes which have tormented philosophers through so many ages are exploded at once by the irrefragable evidence of our eyes, and we are freed from wordy disputes upon this subject, for the Galaxy is nothing else but a mass of innumerable stars planted together in clusters. Upon whatever part of it you direct the telescope straightway a vast crowd of stars presents itself to view. . . ."

"But that which will excite the greatest astonishment by far," he announced, "and which indeed especially moved me to call the attention of all astronomers and philosophers, is this namely, that I have discovered four planets, neither known nor observed by any one of the astronomers before my time, which have their orbits around a certain bright star." These were actually the four satellites of Jupiter.

Each of his simple observations shook another pillar of the Aristotelian–Ptolemaic universe. Now, with his very own eyes, Galileo had seen fixed stars beyond his capacity to count them (Was the Universe infinite?). He had seen that the moon was no more perfect in shape than the earth itself (Was there perhaps no difference, after all, between the substance of celestial bodies and that of the Earth?). The Milky Way then proved to be simply a mass of countless stars (Was there nothing, after all, to the Aristotelian theory of celestial exhalations? Were heavenly processes not essentially different from those on Earth?). While these brief and casual observations began to remove the traditional obstacles of dogma, yet none of them would actually confirm Copernicus. . . .

To him the four newly discovered satellites circulating around Jupiter seemed his most important discoveries, for they were the most obvious evidence that the earth might not be unique in the universe. How many other planets had satellites of their own? And it proved that a body like the Earth with another body circulating around it could itself circulate around still another. . . .

Galileo was invited to Rome, where he enjoyed a quite unexpected triumph. Arriving on April 1, 1611, he was promptly received in audience by the Borghese Pope Paul V who showed him rare deference by refusing to let him remain kneeling. The Jesuit fathers held a special meeting in the Collegio Romano where the encomium was entitled "The Starry Messenger of the Roman College." Galileo persuaded some of the Church authorities to look through his telescope. They enjoyed what they saw, but still did not accept Galileo's interpretations. . . .

Galileo himself, back in Florence, began marshaling arguments for the simultaneous truth of the Bible and the Copernican theory. Anxious to preserve his orthodoxy, he offered an ingenious explanation of the apparent disagreements between the words of Scripture and the facts of Nature. There is only one Truth, he said, but it is communicated in two forms—the language of the Bible and the language of Nature. Both are God's languages. . . .

Meanwhile, in Rome the Jesuit fathers were not so easily satisfied. Prodded by the Pope's champion, the brilliant and belligerent Cardinal Robert Bellarmine (1542–1621), they sniffed heresy. And Bellarmine, the master of theological polemics and Aristotelian orthodoxy, had common sense on his side. He reminded his tempted brothers that Saint Augustine himself had argued that the literal meaning of Scripture should always be taken as correct, unless the contrary was "strictly demonstrated." Since man's everyday experience "tells him plainly that the earth is standing still," and, from the nature of the case, the rotation of the earth and its revolutions around the sun could not be "strictly demonstrated," the literal Scriptures must be defended. King Solomon's observation that the sun "returns to its place" must mean precisely what he said. . . .

When Galileo returned to Florence, he spent the next six years on his Dialogue on the Two Chief World Systems. . . .

The reception of Galileo's Dialogue, published in Florence on February 21, 1632, encouraged him to think that his campaign of publicity was succeeding. In Europe most scientific works were still written in Latin, but to reach a lay audience Galileo had offered this work in Italian. By midsummer he was flooded with fan letters. . . .

Causes that had nothing to do with astronomy conspired to defeat his hopes of converting the Church of Rome. Galileo would be caught in the cross fire between Catholics and Protestants. The rising attacks of Protestantism made it necessary that Pope Urban VIII respond by showing the determination of the Church of Rome to preserve the purity of ancient Christian dogmas. Protestants must have no monopoly on fundamentalism. To put down an old favorite of his like Galileo would dramatize the Pope's apostolic zeal. . . .

The story of Galileo's brutal trial by the Inquisition is familiar. When the Pope's summons reached Galileo in Florence, he was in bed, gravely ill. Medical certificates declared that his removal to Rome might prove fatal. Nevertheless the Pope threatened to remove Galileo in chains if he did not come of his own accord. The Grand Duke of Florence provided a litter, and Galileo was carried all the way to Rome in the wintry February of 1633. The trial focused on technicalities, on what Galileo had or had not been told by Cardinal Bellarmine back in 1616, on how clearly he had known the papal disapproval of Copernican doctrines. To ensure the truthfulness of his testimony, Galileo was threatened with torture, although it was never actually applied. The Pope's verdict, recorded on June 16, chose the most humiliating of all the alternatives. The Pope might merely have prohibited the Dialogue until it was "corrected" or might have condemned Galileo to private penance and house arrest. Instead, the Dialogue was totally forbidden, Galileo was to make public and formal abjuration, and also to be imprisoned for an indefinite period. . . .

Confined in a secluded house in Arcetri outside Florence, he was allowed no visitors except with the permission of the Pope's delegate. . . .

During his last four years Galileo was blind, perhaps from hours spent peering at the sun through his telescope. It was during these years that John Milton visited him, and found additional inspiration (besides his own blindness) for Samson Agonistes. Eventually the Pope allowed him the companionship of a young scholar, Vincenzo Viviani, who reported Galileo's death on January 8, 1642, a month before his seventy-eighth birthday. "With philosophic and Christian firmness he rendered up his soul to its Creator, sending it, as he liked to believe, to enjoy and to watch from a closer vantage point those eternal and im-

mutable marvels which he, by means of a fragile device, had brought closer to our mortal eyes with such eagerness and impatience."

6. Invite students to free write some notes in reaction to any aspect of the reading selection for three to five minutes. Emphasize open, stream-of-consciousness jottings—just words and phrases, if people prefer. This is not meant to be an organized or edited piece of writing.

7. Students should now join in small groups (different from the groups that were formed in step 3 so that students compare more points of view). First, they should share around the circle something of what each person has written, either reading their notes aloud or explaining what topics the notes touched upon. Then, they should discuss freely whatever aspects of the reading the group wishes to explore, whether they be matters of science, religious issues, questions about how something can be proven, how change is resisted, or any other concerns the passage inspires.

8. Regather in the whole group and take quick reports from each small group about the issues they discussed.

9. Now ask that each student write a one-sentence statement—an assertion about one thing he or she believes, on any aspect of this topic. It might be something about astronomy or Galileo, about religion or science, about the student's own personal feelings or reactions to the whole topic, or some related memory or incident in his or her own life. What is called for is a single statement of something the student feels strongly about, after having gone through these experiences today.

10. Have everyone read the assertions aloud, without comment or evaluation from the rest of the class. Point out how finely crafted and thoughtful these statements are (for they will be). And, of course, these are really topic sentences, ready-made, for people to build into a more extended piece.

11. On the board, brainstorm a list of topics, possibilities for the longer pieces that students will be writing. This will of course start with the topics embedded in everyone's assertions, but you can also invite the group to add other subjects that occur to them as this listing goes along. The goal is to show the largest possible range of choices.

12. Now ask students to each pick one idea for writing that is the hottest, the most interesting and attractive, and have them spend about thirty minutes starting a draft of the piece. For some, this may involve consulting reference works, books on the history of science or on the scientific concepts themselves. Tell students that after thirty minutes of work time, they'll regather to read aloud whatever rough draft they've started or to report on the information they are finding.

13. After thirty minutes, students share their drafts in groups of three, and then a few volunteers can be encouraged to read to the whole class. The pieces can be revised outside of class and final versions shared in groups or published in some other way.

14. It is valuable, finally, to debrief the class when the project is finished, to ask students how the work went, what parts of it they found helpful, what parts difficult, and what these realizations tell them about the process of studying a particular scientific principle. This reflection step is important because it helps students to become more aware of what they are learning and to apply the same methods consciously in other study situations.

We might ourselves reflect on the significance of this activity for a moment. It's designed to involve students quickly, without much introduction or prior study, in an intense problem-solving task. It presumes that most participants *don't* know the answer to the question being posed but can learn something about the process of seeking it. Thus, it is probably most useful as an introductory activity, in this case for a unit on astronomy.

Examining any catalogue of thinking skills, one would find that the activity involves a number of types of tasks. Using Raths' categories, we would notice that the overall task is what Raths calls designing an investigation. The discrete steps will include hypothesizing, summarizing, comparing, criticizing, and looking for assumptions. In other words, instead of just presenting facts or even concepts, this kind of exercise asks students—or rather, it doesn't ask, but simply starts them right off—to evaluate concepts and discover what makes them meaningful.

Translating this activity to other topics shouldn't be difficult. Any modern scientific concept that is commonly known but not commonly understood would do nicely. The working of DNA to control particular characteristics of living things, for example, is a topic much in the news. As an introduction to a unit on embryology or DNA, the teacher could pose the question "A baby begins from a one-celled egg, and is born with a complex body in which the cells that make up its muscles, bones, and nerves are all very different from one another. How does that miracle happen?"

Loneliness—A Social Studies Topic

Those who have read our previous book, *A Writing Project*, will recognize the first piece of data used in the following activity. It's recycled here, but much elaborated, in part to show how a teaching idea can be refined over time, and in part just because it's fun. The task differs from the activity we just described, particularly because it asks students to analyze and then compare more explicit data items. And it probably works best after the students have learned something about the topic it relates to, rather than before.

This activity would be relevant for a class examining the history or social experience of immigration by various ethnic groups to the United States. By choosing different sets of data, you can easily shift the focus to other similar historical topics.

1. Hand out a sheet such as Figure 18–1 without comment and let students study it. (If you are concerned about using socially controversial material in class, it's easy to find less racy personal ads in a local paper.) If you simply allow it, spontaneous and humorous discussion will spring up for the purpose of clarifying acronyms and abbreviations.

2. Students are then to free write a reaction to the document, connecting as directly as possible to their own stream of consciousness, feelings, associations, questions, and so forth. After three to five minutes of writing, ask a couple of people to read their writing aloud. Do not comment on correctness or insight, but merely note the range of different approaches and reactions. Variety is important.

3. Hand out a second sheet, such as Figure 18–2, containing matrimonial ads from an ethnic paper. Invite students to do a second free-write (or use clustering for variety). People can either react to the new ads or compare the sets, whichever they prefer.

4. Form small groups for open discussion of the documents. People can use their free writing as a guide or read it aloud if they wish. The agenda should be open, with no need to reconcile the two documents. Just encourage everybody to get their oar in. When discussion time is up, get quick reports from each group on what they discussed.

5. Now ask each student to list five or six topics for possible writing based on the materials. If your students are not as confident as they might be, this listing can be done by the whole group, on the chalkboard, rather than individually.

6. Each student is then to pick one topic that seems most promising and restate it as an assertion, something the writer believes about one or both documents, about some item that came up in the discussion, or about the situation of the people advertising. When students are finished writing, have them read their assertion aloud, around the class.

7. Students now write a draft of an essay based upon their assertion. Allow thirty minutes in class to get the draft started. Share and discuss these draft beginnings. Students can then continue to work on the essays on their own.

Figure 18–1 *Personal Ads*

'MS. OLD FASHIONED', SWF, 26, slender, long dark hair, green eyes, believes in sharing and growing together. Appreciates the simplicity as well as the excitement in life. Seeking a SWJM, 27-34, who desires a 'real relationship' and not a one night 'hot potato'. Photo a must. Please reply to S.C.

VIRGIN OR NON-PROMISCUOUS female wanted by caring, gentle, attractive, white, currently monogamous professional man. We could share hours of satisfying pleasure without risking disease or pregnancy. Prefer thin nonsmoker. Married acceptable. No drugs. I hesitated 1 year to place this ad. If you hesitate we've lost. Matchbox expires this week. Include phone and time to call. Matchbox no M4919./

DESCRIPTION: AVERAGE-LOOKING, old fashioned, quiet, well off, 37, 6'2", 250, workaholic DWM, having lost interest in almost everything, needs a purpose, someone to provide for and share with. Qualifications: the successful applicant will be 27-35, above average in appearance, trim, intelligent and imaginative, with a strong sense of self and personal worth. Integrity, decency and responsibility must be something you value as well as possess. Compensation: Love. With continuous merit raises. Security, stability and dignity. A warm home and a pleasant sense of well-being. Overseas travel, if you're interested, NW suburbs. Photo and phone with letter please. Matchbox no M0124./

HELP! ATTRACTIVE, INTELLIGENT GWM, 24, drowning in sea of jerks. Recent dates had codfish for brains, style like seaweed. Seeking social lifesaver GWM, 23-29; attractive, sensitive cognizant enjoys arts, dancing, conversation. Matchbox no M0122./

THE IMPOSSIBLE DREAM? A positive mutually supportive relationship with a compatible female. I'm a sensitive, handsome MWM, thirties, with no preconceived ideas. Please tell me about yourself. Complete description and telephone needed for reply.

WORKING GRADUATE STUDENT, irreverent, leftish, attractive SWM, 35, eclectic cultural interests, loves dancing/new music, seeks similar S/DF looking for emotional entanglement, ethnicity unimportant, letter, photo? Matchbox M5014./

SWM, 39, 5'8", 165, good looking, fit, active, smart, and successful, Lincoln Park nr lake, enjoys bicycle, lake, travel, seeking very special SDWF who wishes to share laughter, life, dreams, love. To meet me send letter & phone number. Matchbox no M0137./

HANDSOME, BI-CURIOUS SWM, 6'1", 190#, 25, blonde, happy, intelligent, easy going, successful seeks like minded singles and couples for discreet, intimate encounters and relaxed good times. Photo appreciated, all answered. Matchbox no M0144./

IDEALISTIC SWM, 34, nonmaterialistic, sincere, eccentric. Enjoys pizza, beer, flea markets. Loves music (Beatles, U2, Police, Feat, Mitchell, Dead). Interested? Please reply P.O. Box

MULTI-FACETED DWM, 39, 6'1", attractive, professional, athletic, giving, affectionate, lot-o-fun, nonsmoker, healthy, emotionally secure, possessing high level of integrity. Likes: tennis, all kindsa music, going out, staying in, dancing, ethnic food, flora, fauna, creativity, travel, romance, metaphysics, adventure. You: SDWOF, 27-39, with some similar attributes. Never thought I'd advertise. If you never thought you'd answer, change your mind: you'll be pleased! Matchbox no M0138./

ATTRACTIVE, WELL-BUILT SWF, 26, seeks joys of woman relationship with and without male partner. You are SWF, 30-40, feminine looking and discreet. Photo please. Write soon! Matchbox no M0136./

TALL, ATTRACTIVE, RELATIVELY inexperienced SWF, 25, seeking clean WM to guide me along the road to passion. Creative note, photo, phone please. Matchbox no M0113./

SWM 27, 5'9", REASONABLY attractive U of C graduate student dedicated to his work, seeks intelligent, sincere, independent, career oriented SWF to enjoy Chicago's urban pleasures. Matchbox no M0123./

SWM, 51, SEEKING a couple who shares my interest in massage. I'm one who believes sensuality can be safe, friendships rewarding.

MENS SANA IN Corpore Sano: Intellectually passionate ad exec, physically and financially fit SWM, 33, 180, 6'3" is searching for an attractive, slender, perspicacious SWF professional with champagne personality to share intellectual, emotional and spiritual adventures. Interests include Jung, Mozart, blues and bikes. Letter with photo if possible. Downtown or North Shore. Reply to P.O. Box

VALUE COMMUNICATION, CARING, affection? Childless physician, 45, DWM, attractive, in-shape, fair-minded, seeks soulmate to start or expand family: slim woman, nonsmoker. P.O. Box

REMEMBER ME? I am the cute, white, petite, 30, very bi, looking for same bi (or wanting to be) female who wishes the best of both worlds. Since '86 many applicants, but no graduate. A descriptive letter, recent picture (a must) and phone no. will get you a first date over dinner or drinks. If no sparks, bye-bye. If we like each other, this could be the beginning of...heaven on earth. Be an 'angel' and write me. Matchbox no M0118./

SINCERE, ATTRACTIVE, SBM, 28, HIV tested (negative) seeks to 'develop intimacy' with warm, attractive SWF or SBF. Please send letter, photo, phone. Matchbox no M0139./

ATTRACTIVE MWM, SUCCESSFUL, wealthy businessman enjoys spoiling, being supportive and generous with very attractive single female, 21-39, info to Matchbox no M4916./

TALL, TRIM, HEALTHY, secure SWM, professional, 34, enjoys jazz & new age, tennis, exploring restaurants, discovering. I'm in Chicago often and am seeking a trim, conservative SWF for friendship & fun. P.O. Box

AM I UNREALISTIC? All I want is someone to love and to love me. I'm 36, SM, little gelt. Seeking down to earth, unpretentious SF, 34-38, Lincoln Park area, who likes lakefront walks, movies and cuddling. Matchbox no M0130./

GWM 24, 5'10", 175, BLONDE. I smoke, drink, work too much, can't stand 'queens' and don't love Jesus. But, I am intelligent, muscular, straight-acting, non-promiscuous, clean cut, honest and friendly. I'm looking for a compatible, good-looking GWM, 20-26, for friendship and possible relationship. Send whatever, photo helpful. Matchbox no M0131./

LEGAL LAD OF 25, seeks young beauty not contrived, south side quarters off the stream, cares not for material scheme, athletic 5'8 hombre, offbeat woman s'il vous plait. Matchbook no M5006./

ATTENTION: IF YOU'RE nonsmoking, petite, slim, 18-30 y/o female who enjoys rock, sports, blue jeans, and just being together, then this honest, nice, fun, slim SWM professional has much to offer! Matchbox no M0107./

SWM, 5'7", 30, GRAPHIC artist, nonsmoker, college educated, enjoys city, movies, travel, classes, and fine arts. Seeks single female counterpart. Send letter, etc. Matchbox no M0135./

ADDICT WANTED. TRAVEL type for worldly argonaut SWM, 52, 6', 180. If you're a SWF, 38-60, like geography, classic cars, adventure. Send letter, photo. Matchbox no M0140./

Figure 18–2 *Matrimonial Ads*

Matrimonial–Male

Gujarati Brahmin veg., nonsmoker, nondrinker, 6′, 175 lbs., Green Card, well established, self employed, 33 yrs., divorced no children, invites biodata and returnable photographs from sincere, fun loving, unmarried, Gujarati girls with high moral value.   N

Gujarati Brahmin parents invite correspondence for their son 32, 6′1″, CPA, well settled, from educated Gujarati girls. Reply with biodata and returnable photo.   N

Gujarati Jain, Engineer, 32, 5′7″, 160 lbs., seeking correspondence from good looking & new qualified girls. Reply with photographs. No bar.   W

Gujarati, Six Village Patel (Nadiad) parents invite correspondence for their handsome son, 23 yrs., well educated, MBA. Send particulars and photo.   N

Hello there! Are you that educated, attractive, self-confident Indian girl, aware of and interested in the world around. I am Gujarati Computer Engineer, M.S. (Eng.), MBA, early thirties, 5′7″, 140 lbs., never married, intellectual with healthy sense of humor and zest for life, good looking, progressive yet respectful of good traditions, Indian nationalist. Let's talk! Mich.

Iyengar girls reply with details to boy 32, permanent resident.   N

Iyengar male, M.D., 39, divorced, immigrant seeks alliance from Brahmin girls horoscope.

Jain North Indian, 27/5′7″, M.Sc., computer programmer, immigrant, handsome, doing M.S., well settled.

Jain parents invite correspondence from girl for 28 years Matriculate Gujarati boy settled in New Jersey.

Karmarkar family invites matrimonial proposal for their son from a beautiful, Maharashtrian, US resident girl. Call:

Correspondence invited from U.S. resident girls for Patel family, 31 yrs., 5′4″, fair, handsome, fluent English. Contact: (evening) for early marriage.

Match for 31, 5′7″, Khatri near Toronto. Wanted homely girl. Reply to: C

Match for Canadian divorcee Sikh Engineer, 54, 5′8″, for early marriage.   C

Match for Lab. Tech. citizen, Gujarati, 41, 5′2″, divorced, no kids. No bar. Early marriage.   M1189 E

Matrimonial–Male (Contd.)

Matrimonial correspondence invited from girls educated, over 5′3″ tall, attractive and not over 28, for a young Bengali Hindu Engineer, well-settled in U.S.A. Please write positively with photograph to: Texas

Matrimonial correspondence invited for Indian Catholic young man aged 26, from good family currently working in Saudi Arabia. Reply to:

Parents invite correspondence from well settled Hindu Punjabi family for their only son 25, 5′10″, very handsome, finishing accounting degree Dec. 88, earning 32K part time. Preference for cultured student girl (20-23) in degree program. Returnable photograph requested.   N

Parents invite correspondence for son 31, 5′9″, well settled, immigrant Engineer. Prefer attractive, affluent, Telugu professionals. Biodata/photo essential.   W

Matrimonial–Female

Traditional, academic Kayastha family invites correspondence from Kayastha gentlemen for charming daughter, 26, traditional but well-adjusted, educated in India and US and presently working. Please call:

evening or weekends.

Correspondence invited from professionals with similar background for pretty, talented, Bengali Hindu girl, 23, US raised, BS professional, employed. Returnable photograph requested. State no bar.   E

Correspondence invited for very good looking Bengali Hindu girl around mid-thirty doing professional job, divorced with one child. Person well settled, seriously marriage minded only need to write. No bar.   E

Correspondence invited from Sikh professionals for 25 years, 5′4″, attractive, slim niece, presently visiting U.S.A., enrolled in Ph.D. program in India.

Correspondence invited for convent educated, attractive, smart, 22 year old, tall Punjabi girl. Please write with photograph.   E

Correspondence invited from Christians here or India for well educated pretty immigrant sister 36.   MW

Matrimonial–Female (Contd.)

Sikh Saini family seeks well settled, educated boy for daughter 24, with business degree. Federal government employee. Reply: Toronto

Hindu parents invite matrimonial correspondence from U.S. educated doctors only for their beautiful daughter, U.S. born, completing final year law. Apply with full details and photograph. Maryland

Brother invites correspondence from South Indian Hindu gentlemen here/India, 35-38, for sister 33, permanent resident, pretty, high school. Early marriage here/India. Photograph appreciated. Reply to Box: N

Brother invites correspondence for never married, 35 year old sister, permanent resident, well educated, family settled in States. Caste no bar. Please send details.   N

Career oriented, good looking divorcee invites correspondence from very mature person, high moral values, 38-45, nonsmoker, preferably Jat Sikh, Toronto or vicinity only.

Charotar Patel parents invite correspondence for daughter, 26, 5′, B. Com., technician, well settled, smart, beautiful, citizen, from Charotar Patels only. Contact: N

Correspondence only with photo from Hindu doctor for beautiful, fair, 27, 5′3″. finishing D.D.S. in May next year. Tex.

Correspondence invited from professional, educated boys in early 30's for a 31 year old Physician, Punjabi, innocently divorced. Reply soon with returnable photograph.   MW

Correspondence invited from professionals for attractive, slim, Sindhi girl, 22, 5′3″, holding degrees in accounting and law.

Correspondence welcome with photograph from educated Gujarati guys, 30-35, for professional Gujarati Patel lady, divorced, educated in England, settled U.S.   MW

Correspondence invited from tall, handsome North Indian professionals for beautiful, working mgmt. analyst, Hindu Punjabi girl, 27, 5′3″. Write with photo. No divorcee.

Correspondence invited for 28 years, 5′1″, beautiful Punjabi girl, B.A. and diploma in Cosmetology, temporarily settled in U.S.A. Write Zambia.

Correspondence invited for Gujarati Vaishnav girl, 30, 5′1″, slim, beautiful, never married, computer programmer, visiting U.S. now. Reply with photograph.   N

8. After reading final versions in groups or in the whole class, debrief—discuss the activity itself, how people handled the work, and how their ideas may have changed as they explored the topic more thoroughly.

John Hersey's Hiroshima—A More Extended Unit

All of our integrated activities thus far have involved fairly brief readings or data sets. But what happens when the same approach is used in the study of an entire text or novel? Sue Suchor of Carl Sandburg High School has developed the following sequence of activities for John Hersey's book *Hiroshima*.

1. Since the novel is divided into four sections, discussion and writing activities are arranged in four steps, to be completed as students finish each section. After reading the first section, students can be given a set of questions to answer in writing as they continue reading, to help them focus on the events of the story. The questions should concentrate on what happens to each character that Hersey follows.

2. After the second section has been read, the teacher brings to class a collection of news clippings on recent events, particularly articles about accidents, fires, and other incidents in which questions about responsibility and human error could arise. Students select a news story of interest and rewrite it in Hersey's style—that is, without editorializing, but using point of view to imply their views and judgments. Volunteers read aloud to the class, and the group uses the readings to discuss Hersey's style and approach.

3. When students have completed the third section of the book, they are instructed to interview parents or grandparents about their memories of World War II, particularly their own recollections and beliefs about the question of whether the United States should have dropped atomic bombs on Japan. If family members aren't forthcoming, students are free to use the library to obtain data. The interviews are written up and shared in class.

4. The students go to the library to find news articles from the period, particularly on the dropping of the bomb and aspects of the war with Japan, such as revelations about American POWs on Bataan, articles showing the bitterness people felt toward the Japanese, and so forth. The class is then divided into small groups that present information to the class based on the articles they've found.

5. After the small-group presentations, the class is divided into two sides—those who believe the bomb should have been dropped and those who think it shouldn't have—for a semiformal debate. The groups sit on opposite sides of the room and take turns presenting arguments, with brief group consultations after each turn to discuss strategy. The debate itself will be intense, but to help students reflect on it and understand it better, the teacher can keep a list of the pros and cons on the board as the groups present them, to be analyzed when the debate is over. (In fact, the groups will usually find that the "pro" side draws heavily on arguments of strategy and cost, while the "con" group depends on moral arguments.)

6. As a final project, when the students have finished the book, they use a medium or mode of their own choice to express their reactions. Sue says that students have written imaginary letters and diaries of survivors, have composed open letters from fictitious Japanese persons to the people of the United States, and have even made very moving videotapes.

A SUPPORT ACTIVITY AND A VARIATION

Helping Students Learn to Create Good Discussions

Talk is an important element of integrated activities, and we've all had classes that dive eagerly into discussions while others make us feel like we're single-handedly lifting a truck out of a ditch. Elaine Giermak, of Deerfield High School, uses a carefully structured questioning and discussion method to help her students learn to pose good questions about their reading and respond to them. She observes that the technique results in exciting discussions, serves as effective prewriting, and offers students a pattern for thinking about their subject as they write about it. While those interested can learn more about such methods from programs like the Great Books Foundation, it's valuable to briefly review the method, because it echoes many things we've learned about writing.

The core of the discussion is the interpretive question. Interpretive questions are neither factual nor value questions (for a helpful explanation, see Elaine Giermak, "Structuring Open-Ended Discussions for the Gifted and the Not So Gifted," *Illinois English Bulletin*, Winter, 1988). Elaine says she finds that most interpretive questions begin either with "Why" or with "What does the author mean when s/he says. . . ." They are questions the asker truly cares about and finds to be unresolved. They need to be specific and clear and refer to information in the reading selection. Discussions also involve follow-up questions, aimed at clarifying what people have said, seeking support for their statements, or pursuing a line of reasoning. Though these question definitions keep students focused on the reading, their own values and beliefs will emerge anyway, if the climate of the class is open; but they are explored through the text, rather than digressing more widely.

Two interpretive questions on Hersey's *Hiroshima* would be the following:

- What does Tamimoto mean when he refers to the patriotism of his countrymen who faced death at the bombings?
- In his explanation of his use of the atom bomb, why did President Truman omit the fact that the two cities hit had no military installations?

At the start of a discussion, students are asked to free write a brief answer to the first interpretive question, which is posed by the teacher. Responses should not refer to expert opinions or books others haven't read. And most important, the teacher can only ask questions, not make statements. After one or two initial discussions in which the teacher poses the questions, Elaine provides the criteria for interpretive questions to her students and asks them to write their own questions.

Elaine comments, "It looks like a simple system, but profound things happen. I'm amazed at the ideas that emerge, and the kids are too." She uses this technique with remedial students as well as more advanced classes.

While such discussion is obviously just one part of an integrated reading-talking-writing activity, it's a larger part than might first appear. Reading is supported because students must refer back and reread as they try to clarify and support what they have to say. As various points and alternatives emerge, these can be listed as possible topics for writing. Because the questions must be real ones that have more than one possible answer, any writing about them is likely to involve real thought and not just lifeless summary.

Turning the Structure Over to the Students

The following improvement on the integrated activity structure has been used by Bruce Bandy, at Downers Grove South High School. Bruce explains the structure of integrated activities to sophomores and then sets up student panels whose job it is to teach a story or poem to the rest of the class, using the very techniques we've outlined. Each panel must first plan its unit, including the following items:

- A journal-writing question that invites affective response to the literature.

- Small-group discussions and reports to the class on what was discussed.
- Steps to help the class develop writing topics from this activity.

Bruce points out that students not only get to see what teaching feels like, but weaker students both in the panel and in the audience are enabled by the stronger ones to learn more than they otherwise would about the literature being studied.

Chapter 19

Collaborative Research and Term Papers

One of the great ritual mysteries of American schooling is the Term Paper. At some arbitrary moment in their schooling, kids suddenly are presented with a long list of dittoed specifications commanding them to write an example of a highly formalized genre of prose, of which they have almost certainly never read a sample. For most, the project consists of a series of detailed, formulaic steps using 3-by-5-inch note cards, MLA bibliographic notation rules, a liberal peppering of footnotes, and an awkwardly patched-together collection of summaries of articles the student has managed to scrounge up at the local library.

Almost all American students must complete at least one Term Paper in the course of their careers, and in many places the grade level at which this ceremony is performed is going down. It's not at all unusual, amid the writing crisis of the late 1980s, to hear of junior high school—or even elementary-school—students plugging away at a library research project.

Teachers dread term papers as much as students do. They have to check and recheck the work every step of the way, knowing that if they don't, the kids will leave everything to the last minute, making the outcome an even more impossible hodgepodge. They pound home the same stricture repeatedly: NARROW YOUR TOPIC. Students either don't, and string together vague, useless generalizations; or they do, and get bogged down in some unrevealing byway in the subject. At the end of the ritual, teachers trudge home for a lost weekend with huge stacks of sterile rehashes of topics done again and again over the years: lowering the drinking age, abolishing or reinstating capital punishment, legalizing drugs, UFOs.

Everyone stumbles on with the endeavor because "YOU WILL BE REQUIRED TO DO THIS IN YOUR COLLEGE COMPOSITION COURSE." Some (but by no means all, these days) college writing courses, in turn, require term papers because "YOU WILL BE REQUIRED TO DO THIS IN UPPER-LEVEL COURSES." Of course, many upper-level college course instructors don't want to take the time to read all those term papers. Some have stopped assigning them because they find students learn little from the task and have concluded that the expense of time yields too little return. Many teachers get angry at students for their failure to perform, or blame the teachers at lower levels of schooling for not teaching the necessary skills and attitudes. And some caring teachers struggle mightily to help their students overcome their old notions about term papers, begin to ask real research questions, and go through real inquiry and learning processes.

As we consider the possibility of rehabilitating research assignments, it's vital that we fully respect the enormous challenge this kind of writing poses to students. Doing formal academic research is a tremendously demanding intellectual process, which is the main thing that kids' consistent failure at it should tell us. Cognitively speaking, we believe that the task of doing formal library research and coping with note taking, paraphrasing, summarizing, quotations, attribution, documentation, footnoting, and bibliographies is the most challenging academic exercise that's taught in school. As two people who have written or edited a half-dozen books between us, we know that this is the most complex, abstract, and taxing skill we've ever developed.

Yet it seems reasonable to think that research projects could offer wonderful opportunities for writing. Here's a chance for individual students to choose topics that really interest them and begin to make a piece of intellectual territory their own. Students can be active learners, not just listening to lectures and reading textbooks, but gathering material and attempting to explain it to someone else. The benefits of personal involvement, engagement with an audience, and analysis of transactional data can all be combined in one writing activity. In fact, more and more good teachers are finding ways to recast this task in a more worthwhile form.

Two kinds of improvement are needed if we are to teach research writing and/or term papers in a more constructive way. The first change is that when we assign such projects, they must be redesigned as process writing assignments. This means that the teacher must select and sequence the instructions and activities in the project to help kids, not to be rigorous or daunting. One reason why term-paper assignments usually fail is because the way they are typically assigned is too enormous and detailed for students to absorb at once. It is ironic but true that the teacher who carefully prepares a huge, typed packet of instructions and distributes these at the start of a research writing project is probably doing more harm than good.

For exactly the same reasons that we outlined in Chapter 9, skillful teachers break the term-paper assignment into manageable stages and chunks. This means, among other things, that they plan activities to help students find and take genuine ownership of a topic, provide a variety of prewriting experiences to assist students in gathering and organizing material, structure time and help for getting drafts started, help students get early response from readers and revise their texts accordingly, provide outlets for kids to publish their final products, and so forth. Later in this chapter, we'll share two versions of process-model research writing that provide such selection and sequencing.

The second thing that needs to change is that kids must be prepared over time for research writing. As they move up through the grades, students need to be led through a gradually escalating series of research experiences. They should move steadily from working with concrete and familiar material toward more distant and abstract data. Figure 19–1 reminds us of the natural sequence in kids' developing ability to gather information by looking outside themselves, starting with people and phenomena nearby and gradually expanding out into the wider world. We need to tap into this pattern of growth, use it, and stretch it by designing activities that help kids practice doing research in natural, developmentally appropriate ways. If we do, kids can get plenty of experience in the fundamental underlying processes of research—which are not, after all, so terribly alien. Research is just gathering and organizing material from out in the world and then incorporating it into pieces of writing.

Now ideally, this kind of developmental, sequential exposure to research-writing tasks would take place throughout a student's whole academic career, so that we would not be surprising anyone, as we now do, with the huge jolt that research papers currently represent for most secondary-school kids. But even if such groundwork hasn't been created over a period of years, teachers looking toward a term-paper assignment for their students can still lay some foundation by providing experiences that lead kids to the later, formal assignment.

PRELIMINARY ACTIVITIES

Below we list a series of pre-research-paper writing activities that teachers might select from, either as part of a long-term effort to build a foundation, or as immediate preparation for a formal research-writing activity.

1. Engage in autobiographical writings. Use personal source materials, explore in the library of one's own experience. Seek and organize data about one's family.

2. Describe objects—potatoes, sea shells, meaningful personal possessions.

Figure 19–1 *Relating Information Sources to Student Experience (from Frances Zaniello, based on a talk by Gordon Pradl)*

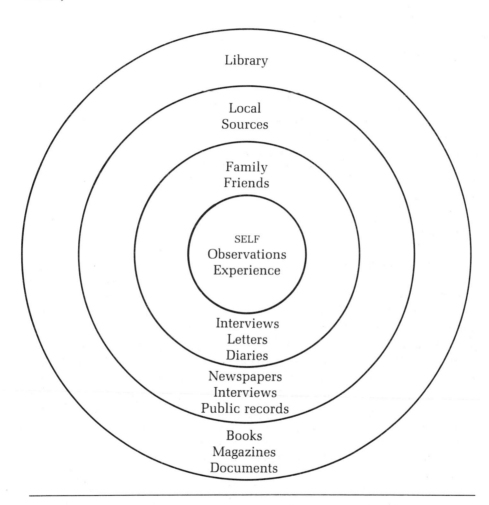

3. Describe places—a room, a place in nature, elsewhere in space or time.

4. Describe a person, a friend, or a classmate from observation and notes; from an interview.

5. Write how-to papers: explain a process or activity you know how to

do. Find others who share this skill and interview them; add their insights to your own.

6. Compose instructions and directions: how to get from here to the school office, the police station, your house.

7. Interview friends, relatives, elders to elicit information. Practice making up interview questions first.

8. Interview strangers (businesspeople, local officials, experts) for a specific expository purpose.

9. Conduct written surveys or questionnaires, in school or in the neighborhood.

10. Do on-the-hoof research on local issues or problems. Travel to people, places, libraries as needed.

11. Do some consumer research on everyday products—gum, shampoo, potato chips, bicycles, and the like. Use real samples, set criteria, test, report results. Look up model consumer reporting in library. (More about this below.)

12. Gather data from the school library to answer simple, quick questions related to course content.

All of these activities compel students to actively explore a topic, formulate questions that matter, figure out how to get information, gather material, and put together a complex variety of data using live, concrete, tangible, primary-source material, rather than information from books. This eases the difficult and often discouraging task of locating worthwhile written information, a task that can easily discourage even the most diligent graduate student. It also helps cope with the fact that junior-high and high-school students will rarely have the chance to read enough about a particular subject to interpret and relate pieces of information with any real skill—something people acquire only through extended study and professional experience.

The above list suggests just a few promising research activities using real-life information students can gather and write about effectively. Most of them are not unfamiliar to veteran teachers. Social-studies teachers have long been aware of activity 7, asking their students to interview parents or grandparents about growing up in an earlier decade, about memories of war, the Depression, or work experience. Marge Kusterman at Evanston Township High School asks students to search their rooms, attics, and closets for old school assignments, from which they reconstruct the history of their own growth as writers. All of this data gathering is *research*, and writing about it calls on all the same thinking skills, organizational tasks, and audience concerns that go into more traditional library research projects.

THE PRODUCT RESEARCH PROJECT

One particularly helpful transitional research assignment, listed as activity 11 above, deserves special attention here, since so many teachers have used it with delight. Most of us are thoroughly familiar with product reviews. It used to be that they were found only in consumer magazines or in the specialized magazines and journals of particular industries, fields, or hobbies—comparisons of new forklift equipment, brass cymbals, or cameras. Now even daily newspapers, in the scramble to maintain readership, review restaurants, new automobiles, books, movies, TV shows, and computers. Many students will recognize the genre immediately. Depending on the time available and the level of the students, this research task can range from a simple comparison of toothpaste tastes and tubes to a study of how national health problems are affected by food additives.

• *Step 1: Introduce the concept.* If possible, bring in several brands or models of an item you own—hair driers, portable radios, or magazines, for example. If one model is clearly better than the other, of course, the point will be obvious. If there are trade-offs between several models, all the better. If you don't own two of anything, students can bring in some category of possessions to compare. A general examination, operating or looking over the samples, will probably incite plenty of spin-off stories about toys and electronic devices that broke down within a week after Christmas. If there's time, students can use focused free writing to compose these stories and then read them aloud.

• *Step 2: Identify topics.* Next the class brainstorms a list of items they'd like to see compared. These may include things they already own as well as those they might purchase in the future. Students can write their own lists first, so they have something to contribute, or the whole group can create the list from the start. Once the list is nice and long, you can go back and help the class to eliminate any items that would be difficult to research because of cost or availability. When this project moves on to the actual doing stage, kids will probably have to pick products that are cheap and easily available in multiple brands, like chewing gum, potato chips, shampoo, yogurt, or spiral notebooks; or commonly owned appliances like hair driers or radios. Special interest groups, however, might evaluate sports equipment, musical instruments, or other more unusual items.

• *Step 3: Form groups.* Students can then be grouped by interest, if their preferences aren't too disparate. Otherwise, they can simply be organized just as peer critiquing groups are. It's extremely important to take time for sensitizing students to the process of working in groups, using activities outlined in Chapter 14 (or see the variation described in step 1 of the library research activity, below). This is the step teachers most often skip over, and it's the element perhaps most important for the success of the activity.

The groups will have to take some time to decide on a specific product to review and to focus on some relatively specific version (or versions); obviously, "food" or even "snack foods" would present far more choices than they could possibly study over a several-week period. Remind students that they've got to choose their audience as they make these decisions: are they going to be reviewing the products for the rest of the class or for fellow afficionados (of electronic keyboards, motorcycles, running shoes or whatever)?

• *Step 4: Read articles from* Consumer Reports. In order for students to internalize the nature of product evaluations, they should have a chance to read several examples from *Consumer Reports* and other sources. These articles tend to have a very obvious and easily-followed structure: the basic purpose or key quality of the product in question is defined in detail, criteria for evaluation are set, testing data is presented and interpreted, and recommendations are made.

• *Step 5: Groups develop criteria.* Students must now decide what characteristics they will use to judge the products. This is likely to be a complex issue. Take ten-speed bicycles, for example. How much increased expense and decreased durability will they want to trade off for a lighter frame? How much will they consider the brakes, or the type of derailleur? If you think the groups will have trouble with this step, you can model such analysis with the whole class, using a product no group has chosen. One good way to conduct this analysis is to brainstorm a list of characteristics and then make a chart with the brands or models forming one axis and the characteristics the other.

The groups will discover that they need to talk over this matter quite a bit, and if there's enough time they'll probably need to do some firsthand research, trying out models, perhaps visiting stores to let the salespeople give their pitch, or even contacting manufacturers to obtain brochures and spec lists. Another approach would be to survey schoolmates who use the product to see what qualities *they* find crucial. The most in-depth approach of all would be to include some reading and library research. Many products have received careful scrutiny and have involved major national controversy. A group that decides to compare artificial sweeteners, for example, will find that there's a lot more to consider than just the taste.

• *Step 6: Doing the comparison.* Depending on the type of product, evaluation may involve sitting down to taste all the brands using a blindfolded panel, or poring over the literature to compile various specifications for each brand.

• *Step 7: Writing the report.* Once the products are tested, the groups will find that they need to organize the data somehow and decide which characteristics to explain first. They'll need to think about introductions and conclusions. Before they start writing students may wish to review the sample articles from *Consumer Reports.*

• *Step 8: Publication.* When the reports are revised and polished, they can be bound together as a consumer journal to be put in the reference section of the library (where a growing collection of these could become a significant resource for other students). And/or you could stage a panel day in class, at which time each group comes forward to field questions and give advice about buying the product.

THE LIBRARY RESEARCH PROJECT

Students *can* learn a great deal from library research, once they have a sense of what real research is about and once they have a meaningful context for their writing and plenty of support. Judy Johnstone, at Carl Sandburg High School, has developed a highly successful plan for carrying out collaborative library research projects, which we'd like to describe here. What makes the plan work well, we believe, is a combination of: (1) training in how to work in groups before the actual project begins, (2) support for important steps in the process, (3) a heightened awareness of substantive and stylistic issues created by discussion within the groups, and (4) thorough reflection on the process after it is finished. Here's how it goes.

• *Step 1: Training.* To prepare people to work effectively in small groups, begin with a "fishbowl" exercise, as follows. Divide the class into groups of about eight. Within each group, four will be given a problem to solve, and the other four will be asked to observe the problem-solving group. The "problem" Judy usually sets up is to give the group a list of occupations, ranging from physician to undertaker, to be ranked in terms of the prestige each occupation commands in the United States. Each observer is assigned to watch for the use of a particular role in the problem-solving group, based on the list of roles one can find in any group dynamics text—roles such as establisher of procedures, summarizer, gatekeeper, mediator, dominator, and so forth. Observers must also watch to see how decisions are made in the group—by majority vote, consensus, compromise, or minority domination. The observers must be reminded to keep from thinking too much about the issues the problem solvers argue over, and concentrate on the group processes instead.

After the groups go through the exercise, the observers are asked to report, and discussion about the group processes ensues. Judy has observed that the central controversy turns out to be the difference between consensus and compromise. Many group members will passively agree to a decision they don't really support and then lose interest in the outcome. Judy helps the students understand that this is not consensus, but a form of compromise that only undermines group work. As the losers withdraw, one or two students end up dominating and doing all the work. As they realize this, students begin to figure out what it will take to really work together.

• *Step 2: Forming groups.* Groups are now formed to do their research together, four to a group, using one of the methods described for organizing peer critiquing groups (see Chapter 14). One factor Judy considers especially important in constructing the groups is learning style. As much as possible, she tries to make sure each group includes one relatively organized student and one divergent thinker. The skills of each will be needed as the project proceeds.

• *Step 3: Brainstorming topics.* The groups are asked to make lists of topics they might like to work on, topics they think students in the class would like to know about. The rest of the class, they are told, will be the audience for the final report. Help is provided to the groups in the form of various prewriting activities, such as formal brainstorming and free writing on successively associated topics on 3-by-5 cards. Each group must find a topic that everyone in the group wants to research.

• *Step 4: Question generating.* The next task for the groups is to brainstorm as many questions as possible about their chosen topic. Judy provides various questioning rubrics: the news reporter's "Wh" questions, Burke's "pentad" of inquiry probes (act, scene, agent, agency, and purpose); and so forth. Once the question lists are of good length, each student in a group chooses one question or a group of related questions (the size of the task depends on the length of the project and the level of the students) to research in the library.

• *Step 5: Technical instruction.* Before students begin their actual research, Judy provides instruction in creating bibliography cards—how to take notes so that students will have the information they need. This is the point at which students are helped to grapple with the concept of summarizing and with the realization that they can be selective and emphasize what they consider important. To encourage students to begin the process of summarizing and making sense of their data (and thus to prepare them to work with their groups later on), Judy emphasizes that they will not be able to bring actual texts to class when writing time comes, but must use their notes.

•   *Step 6: Library work.* Now that the students are ready, they can spend time in the library, with the teacher providing group instruction and individual help finding items as needed. One can economize on time by devoting some class meetings to other topics while the research is going on. When the research time is up, Judy collects the bibliography cards and gives credit for work done to this point.

•   *Step 7: Drafting.* The main work of drafting is done in class, over a span of three to five days (depending on the size of the project). Judy first gives out a sheet listing the criteria she'll use to evaluate the finished papers. Then the groups get to work. Judy does not tell them how they should proceed, but she has observed that many groups generally operate the same way, although there are some interesting variations. The first period is usually spent organizing and comparing the information each person has found. The teacher circulates and is available to help when groups are having trouble; but the most important thing the teacher can do is to listen and observe to see what students are discovering as they move through the composing process.

In the course of the second day, the typical group has decided on a thesis statement, begun to decide on an order for the material, and discovered that some people's data fits the chosen focus better than others'. A crisis often occurs, as the group realizes that someone's data will have to be omitted or the thesis changed. To help ease this problem, students are given credit for their research whether it is included in the final paper or not. However, the group tends to consider far more carefully than do most students working alone the question of how the pieces fit together.

By the end of the second or third day, the groups are usually assigning individual members writing tasks to be done at home—a phenomenon rarely seen in schools, but which Judy says happens all the time with collaborative research projects. Then, as people bring in their pieces, the groups turn to the task of revising them so that they fit together and the ideas and the tone are consistent. Again, this issue usually comes up in the groups; the teacher needs to do little or no instructing. "The whole endeavor teaches so much," Judy says. "I couldn't begin to teach it all myself. But this way, all I have to do is just confirm what they're learning." The writing period ends with a weekend during which a final revised version is typed, often after a last at-home revising meeting held by the group.

•   *Step 8: Reflection.* Judy uses several evaluation forms to help students become more conscious of what they've learned after the process is over. First, students consider the work of their group and each individual within it. Then they look at themselves, responding to such questions as:

- What did you learn about groups?
- What role(s) did you take in your group?
- What would you do differently if you were to do such a project again?
- What did you learn about writing?
- What did you revise most?
- What was your biggest problem?

Judy observes that most students start off very skeptical about group projects. Through this experience, they realize their value for the first time.

- *Step 9: Publication.* The projects can be shared with the whole class in a variety of ways. The groups can act as panels, with the rest of the class asking questions about the subject. Groups can serve as readers for other groups. The reports can be put together to form a magazine to be bound and placed in the library—not too difficult, since there will be only about eight reports per class. Often, Judy says, the data collected in this project becomes the basis for the next assignment: an argumentation paper in which individual students must take a stand on an issue they consider important.

When we asked Judy what problems a teacher might anticipate in conducting this sort of writing activity, she hesitated and then patiently explained that we were asking the wrong question. Solving problems, she pointed out, is the purpose for which the *groups* exist. She makes clear to her students that the whole activity is meant both to help them write about research *and* to learn how to work in groups, so most problems simply become part of the learning process.

The one difficulty she does struggle with is time. The project requires enough time for the groups to develop a working relationship and to reach consensus on basic decisions. Absenteeism complicates this, so on the days when crucial work takes place in the groups, Judy awards extra credit just for attendance—not a lot of credit, but enough to symbolize the importance of being there.

We hope it is clear that even more than in some other forms of writing, the focus in these projects is on the processes—question generating, data gathering, analyzing, organizing, and explaining—because these are the thinking skills we want students to learn from research. This is why collaborative small-group work is so well suited to the task. It forces students to talk over alternatives and argue out issues. And the possibilities are endless—surveys of student attitudes and goals throughout the school, comparative studies of TV programming or commercials, learning about careers. It's all research.

We think it's also clear that the reason Judy Johnstone's students succeed so well in their collaborative research projects is that Judy has recreated an old assignment under the new paradigm. Even though the kids are writing real term papers, they are working not as competitors grinding out verbiage for a grade, but as cooperating members of a community of writers seeking to make sense of their world and find their own voices. And that makes all the difference.

Chapter 20

Looking Ahead

We can summarize what we've said in this book quite simply. The fifteen key elements of the process approach to teaching writing, which we introduced at the very start of the book and have been elaborating upon ever since, can be restated plainly:

- Believe in your students. They *can* write.
- Give students plenty of writing time. All writers need practice.
- Help kids internalize and use a craftsmanlike, staged approach to working at pieces of writing.
- Encourage students to write for personally significant purposes.
- Help students find real and varied audiences for their work.
- Provide rich reading experiences for young writers, both silent individual reading and whole-class reading aloud.
- Be a writer yourself, and help students discover other models of how writers really work.
- Make writing a collaborative, social activity in the classroom.
- Have regular, one-to-one conferences with students.
- Initiate inductive, inquiry-based activities in the classroom that immerse students in raw material, invite them to discover principles, and organize their thinking through writing.
- Teach less formal grammar and spend more time on real writing.
- Teach mechanics in the context of kids' actual texts, not as separate drills.
- Don't expect intensive red-penciled correction to improve proofreading; teach students how to locate and fix their own errors.
- In evaluating student work, balance praise with correction, sustaining students' morale as you challenge them to grow.
- Use writing to teach the content of the English curriculum, and help

your colleagues in other disciplines to see how writing can work for them, too.

If it were really easy to implement these ideas—singly or several at once—books like this one wouldn't be necessary. But it is not easy. When teachers start organizing instruction in these ways, a lot of things change in the classroom and a lot of resistance can be encountered: resistance from kids, from administrators, and from the weight of tradition and community expectations, none of which may even be expressed overtly, but all of which are carried around in the psyche of every American teacher.

So we're not underestimating the challenge. To teach in this new way is demanding and risky; it requires commitment, patience, persistence, and a thick skin. But we should not underestimate the benefits, either. Teaching writing in the ways this book has outlined is not just more effective pedagogy, a more efficient way to get content into students' heads or mold them into some preconceived idea of an educated person. When applied in a true form, this kind of teaching is deeply reformist, progressive, and democratic.

Amid all the current talk about school reform, teachers who congruently implement the strategies outlined in this book are reforming their classrooms in profound ways, ways that are scarcely touched upon in the superficial banalities of blue-ribbon commission recommendations. The writing-process classroom is active and inductive; authority is decentralized; responsibility is vested in students as well as the teacher; instruction proceeds by active engagement and practice, not by presentation; goal structures are not competitive and individualistic, but collaborative; the room isn't arranged in silent, permanent rows, but changes organically every day as students rearrange themselves for active, energetic learning.

As we complete this book in mid-1988, America is clearly on the brink of its next wave of progressive education. The writing-workshop classrooms around our country offer a heartening forecast of what lies ahead. After twenty years, the back-to-basics movement, with its wholesale repudiation of the good and bad innovations of the 1960s, is rapidly petering out. Public concern and energy for improving schools is at a peak, and the first wave of more-of-the-same "school reform" is already backfiring. Many key players in the school renewal movement are learning that tough testing programs and bureaucratic police work may make easy-to-pass legislation, but they don't help kids learn much. Even lionized school gurus and media-hungry politicians are realizing that there aren't any Good Old Days to which schools can return and that simply doing traditional schooling harder and longer and under severer penalties doesn't reform anything. Indeed, as the consensus for regression collapses, we are perched at the onset of a tremendously exciting new era. Americans are getting ready to try something different with their schools.

As we pointed out in Chapter 2, the cyclic vacillations between authoritarian and progressive education are not random pendulum swings, but the advances and retreats along a battlefront—the playing out, over a huge span of time, of the war for the soul of schooling in our society. In the end, the student-centered, humanistic, developmental approach will win out over the authoritarian model because it parallels the direction in which civilization itself progresses. If we look broadly enough, we can see evidence that this direction is already well established: in matters of discipline, teachers no longer whip students in school or crown them with dunce caps. In language arts, we no longer require endless copying of great authors' texts, we no longer have kids stand beside their desks for recitation and enunciation; and sentence diagramming, though far from dead, now occupies far less of the average school day than it did just one generation ago.

Of course there will always be regressions and short-term backslides. Change in schools never follows a straight, steady path, but is more like three steps forward and two-and-a-half steps back. Perhaps tomorrow a movement will spring up to restore the teaching of sentence diagramming to its "rightful, central place in the English curriculum," and such a trend might even catch on for a few years. Indeed, it is just this sort of event that misleads us, as individuals living in a particular brief here and now, into believing that there's always a pendulum swinging back and forth between two eternal, fixed points, ensuring that nothing ever really changes.

But we must not forget the half-step gained in every cycle. The larger, overall direction of the teaching of grammar—and schooling in general —is heading the other way. The slow, long trend always prevails. And each cycle of regression, though probably inevitable, can be shortened if classroom teachers feel the confidence to push back at any pendulums that swing their way.

We believe that the kind of teaching called process writing will be part of the first wave in turning the tide toward a new era of educational innovation in American schools. The young English teachers who are being trained in the late 1980s can begin their careers teaching writing (and literacy in general) in a better way. Unencumbered by years of teaching experience and ingrained habits, they can seize the new paradigm as their own. But even for these young teachers, enacting the new model won't be easy. Their own experience as students in school—which is the most powerful influence on what teachers actually do and feel—will conflict with the new ways of the process model. In order to truly own the new methods and fully enact the values of the next progressive era, even today's youngest teachers will have to struggle against some of their own experience and actively choose, every day, to be a part of something different.

For those of us who are veteran teachers, the process model of writing instruction invites us to remake our teaching and revitalize our commitment to the students we serve. But such a change asks a lot of us. After all, we have already taught, by most definitions successfully, for ten or twenty years. To adopt the new paradigm means overcoming our own inertia, questioning familiar habits, abandoning comfortable routines, filing away some surefire unit plans. But nothing is more deeply energizing than rediscovering, at the age of 35 or 45 or 55, the love and joy in teaching—remembering why we chose this infuriatingly wonderful career in the first place. And as we've watched teachers change, we've observed that there is no quicker way to reconnect with that spirit of idealism than to try out methods like those described in this book; to stop being a writing teacher and become part of a community of writers.

And we oldsters can also look forward to this: we will be retiring at the peak of the longest, the strongest, and the greatest era of progressive education this country has ever seen. We're starting to make it happen right now. And someday, as we rock back and forth on the porch of the Old Teachers' Home, we'll be able to recollect with pleasure, and perhaps tell a few tales, about what it was like to be there back in the late 1980s, when it all started.

Appendix

Teachers Who Contributed Ideas to A Community of Writers

Bruce Bandy
Downers Grove South High
  School
1436 Norfolk
Downers Grove, IL 60515

Linda Cannon
Fremd High School
1000 South Quentin Road
Palatine, IL 60067

Barbara Dill
Glenbard West High School
670 Crescent Drive
Glen Ellyn, IL 60137

Elaine Giermak
Deerfield High School
1959 North Waukegan Road
Deerfield, IL 60015

Mark Huegelmann
Orland Junior High School
14855 South West Avenue
Orland Park, IL 60462

Judy Johnstone
Carl Sandburg High School
131st and LaGrange Road
Orland Park, IL 60462

Robin Kacel
Wheeling High School
900 South Elmhurst Road
Wheeling, IL 60090

Margaret Kusterman
Evanston Township High School
1600 Dodge Avenue
Evanston, IL 60204

Jim Langlas
Wheaton North High School
701 West Thomas Road
Wheaton, IL 60187

Shirley Meier
Hoffman Estates High School
1100 West Higgins Road
Hoffman Estates, IL 60195

Steve Ogilvie
Elmwood Park High School
8201 West Fullerton Avenue
Elmwood Park, IL 60635

Shelly Reece
English Department
Portland State University
Portland, OR 97207

Bob Runtz
Hersey High School
1900 East Thomas Street
Arlington Heights, IL 60004

Phyllis Stimac
Seventh Avenue School
701 South Seventh Avenue
LaGrange, IL 60525

Sue Suchor
Carl Sandburg High School
131st and LaGrange Road
Orland Park, IL 60462

Elaine Taylor
Wauconda Junior High School
215 Slocum Lake Road
Wauconda, IL 60084

Jim Vopat
English Department
Carroll College
Waukesha, WI 53186

Bibliography

RESEARCH ON WRITING

Applebee, Arthur N., Judith Langer, and Ina Mulles. *Writing Across the Decade, 1974–84.* Princeton: Educational Testing Service/National Assessment of Educational Progress, 1986.

Bereiter, Carl. "Development in Writing." In *Cognitive Processes in Writing,* edited by Lee W. Gregg and Erwin R. Steinberg. Hillsdale, N.J.: Lawrence Erlbaum Associates, 1979.

Bissex, Glenda. *GNYS AT WRK: A Child Learns to Write and Read.* Cambridge, Mass.: Harvard University Press, 1980.

Britton, James, et al. *The Development of Writing Abilities 11–18.* New York: Macmillan, 1975.

Cooper, Charles, and Lee Odell. *Research on Composing.* Urbana, Ill.: National Council of Teachers of English, 1978.

Emig, Janet. *The Composing Processes of Twelfth Graders.* Urbana, Ill.: National Council of Teachers of English, 1971.

———. "Writing, Composition, and Rhetoric." In *Encyclopedia of Educational Research.* 5th ed. Vol. 4, pp. 2021–36. New York: Free Press, 1982.

Goswami, Dixie, and Peter Stillman, eds. *Reclaiming the Classroom: Teacher Research as an Agency for Change.* Portsmouth, N.H.: Boynton/Cook, 1987.

Hillocks, George, Jr. *Research on Written Composition: New Directions for Teaching.* Urbana, Ill.: National Council of Teachers of English, 1986.

Newkirk, Thomas, and Nancie Atwell, eds. *Understanding Writing: Ways of Observing, Learning, and Teaching.* 2d ed. Portsmouth, N.H.: Heinemann, 1988.

Rose, Mike. *Writer's Block: The Cognitive Dimension*. Urbana, Ill.: National Council of Teachers of English, 1984.

PHILOSOPHY AND BACKGROUND

Applebee, Arthur N. *Writing in the Secondary School: English and the Content Areas*. Urbana, Ill.: National Council of Teachers of English, 1981.

Applebee, Arthur N., et al. *Contexts for Learning to Write: Studies of Secondary School Instruction*. Norwood, N.J.: Ablex, 1984.

Bandler, Richard, and John Grinder. *Frogs into Princes*. Moab, Utah: Real People Press, 1979.

Berthoff, Ann, ed., *Reclaiming the Imagination: Philosophical Perspectives for Writers and Teachers of Writing*. Portsmouth, N.H.: Boynton/Cook, 1984.

Britton, James. *Language and Learning*. Coral Gables, Fla.: University of Miami Press, 1970.

———. *Prospect and Retrospect: Selected Essays*. Portsmouth, N.H.: Boynton/Cook, 1983.

Burling, Robbins. *English in Black and White*. New York: Holt, Rinehart and Winston, 1973.

Cedaline, Anthony. *Job Burnout in Public Education: Symptoms, Causes, and Survival Skills*. New York: Teachers College Press, 1982.

Daniels, Harvey. *Famous Last Words: The American Language Crisis Revisited*. Carbondale, Ill.: Southern Illinois University Press, 1983.

Dixon, John. *Growth Through English: Set in the Perspective of the Seventies*. London: Oxford University Press, 1975.

Donovan, Timothy, and Ben W. McClelland, eds. *Eight Approaches to Teaching Composition*. Urbana, Ill.: National Council of Teachers of English, 1980.

Eiben, Ray, and Al Millren. *Educational Change: A Humanistic Approach*. San Diego: University Associates, 1976.

Elbow, Peter. *Writing With Power*. New York: Oxford University Press, 1981.

———. *Writing Without Teachers*. New York: Oxford University Press, 1973.

Farr, Marcia, and Harvey Daniels. *Language Diversity and Writing Instruction*. Urbana, Ill.: National Council of Teachers of English, 1986.

Gere, Anne Ruggles, and Eugene Smith. *Attitudes, Language and Change*. Urbana, Ill.: National Council of Teachers of English, 1979.

Glasser, William. *Control Theory in the Classroom*. New York: Harper and Row, 1986.

Glatthorn, Alan. *Writing in the Schools*. Reston, Va.: National Association of Secondary School Principals, 1981.

Halliday, M. A. K. *Explorations in the Function of Language*. London: Edward Arnold, 1973.

Heath, Shirley Brice. *Ways With Words*. New York: Cambridge University Press, 1983.

Knoblauch, C. H., and Lil Brannon. *Rhetorical Traditions and the Teaching of Writing*. Portsmouth, N.H.: Boynton/Cook, 1984.

Labov, William. *Language in the Inner City: Studies in the Black English Vernacular*. Philadelphia: University of Pennsylvania Press, 1972.

Martin, Nancy. *Mostly About Writing: Selected Essays*. Portsmouth, N.H.: Boynton/Cook, 1983.

Mayher, John, Gordon Pradl, and Nancy Lester. *Learning to Write/Writing to Learn*. Portsmouth, N.H.: Boynton/Cook, 1983.

Moffett, James. *Coming on Center*. 2d ed. Portsmouth, N.H.: Boynton/Cook, 1988.

————. *Teaching the Universe of Discourse*. Portsmouth, N.H.: Boynton/Cook, 1983.

Murray, Donald. *Learning by Teaching: Selected Articles on Writing and Teaching*. Portsmouth, N.H.: Boynton/Cook, 1983.

Myers, Miles, and James Gray. *Theory and Practice in the Teaching of Composition*. Urbana, Ill.: National Council of Teachers of English, 1983.

Ohmann, Richard. *English in America*. New York: Oxford University Press, 1977.

Perl, Sondra. "Five Writers Writing: Case Studies of the Composing Processes of Unskilled College Writers." Ph.D. diss., New York University, 1978.

Perl, Sondra, and Nancy Wilson. *Through Teachers' Eyes: Portraits of Writing Teachers at Work*. Portsmouth, N.H.: Heinemann, 1986.

Rogers, Carl. *Freedom to Learn*. Columbus, Ohio: Charles E. Merrill, 1983.

Siegel, Muffy, and Toby Olson. *Writing Talks: Views on Teaching Writing from Across the Professions*. Portsmouth, N.H.: Boynton/Cook, 1983.

COMPREHENSIVE APPROACHES

Atwell, Nancie. *In the Middle: Writing, Reading, and Learning with Adolescents*. Portsmouth, N.H.: Boynton/Cook, 1987.

Bechtel, Judith. *Improving Writing and Learning: A Handbook for Teachers in Every Class*. Boston: Allyn and Bacon, 1985.

Calkins, Lucy McCormick. *The Art of Teaching Writing*. Portsmouth, N.H.: Heinemann, 1986.

Camp, Gerald. *Teaching Writing: Essays from the Bay Area Writing Project.* Portsmouth, N.H.: Boynton/Cook, 1983.

Coles, William E., Jr. *The Plural I—And After.* Portsmouth, N.H.: Boynton/Cook, 1988.

Daniels, Harvey, and Steven Zemelman. *A Writing Project: Training Teachers of Composition from Kindergarten to College.* Portsmouth, N.H.: Heinemann, 1985.

Graves, Donald H. *Writing: Teachers and Children at Work.* Portsmouth, N.H.: Heinemann, 1983.

Graves, Richard, ed. *Rhetoric and Composition: A Sourcebook for Teachers and Writers.* Portsmouth, N.H.: Boynton/Cook, 1984.

Kirby, Dan, and Tom Liner. *Inside Out: Developmental Strategies for Teaching Writing.* Portsmouth, N.H.: Boynton/Cook, 1981.

Klaus, Carl, and Nancy Jones, eds. *Courses for Change in Writing.* Portsmouth, N.H.: Boynton/Cook, 1984.

Koch, Carl, and James M. Brazil. *Strategies for Teaching the Composition Process.* Urbana, Ill.: National Council of Teachers of English, 1978.

Macrorie, Ken. *Telling Writing.* 4th ed. Portsmouth, N.H.: Boynton/Cook, 1985.

———. *Writing to Be Read.* 3d ed. Portsmouth, N.H.: Boynton/Cook, 1984.

Moffett, James. *Active Voice: A Writing Program Across the Curriculum.* Portsmouth, N.H.: Boynton/Cook, 1981.

Moffett, James, and Betty Jane Wagner. *Student-Centered Language Arts and Reading, K–13.* Boston: Houghton Mifflin, 1976.

Murray, Donald. *A Writer Teaches Writing.* Boston: Houghton Mifflin, 1968.

Newkirk, Thomas, ed. *To Compose: Teaching Writing in the High School.* Portsmouth, N.H.: Heinemann, 1986.

Ponsot, Marie, and Rosemary Deen. *Beat Not the Poor Desk: Writing—What to Teach, How to Teach It, and Why.* Portsmouth, N.H.: Boynton/Cook, 1982.

Proett, Jackie, and Kent Gill. *The Writing Process in Action: A Handbook for Teachers.* Urbana, Ill.: National Council of Teachers of English, 1986.

Romano, Tom. *Clearing the Way: Working with Teenage Writers.* Portsmouth, N.H.: Heinemann, 1987.

Tchudi, Steven, and Susan Tchudi. *An Introduction to the Teaching of Writing.* New York: Wiley, 1981.

JOURNALS, PREWRITING, AND GUIDED IMAGERY

All About Letters. Urbana, Ill.: National Council of Teachers of English and the U.S. Postal Service.

Fulwiler, Toby, ed. *The Journal Book.* Portsmouth, N.H.: Boynton/Cook, 1987.

Gawain, Shakti. *Creative Visualization.* New York: Bantam, 1978.

Grinder, John, and Richard Bandler. *Trance-Formations.* Moab, Utah: Real People Press, 1985.

Hillocks, George. *Observing and Writing.* Urbana, Ill.: National Council of Teachers of English, 1975.

Johannessen, Larry R., Elizabeth A. Kahn, and Carolyn Calhoun Walter. *Designing and Sequencing Prewriting Activities.* Urbana, Ill.: National Council of Teachers of English, 1982.

Koch, Kenneth. *Wishes, Lies and Dreams.* New York: Vintage Books, 1976.

Leuner, Hanscarl, Gunther Horn, and Edda Klessmann. *Guided Affective Imagery with Children and Adolescents.* New York: Plenum Press, 1983.

Paivio, A. *Imagery and Verbal Processes.* New York: Holt, Rinehart and Winston, 1971.

Progoff, Ira. *At a Journal Workshop.* New York: Dialogue House, 1975.

Purkel, W., and M. H. Bornstein. "Pictures and Imagery Enhance Children's Short-Term and Long-Term Recall." *Developmental Psychology* 16 (March 1980): 153–54.

Rico, Gabrielle. *Writing the Natural Way.* New York: Tarcher, 1983.

Shaw, G. "The Use of Imagery by Intelligent and by Creative Children." *Journal of Counseling Psychology* 112, pt. 2 (April 1985): 153–71.

Sheikh, Anees, ed. *Imagery: Current Theory, Research, and Applications.* New York: Wiley, 1983.

Shorr, Joseph, et al. *Imagery: Its Many Dimensions and Applications.* New York: Plenum Press, 1980.

Staton, Jana. *Dialogue Journal Communication: Classroom, Linguistic, Social and Cognitive Views.* Norwood, N.J.: Ablex, in press.

Strosahl, K. D., and J. C. Ascough. "Clinical Uses of Mental Imagery: Experimental Foundations, Theoretical Misconceptions, and Research Issues." *Psychological Bulletin* 89 (May 1981): 422–38.

Waters, H. S. "Memory Development in Adolescence: Relationships Between Metamemory, Strategy Use and Performance." *Journal of Experimental Child Psychology* 33 (April 1982): 183–95.

GROUP DYNAMICS AND COLLABORATIVE LEARNING

Alvermann, Donna, Deborah Dillon, and David O'Brien. *Using Discussion to Promote Reading Comprehension.* Newark, Del.: International Reading Association, 1987.

Benjamin, Alfred. *Behavior in Small Groups.* Boston: Houghton Mifflin, 1978.

Bradford, Leland, ed. *Group Development.* San Diego: University Associates, 1976.

Bruffee, Kenneth. *A Short Course in Writing.* 2d ed. Cambridge, Mass.: Winthrop, 1980.

Fader, Daniel, et al. *The New Hooked on Books.* New York: Berkeley, 1976.

Freedman, Sarah W. *Peer Response Groups in Two Ninth-Grade Classrooms.* Berkeley, Calif.: Center for the Study of Writing, 1987.

Giermak, Elaine A. "Structuring Open-Ended Discussions for the Gifted and the Not So Gifted." *Illinois English Bulletin* 75 (Winter 1988).

Hanson, Philip. *Learning Through Groups: A Trainer's Basic Guide.* San Diego: University Associates, 1981.

Hawkins, Thom. *Group Inquiry Techniques for Teaching Writing.* Urbana, Ill.: National Council of Teachers of English, 1976.

Jacobsen, Sid. *Meta-Cation.* Cupertino, Calif.: Meta Publications, 1983.

Johnson, David, et al. *Circles of Learning.* Alexandria, Va.: Association for Supervision and Curriculum Development, 1984.

Pfeiffer, William, and John Jones. *A Handbook of Structured Experiences for Human Relations Training.* Rev. ed. Vols. 1 and 4. San Diego: University Associates, 1969.

Schmuck, Richard, and Patricia Schmuck. *Group Processes in the Classroom.* Dubuque, Iowa: William C. Brown, 1983.

Sommer, Robert. *The Mind's Eye.* Palo Alto, Calif.: Dale Seymour, 1978.

Spear, Karen. *Sharing Writing: Peer Response Groups in English Classes.* Portsmouth, N.H.: Boynton/Cook, 1988.

Thayer, Louis, ed. *Fifty Strategies for Experiential Learning: Book One.* San Diego: University Associates, 1976.

———, ed. *Fifty Strategies for Experiential Learning: Book Two.* San Diego: University Associates, 1981.

WRITING TO LEARN/WRITING ACROSS THE CURRICULUM

Clarke, Mark. "Don't Blame the System: Constraints on Whole Language Reform." *Language Arts* 64 (1987): 384–96.

Emig, Janet. *The Web of Meaning: Essays on Writing, Thinking, Learning, and Teaching.* Portsmouth, N.H.: Boynton/Cook, 1983.

Fulwiler, Toby, and Art Young, eds. *Language Connections: Writing and Reading Across the Curriculum.* Urbana, Ill.: National Council of Teachers of English, 1970.

Gere, Anne Ruggles, ed. *Roots in the Sawdust: Writing to Learn Across the Disciplines.* Urbana, Ill.: National Council of Teachers of English, 1985.

Golub, Jeff. *Activities to Promote Critical Thinking: Classroom Practices in Teaching English, 1986.* Urbana, Ill.: National Council of Teachers of English, 1986.

Macrorie, Ken. *Searching Writing.* Portsmouth, N.H.: Boynton/Cook, 1980.

Martin, Nancy, et al. *Writing and Learning Across the Curriculum 11–16.* Portsmouth, N.H.: Boynton/Cook, 1976.

Newman, Judith, ed. *Whole Language: Theory in Use.* Portsmouth, N.H.: Heinemann, 1985.

Parker, Robert P., and Vera Goodkin. *The Consequences of Writing: Enhancing Learning in the Disciplines.* Portsmouth, N.H.: Boynton/Cook, 1987.

Raths, Louis. *Teaching for Thinking.* Indianapolis: Bobbs Merrill, 1976.

Tchudi, Stephen. *Teaching Writing in the Content Areas.* Volumes 1–3: Elementary (with Susan Tchudi); Middle School (with Margie Huerta); High School (with Joanne Yates). Washington, D.C.: National Education Association, 1983.

Wolsch, Robert A., and Lois Wolsch. *From Speaking to Writing to Reading: Relating the Arts of Communication.* New York: Teachers College Press, 1982.

Walvoord, Barbara. *Helping Students Write Well: A Guide for Teachers in All Disciplines.* New York: Modern Language Association, 1986.

REVISING, EDITING, AND GRAMMAR

Brannon, Lillian. "The Role of Authority in Teacher-Student Writing Conferences." Paper presented at conference of Commission on College Composition and Communication, 1985.

Brannon, Lillian, Melinda Knight, and Vara Neverow-Turk. *Writers Writing.* Portsmouth, N.H.: Boynton/Cook, 1982.

Bridwell, Lillian S. "Revising Processes in Twelfth Grade Students' Transactional Writing." *Research in the Teaching of English* 14 (1980): 197–222.

Cooper, Charles R., ed. *The Nature and Measurement of Competency in English.* Urbana, Ill.: National Council of Teachers of English, 1981.

Cooper, Charles, and Lee Odell, eds. *Evaluating Writing.* Urbana, Ill.: National Council of Teachers of English, 1977.

Daiker, Donald A., Andrew Kerek, and Max Morenberg. *The Writer's Options.* New York: Harper and Row, 1982.

Diederich, Paul. *Measuring Growth in English.* Urbana, Ill.: National Council of Teachers of English, 1974.

Harris, Muriel. *Teaching One-to-One: The Writing Conference.* Urbana, Ill.: National Council of Teachers of English, 1986.

Hays, J. N. "The Effect of Audience Considerations Upon the Revisions of a Group of Basic Writers and More Competent Junior and Senior Writers." Paper presented at conference of Commission on College Composition and Communication, 1981.

Killgallon, Don. *Sentence Composing: The Complete Course.* Portsmouth, N.H.: Boynton/Cook, 1987.

Mohr, Marian. *Revision: The Rhythm of Meaning.* Portsmouth, N.H.: Boynton/Cook, 1984.

Shaughnessy, Mina. *Errors and Expectations.* New York: Oxford University Press, 1977.

Strong, William. *Creative Approaches to Sentence Combining.* Urbana, Ill.: National Council of Teachers of English, 1986.

Weaver, Constance. *Grammar for Teachers: Perspectives and Definitions.* Urbana, Ill.: National Council of Teachers of English, 1979.

Index